MURDER in the HIGH HIMALAYA

MURDER IN
THE HIGH
HIMALAYA
LOYALTY, TRAGEDY, AND ESCAPE FROM TIBET

— · —

JONATHAN GREEN

PUBLICAFFAIRS
New York

Copyright © 2010 by Jonathan Green.

Published in the United States by PublicAffairs™,
a member of the Perseus Books Group.

All rights reserved.

Printed in the United States of America.

No part of this book may be reproduced in any manner whatsoever
without written permission except in the case of brief quotations
embodied in critical articles and reviews. For information, address
PublicAffairs, 250 West 57th Street, Suite 1321, New York, NY 10107.

PublicAffairs books are available at special discounts for bulk
purchases in the U.S. by corporations, institutions, and other organizations. For more information, please contact the Special Markets
Department at the Perseus Books Group, 2300 Chestnut Street,
Suite 200, Philadelphia, PA 19103, call (800) 810-4145, ext. 5000,
or e-mail special.markets@perseusbooks.com.

Book design and production by Eclipse Publishing Services
Maps by Chris Erichsen

Library of Congress Cataloging-in-Publication Data

Green, Jonathan.
  Murder in the high Himalaya : loyalty, tragedy, and escape from Tibet /
Jonathan Green. — 1st ed.
    p. cm.
  Includes bibliographical references and index.
  ISBN 978-1-58648-714-0 (hardcover)
  1. Human rights—China—Tibet—Case studies. 2. Civil rights—
China—Tibet—Case studies. 3. Freedom of religion—China—Tibet—
Case studies. 4. Murder—China—Tibet—Case studies. 5. Refugees—
Crimes against—China—Tibet. I. Title.
  JC599.C62T53455 2010
  323'.0440922515—dc22
                          2010002571

First Edition

10 9 8 7 6 5 4 3 2 1

This book is dedicated to my parents,
Anthony and Sarah Green.
They taught me the importance of justice and truth, no matter the cost.

And Keisha.
Love of my life, my strength and my foundation.

CONTENTS

—·—·—

CONTENTS

AUTHOR'S NOTE

—·—·—

Writing about Tibet offers myriad problems for any reporter. The truth and those prepared to speak it are dismayingly hard to discover. Misrepresentation, conspiracies of silence, and the hijacking of the truth for political and personal agendas are certain obstacles for anyone engaging in serious investigation into modern-day Tibet.

Because the consequences can be severe for any Tibetan caught speaking out about his or her country—certainly for any Tibetan lending information to an investigative reporter like myself—I have made every effort to protect the identities of the individuals in this book. I have changed the names of all of the individuals within the book who remain in Tibet, and I have obscured details when I felt it was necessary to do so in order to protect the rights and privacy of characters whose lives have been affected by the events on the Nangpa La.

The details of the escape were constructed from scores of interviews with escapees, other witnesses, transcripts supplied by the International Campaign for Tibet, and first-hand reporting in the Himalaya. In some cases, reporting action or dialogue, I have relied on single-source accounts.

INTRODUCTION

Tibet is a land of timeless, infinite expanse. The "Roof of the World" soars from the Earth's crust some three miles above sea level. The highest region on the planet is a vast plateau, six times bigger than Western Europe. At such altitude, there is half as much oxygen in the air as there is at sea level. Tibetans call their home "The Land of Snows."

For centuries, Tibet was known as a forbidden, inaccessible, and secretive realm, sequestered from the world by its altitude and bordered by an often impassable mountain range, the mightiest in the world. To the west of Tibet is the scimitar slash of the Karakoram range of northern Kashmir, the high-altitude battleground between Pakistan and India. To the north are the Kunlun and Qilian ranges that separate the country from the desolate Gobi desert. To the south is the empyrean, glacier-draped Himalayan range.

The high plateau is often called the "Third Pole." With forty-six thousand glaciers, it contains the biggest ice fields outside of the Arctic and Antarctic. To the north is Chang Tang, a massive, impassable, and unpopulated salt and borax desert, which resembles a lunarscape. Forests of juniper, oak, ash, spruce, cypress, and jungles of rhododendron lie to the south. This vast wilderness is roamed by snow leopards and Tibetan Blue Bear in the mountains, by monkeys and red pandas in the valleys, and by wild antelope and kiang (wild asses) on the plains. The Tibetan antelope—chiru—roam the grasslands like African wildebeest. Overhead, giant Griffon Vultures and Golden Eagles soar.

Tibetans believe that their genesis took place when their land was once ruled by a peaceful, contemplative monkey. The monkey king lived

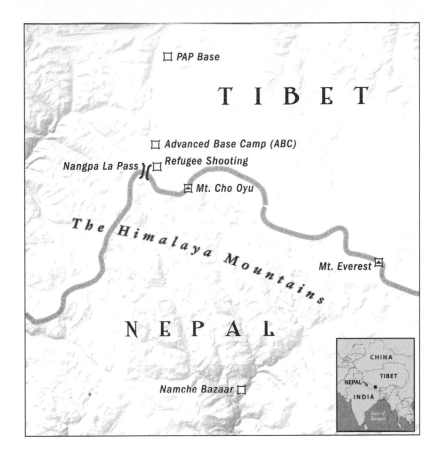

in retreat in a cave but was lured by the mournful cries of a female ogre, who was vindictive and sexually insatiable. Seduced, he fathered six children with her; they became the first Tibetans.

For twenty-five thousand years, humans have lived on the high plateau.

— . — . —

Into the mid-twentieth century, Tibet remained an antiquated theocracy. Even by the 1950s, few Westerners had seen Lhasa, the capital of Tibet.

Life was harsh. Yet nomads, warrior chieftains, monks, and nuns in the vast disconnected land of Tibet were unified in their devotion to the Dalai Lama. Over centuries, in each reincarnation, his mission was to teach compassion. His name meant "Ocean of Wisdom." Tibetans called him "Precious Conqueror" or "Wish-Granting Jewel." Others simply called him Kundun—The Presence.

Today, the Dalai Lama lives in exile in India, and Tibet, his former home, is sometimes mythologized by Westerners as an enigmatic Shangri-La.

For Tibetans, whose homeland is now annexed to China, life is lived in a fiercely patrolled, highly secretive zone on the roof of the world where the Dalai Lama cannot set foot and where pledging allegiance to the spiritual leader of the country can result in a protracted jail term. Hundreds of Tibetan monks, nuns, and laypeople are serving prison terms for flying Tibetan flags, for daring to voice their desire for a free Tibet in public, or for supporting the Dalai Lama publicly or privately. In modern-day Tibet free speech is criminalized. Tibetans can be handed prison terms of fifteen years or more by Chinese Communist Party officials for broadcasting their views on websites or speaking out to foreigners about their country on the telephone or in e-mail. Just downloading songs about the Dalai Lama on the Internet can result in a jail term.

Despite exploding economic and military growth in China, the Communist Party fears separatism and revolt in Tibet—which forms one quarter of China's landmass—as it attempts to consolidate control and assimilate the country into China.

Today, Tibetan cities are being flooded with Han Chinese migrants who are rapidly outnumbering Tibetans, leaving them undereducated with ever-dwindling long-term opportunities. Lhasa, once the Forbidden City, is now fast becoming a booming Chinese capital city replete with karaoke bars, brothels, five-star hotels, and luxury car dealerships.

The Chinese call Tibet, *Xizang*, meaning Western Treasure House. The exploitation of the natural resources of Tibet is under way.[1] Within the plateau lie 40 million tons of copper, 40 million tons of lead and zinc, and more than a billion tons of iron. (Tibetan copper alone amounts to one-third of China's reserves.) Mining revenue from Tibet will top $1.5 billion in the coming years.[2]

The once indomitable peaks of the Himalaya, which have long served to isolate Tibet from its neighbors, have meanwhile become the ultimate test for serious Western mountain climbers. Each year, increasing numbers seek glory and an escape from the drudgery of their lives, an answer to life's eternal riddle in the world's highest mountain range.

Roughly 2,500 Tibetans flee their country annually in a brutal journey over the Himalaya. Some are escaping for a new life in India. All want to meet their exiled spiritual leader, the Dalai Lama.

— · — · —

A Note On Geography

Tibet traditionally comprised three main regions: Amdo (northeastern Tibet), Kham (eastern Tibet), and U-Tsang (central and western Tibet). In 1965 the Chinese government established the Tibetan Autonomous Region (TAR). It includes Tibet west of the Yangste River and part of Kham. The rest of Amdo and Kham were incorporated into Chinese provinces. These areas, where there is a dense Tibetan population, are designated as Tibetan Autonomous Prefectures and Tibetan Autonomous Counties. Chinese authorities still regard most of Qinghai and parts of Gansu, Sichuan, and Yunnan provinces as 'Tibetan.'

Kelsang Namtso photographed near her hometown of Driru. Date unknown.

Dolma at the Tibetan Children's Village School, Suja, Bir, India, March 2008

Luis Benitez in front of the Khumbu icefall, Mount Everest, 2003.
PHOTO COURTESY OF DIDRIK JOHNCK.

Chinese PAP on Cho Oyu, September 2006,
shortly after the murder of Kelsang Namtso.
PAVLE KOZJEK

Dolma and Jamyang at the Tibetan Children's School,
Suja, Bir, India, 2008
AUTHOR'S PHOTO COLLECTION

Tibetan refugee safe house, Nepal December 2006
AUTHOR'S PHOTO COLLECTION

Sergiu Matei and the Dalai Lama, Warsaw,
Poland, December 2008
© SERGIU MATEI

MURDER in the HIGH HIMALAYA

1

Songs to the Precious One

— · — · —

This core of the earth
This heart of the world
Fenced round by snow
The headland of all rivers
Where the mountains are high and the land is pure
A country so good
Where men are born as sages and heroes
And act according to good laws
A land of horses even more speedy
From a ninth-century document describing Tibet

The scouring winds howled in from the plateau. Just above the insistent moaning of the unstoppable gust through the cracks of the spruce door, she heard it again. A rapping and then, faintly, beyond the thick mud wall of the house, voices. Dolma Palkyi's eyes snapped open, and a familiar knotted sense of dread rose in her throat. At 10:30 p.m., an unannounced visit in Chinese-occupied Tibet meant trouble.

The one-room house was thick with the cloying smoke of a yak-dung fire. A single, guttering yak-butter candle lit the room. Eight-year-old Dolma, who had raven black hair and piercing almond eyes set above broad cheekbones, was lying motionless under a yak hide. Her mother, Nyima,* moved quickly in the darkness. The family was used to these intrusions. Sometimes the men from the Public Security Bureau (PSB) left the rural Tibetans alone. Other times, they summarily detained men, women, and children. Nyima slid out of bed and blew out the

---

* "Nyima" and other names throughout the book are pseudonyms to protect the identities of these individuals.

candle. The knocking on the door intensified. "Don't move," she told her daughter. "You're not to say anything if they ask you anything." Dolma's brother Rinzin, a gangly thirteen-year-old, was rousing himself. Nyima strode across the room to pick up her five-year-old daughter Kyizom. Quickly she turned to her children and said, "Remember, say nothing." Outside, snowstorms had buried the highland steppe under a meter of snow. In this exceptionally unforgiving winter, yaks, the mainstay of many Tibetan families, were freezing to death and dying by the hundreds.

Nyima struggled to lift the cumbersome wooden bar across the heavy, warped door. As the door slid open, a blast of minus-thirty-degree air roared into the room. Out of the darkness, three men in long, ill-fitting Chinese overcoats emerged. One mustached man, his hands deep in his pockets, scanned the room and grunted. The other two went to work, lifting pots by the fire, looking inside and underneath before dropping them, irritably, back in place.

"We've come to check to see if you are using an electric stove," lied the man with the moustache to Nyima. There was no electricity during the harsh winter in the tiny village of Juchen. The Nagchu River, a tributary of the mighty Salween, was a frozen highway of ice in the winter months. When the ice choked the river, the Chinese-built hydropower plants couldn't function, and electricity failed.

The men were poorly disguised PSB officials, secret police who arbitrarily snatched people out of their homes and off the streets for activities deemed "unpatriotic" to China and Mao Zedung's Communist legacy. Tonight, they were searching for pictures of the Dalai Lama. Just three years earlier, in 1995, possession of a picture of the exiled spiritual leader of Tibet had been made a crime that could easily be met with torture, grueling patriotic reeducation sessions, a prison sentence, or hard labor.

The three men clumped past the stove in heavy boots, peered behind it, and poked around a pile of smoldering yak dung. Nyima allowed herself only the quickest of glances at the fuel tray of the mud stove. A few hours before, she had stashed images of His Holiness within.

To Westerners, the Dalai Lama is the winner of a Nobel Peace Prize and spiritual head of one of the world's oldest religions. To Tibetans,

Tenzin Gyatso, the fourteenth Dalai Lama, is a god in human form. To the Chinese officials in the Tibet Autonomous Region, the Dalai Lama is a "splittist"—public enemy number one. In the words of Zhang Qingli, head of the Communist Party in Tibet, he is "a wolf wrapped in monk's robes, a monster with a human face but the heart of a beast,"[1] and an advocate of rape, murder and child cannibalism.[2]

Without a word spoken, the men rummaged around pulling the four small beds away from the wall, tearing off still-warm bedding. They lingered by the *choesom,* a beautiful filigreed altar in the corner of the room. Pictures of lamas were displayed, but none of His Holiness. With curt nods to Nyima, the PSB officials abandoned their search, leaving as gruffly as they'd come. They had failed in their mission to catch the family with forbidden pictures at an unguarded hour.

Nyima moved to barricade the door. Snow had whistled in and settled on the kitchen table. Hurriedly, she crossed to the stove and pulled out three pictures of His Holiness. The pictures steamed; one was singed at the corner. In one, the Dalai Lama sat in the lotus position wearing a large yellow hat—resembling a saffron Mohawk hairstyle—denoting his allegiance to the Gelugpa School of Tibetan Buddhism. In another, the Dalai Lama floated above the Potala Palace, his former home in Lhasa. The third, a pendant that Nyima always wore tucked deep into her clothing and hidden out of sight, featured the Dalai Lama making a benediction. Nyima clutched the images to her chest, smiling with relief. Several hours earlier, a neighbor had alerted Nyima that an unmarked PSB car had been spotted heading to Juchen village. Many of the villagers had had just enough time to hide their pictures of His Holiness.

Nyima's children crowded around, hugging their mother tightly. Nyima soothed them with stories of what life was like before the drab, humorless Communists invaded on October 7, 1950, which was the start of a move to violently annex Tibet to the "Motherland."

To the Communists in their shapeless, frog-green uniforms who decried religion and lived according to a mass of party rules, the Tibetan monks and nuns in their swirling maroon robes who spent hours chanting Buddhist mantras were anathema. The Chinese scorned Tibetans as primitive barbarians and the religious elite as lazy. Around 15 percent of the population lived as monks and nuns, devoting their lives to meditation, retreat, and devotion to the Buddha. The Chinese regarded the religious community of Tibet as parasites kept fat by the hard work of the serfs who supported them. They were most disgusted by their unquestioning fealty to the Dalai Lama.

The Dalai Lama, aged twenty-three, eventually fled his hallowed quarters in the Potala Palace after a failed uprising against Chinese rule in 1959. Disguised as a soldier, with seven hundred Khampa guerillas guarding him at the rear, he had successfully escaped to India. Since the Dalai Lama's departure, over 100,000 Tibetans had fled the country.

As the children huddled for warmth, Nyima recounted stories of their grandfather, a warlord chieftain. Dolma listened enraptured, as her mother told of the courtiers in brocade gowns and fur-lined hats who fussed around her grandfather when he visited Lhasa. He was wealthy and always bedecked in centuries-old gold jewelry, his face framed by rare turquoise earrings. Dolma nuzzled closer, comforted by the familiar earthy smell of her mother. Nyima's small hands were callused, and there were dark crescents of dirt under nails from laboring in the fields behind the family's home. But she had a regal aspect—sharp cheekbones and a defiant gaze that set her apart from other villagers.

Nyima told how the invading Chinese army had killed thousands in Kham, marching forward under fluttering blood-red Communist pennants. Nyima whispered, "The Tibetans who were killed came back to life; they became *rolang* [zombies], always roaming the land looking for people to eat." In a low whisper, Nyima continued, "But the Tibetans made doors with high sills and low beams. The rolang could not bend down, so they couldn't get in the houses." The three children turned to observe their own humble door. Indeed, it was small; adults had to stoop when they entered. Nyima went on, "They only jump; they don't walk." The wind continued to batter the door as it rattled against the lock. Nyima chuckled in the half-light. At last, Dolma felt safe. The memory of the uninvited men in their home receded. She felt her eyes grow heavy with sleep.

— · — · —

By the age of ten, when Dolma began to undertake chores outside the home, she was inseparable from her best friend and closest neighbor, Dolkar Tomso. Dolma's and Dolkar's houses faced each other across a patch of bumpy, undeveloped ground near a small pond. Together they headed each day to the little creek behind their houses to get water for their families. (In winter, they had to break the thick ice with an axe.) Dolkar was a capricious ball of energy. Whip-thin, with full crimson lips and large expressive brown eyes, she could also be painfully quiet and secretive. Above all, she was mulishly stubborn.

A year older than Dolkar, Dolma was the perfect foil to her friend's impulsive nature. Even when she walked, Dolma expressed an economy of movement. Her voice was soothing but firm. She was refined, and covered her mouth when she coughed. While other neighborhood children looked worn out from poor diets and heavy workloads, Dolma positively shone with good health and was carefully dressed in bright clothes that her mother made for her.

In Juchen village, a hamlet in Tibet's Driru (Ch: Biru) County, seventy crudely constructed sandstone houses cling to the lower inclines of a mountain. At 14,000 feet above sea level, the village is barely visible from a vast panorama of plummeting gorges and rippling mountains. Forty towering peaks of the Yargong Snow Mountains surround Driru County. In winter, they are capped with blisteringly white snow. For a few short months in the spring and summer, the russet sandstone mountains are carpeted with thick alpine grass.

Juchen lies by a tributary of the mighty Salween, which provides Southeast Asia with fresh water. Tibetans call the Salween the "Nagchu" (Nag means black, chu means water or river); its inky hue derives from black metamorphic rocks near the industrial town of Nagchu. The watershed of Asia, Tibet supplies water to hundreds of millions of the earth's population (in India and Southeast Asia). The headwaters of the Yellow, Yangtze, Mekong, Brahmaputra, and Indus rivers all originate there. They snake over the great plains and grassland steppe through lush valleys as gentle, jade-colored streams before bursting through the Himalaya. Thousands of feet below, with a sound like a cataclysmic rolling thunder, the Salween forms massive, forested gorges thick with rhododendron.

Juchen is one of a nexus of villages that line the banks of the river. It is connected to the main country road leading to the larger town of Driru by an unassuming iron bridge. For any medical emergencies or even simple groceries, people have to head to Driru.

—·—·—

The mountains provided Dolma and Dolkar with a vast playground and an unrivalled refuge. When word arrived that a PSB search was imminent, Nyima loaded Dolma with images and recordings of the Dalai Lama to stash in a cave on Bungga Mountain. (Some families hid such contraband in the village; others placed it in weighted plastic bags that they dropped in the river for later retrieval.)

From the mouth of the musty cave, Dolma and Dolkar could see the Kongpo mountains to the south. The tallest mountain in the range, also called Kongpo, was the protector of Juchen and home of the fearsome female deity, Jomo Kongchoe. The girls prayed to her for their safety. But at heart, they felt safe here in the shelter of the massive mountains. This was their territory.

The Chinese security presence in Tibet was ubiquitous. A military headquarters with whitewashed walls and a corrugated steel roof lay to the southwest of Juchen. Dolma and Dolkar could see into the base when they climbed up the mountain to collect wild onions. Sometimes they saw soldiers running in formation along the roads, chanting in unison. The girls were used to being scrutinized. Everywhere they went, Dolma and Dolkar encountered Chinese roadblocks and checkpoints. Grim-faced officials asked innumerable questions, looking for any infraction of regulations. The two friends had learned early on to give a minimum amount of information.

Driru is the first region of Kham reached when heading northeast from Lhasa. Once run by warlords, Kham was historically a mountainous stronghold. To this day, Khampas are feared by Chinese and Tibetans alike.

After the Chinese invasion of Tibet in 1950, many Khampas, funded and trained by the American CIA, became a fearsome insurgent army, code-named *Chushi-Gangdruk,* the Four Rivers Six Ranges. They rode on horseback with muzzle-loaded flintlocks, mercilessly attacking Chinese convoys and bases. Dressed in sheepskin jackets and fox-fur hats, the Khampas were as rugged as the land they inhabited. The Chinese quickly learned not to tangle with them. While the Chinese brutally suppressed the rest of Tibet, they found the remote regions like Driru harder to control. The Khampas from Driru fought so famously hard against the Chinese that few men were left in the area. To the Khampas, the Chinese authorities were just interlopers in the great passage of history, and the land was too powerful to be owned by anyone.

The Red Guards destroyed 6,000 Buddhist monasteries in Tibet before and during the Cultural Revolution and forbade the building of *stupas* (sacred edifices containing Buddhist relics) and Buddhist monuments. But Juchen's determined villagers shipped in bricks surreptitiously from Lhasa. At night, they carried the heavy stones high up a mountain to the east to construct a stupa. A few weeks before its completion, Chinese officials discovered the two-story structure. Unable to get heavy machinery up the mountain to destroy it, the Chinese had no option but to let this black eye to their authority stand.

The Communist Party closely monitored education in Tibet. Tibetan children were to be educated at a Chinese government-run school where they learned Chinese, English, and the "official" version of Tibetan history. In Juchen, a kind man with a walnut complexion had taught Tibetan. When they were eleven and twelve, Dolkar and Dolma briefly attended classes in a makeshift one-room school. But when the Chinese got wind of the operation, it was quickly shut down.

Most parents refused to send their children to the Chinese school. They worried that they would become corrupted by Communist dogma and end up as prostitutes serving the massive Chinese army in Tibet or that they would be lured away from helping at home to become store clerks. Nyima's refusal to allow Dolma to attend the school was more pragmatic. She worried about the food that was served at the school. All the children who went there came home with food poisoning.

By the time they were adolescents, both Dolma and Dolkar shouldered increasingly harder outdoor chores, beyond the cozy confines of their homes, like taking care of the families' yaks—leading them to pasture before breakfast and herding them back home at dark. During the day, the girls scavenged the mountainsides for firewood, which provided much needed income and fuel for their families.

Dolkar was impulsive. Once, heading home while slumped under the weight of a particularly heavy load of wood, Dolkar bound her bundle tightly, axe and all. Before Dolma could stop her, she impatiently kicked the bundle downhill. It bounced violently and flew open, sending its contents flying. A day's work had been lost. Worse, the axe was gone.

They knew that Dolkar's father, Tsedup, would be furious if his axe was lost. The girls spent three hours combing the mountainside before Dolma triumphantly raised the axe above her head. When they returned home late that night, Tsedup, a tall, mercurial man with little patience for foolishness, was incandescent with rage that a fire could not be lit and that potential income had been squandered due to Dolkar's fecklessness. Sometimes People's Liberation Army (PLA) soldiers from a nearby garrison aggressively demanded fuel for their fires from each household. Villagers without fuel to spare were beaten. Tsedup couldn't risk his supply of yak dung. That night the family shivered under their yak hides, struggling to stay warm.

—·—·—

In the normally hardscrabble life of Juchen, an economic boom was underway Previously dependent on subsistence farming and the few yuan they were able to get selling surplus crops, firewood, and yak products, Tibetans in Driru and the surrounding counties found themselves surrounded by an incredibly lucrative natural resource—caterpillar fungus, or *yartsa gunbu*,* which flourishes in high-altitude grasslands.

Yartsa gunbu had been popular in Asia since the fifteenth century, but in the past two decades, demand for the fungus had boomed. In the 1990s, three Chinese runners broke world records for their running times in the 1,500, 3,000, and 10,000 meter races, and they pointed to

---

* A parasitic fungus (Cordyceps) attacks the larvae of the ghost moth, kills the organism, and produces a mushroom that grows from the head of the larval body. Cordyceps is highly valued by the Chinese as an aphrodisiac and for its curative powers (from fatigue to cancer).

caterpillar fungus as their secret weapon. In preparation for the 2008 Beijing Olympics, the Chinese Olympic team ingested caterpillar fungus in massive quantities. With such voracious demand for the fungus in China, it was more valuable than gold (Tibetans refer to the fungus as "soft gold"). The price had increased 500 percent from 1997 to 2006. In Tibet, Chinese Muslim traders paid from $2,800 to $11,200 for one kilogram of dried *yartsa,* more than enough money for a Tibetan family to live on for a year.

The PSB restricted Tibetans from other areas from taking the soft gold out of Driru because it led to violence. The brother of Dolkar's friend Thinley Wangmo was sentenced to a year in prison after a vicious fight with Hui Muslim traders over mountain territory with a high yield of caterpillar fungus. In the summer months, Dolkar and Dolma headed into the mountains with their families to hunt for the fungus. To Nyima's chagrin, the girls would become lost in play, often missing the precious resource beneath their feet.

The spoils from caterpillar fungus had transformed subsistence villages like Juchen. For the first time in years, villagers had access to real cash flow. They bought shiny motorcycles from booming dealerships made rich by Khampas who took to two wheels with the same élan as they once took to fierce Tibetan horses. Villagers renovated their homes. Dolma's mother spent money on lavish interiors in their home; bright, lacquered colors, firebox red ceilings, ornate pillars, and beautiful blonde wood countertops.

—·—·—

Every year, Dolma and Dolkar enjoyed a few brief respites from their familial duties. During the Tibetan New Year, *Losar,* which ran for fifteen days during February and March, Juchen's villagers held a lavish party, celebrating the dawn of a new year. The night before the festivities, Dolkar and Dolma brought their yaks up the mountain to graze, freeing themselves for a full twenty-four hours. They would drink soda and dance in the courtyard of the town's sole temple.

Juchen was situated on brittle, iron-hard land that was never entirely frost-free. The harsh winters, from November to March, confined most villagers to their homes in dark, endless days. But in the spring and summer months, the warming rays of the high sun brought the landscape to life again and beckoned the girls outside. In the spring, the men circled the fields with holy scriptures, praying for a bumper barley crop. At the harvest festival, they danced in thanks.

In the sun-drugged evenings, Dolma and Dolkar and a half-dozen other girls their age crept away from the merrymaking to a secluded spot out of the village and out of earshot of Communist officials. Beneath a spray of stars in a pasture that felt like velvet underfoot, they sang songs to the Dalai Lama and Tibetan independence. And they danced. It was one of the few times when Dolkar felt free to be herself. There, swelling her lungs with song and shouting into the night air, she found liberation.

Together the girls sang:

> Sitting on the golden throne.
> Is the Precious One, His Holiness Dalai Lama
> We presented him a *kata*
> In return, we got blessings from him.

When they were breathless from singing and dancing, the girls collapsed on the grass and talked about their dreams. Often they discussed escaping to India and seeing the Dalai Lama. Just to touch him and to get his blessing would earn their families merit. A handful of Dolma's and Dolkar's friends had made the dangerous journey to India to the Dalai Lama. In Dharamsala, home of the Tibetan Government in Exile, Tibetans could receive a traditional Tibetan education and be free to practice their faith without fear of persecution.

Several young nuns from Juchen had successfully made the trip. One nun, Monlam Sangmo, sent back snapshots of the Dhauladhar Mountains and the lush green foothills and pastures in the Kangra Valley where she had received a special blessing from His Holiness. Dolkar had seen photos of Dolma Ling, a beautifully landscaped nunnery that was home to 228 nuns near Dharamsala. On the other side of the mighty Himalaya, there was a promise of freedom.

2

SACRED VOWS

—·—·—

Grant the vision of direct enlightenment,
Whose nature is universal voidness!
The disciple should press her palms together,
Praise the mentor and then entreat him:
Great Savior, grant me the vision
Of direct enlightenment,
Free from evolution and birth.
        "Universal Enlightenment," from Nagarjuna's
                Five Stages of the Perfection Stage

In Juchen hamlet, far from the towering summits sought by adventurers, Dolma and Dolkar nursed their fervent dream of escaping over the mountains to India.

Dolkar Tsomo was the sole girl among seven children. With so many hungry mouths to feed, her family struggled to make ends meet. Dolkar's house, a large two-story building, was impossible to heat in winter. Gokarmo, Dolkar's mother, had developed severe, debilitating arthritis. Cooking and cleaning had fallen to Dolkar at age ten. Often Dolkar fended off gnawing hunger. Her clothes were threadbare. But, no matter the season, she wore her favorite scarf, fawn-colored and striped with white and silver.

To her delight, when Dolkar was fourteen, her mother gave birth to a baby girl. But the baby was sickly from the first day. A rudimentary incubator (a glass box) was brought from Lhasa, but that was the extent of her care. In rural Tibet, there are few doctors, and deaths during childbirth are not uncommon. Fifteen months after her birth, Dolkar's sister died. Earlier in the year, the family had mourned the death of a beloved aunt. The two events cast an inescapable pall over a household already stretched thin. After the death of her sister, Dolkar often took refuge at Dolma's house.

In contrast to Dolkar's life of work and family pressure, Dolma's home life was relaxed. In the evenings, Nyima would sit and weave wool on a loom, recounting stories of her pilgrimages to Lhasa or folkloric tales of the ancient land of Tibet.

Nyima, who offered Dolkar an inspiring model of religious devotion, was proud of her Tibetan ancestry. She dressed brightly in traditional Tibetan clothes: red cardigans, boldly patterned aprons, and ornate jade earrings. She refused to marry, telling her children that she didn't want to be subservient to any man or to "become a bride in some man's house." Tibetan women are famously independent. Nyima maintained that her father had, despite his standing in the community and tough reputation, not treated her well. Dolma never knew her own father, Lobsang, who had died in a car accident when she was small.

Nyima was strongly rooted in her Tibetan identity. When fellow villagers put up pictures of Chairman Mao or Chinese premier Hu Jintao, as they were encouraged to do by the local authorities, she made sure that they also put up pictures of Tibetan lamas or kings.

Yet despite her sometimes fiery temperament, she could display true generosity of spirit, even to the Chinese occupiers. In 2002, when work on a hydropower station northeast of Juchen began, Chinese from various cities in mainland China worked on the plant. The building site swallowed precious local farmlands as it constantly expanded. The Chinese workers were a sad and malnourished lot, their hands rubbed raw by hard labor. Nyima often arrived with tea and biscuits to dole out to them when they were at work building roads or putting up telegraph poles near her village. The Chinese workers bowed their heads gratefully, unaccustomed to such largesse. Nyima disabused the notion that the Chinese were malevolent. "They are poor people like us," she told her daughter.

When Nyima wasn't out in the fields tending her barley and vegetables, she was often away on pilgrimages. Every year, she headed to Lhasa to pay her respects at the Jokhang Temple, the holiest place in all of Tibet.

—·—·—

Over the years, Dolma had noticed a change in Dolkar. She rarely complained about her heavy workload, thin clothes, or her unhappy home life. Yet, it was clear to Dolma that her friend was gravely unhappy. The death of Dolkar's baby sister, her mother's misery, coping with such a large family, and a foul-tempered father had etched an unflattering portrait of family life in Dolkar's young mind. Marriage, she concluded, wasn't for her. Unlike Dolkar's mother, Nyima was a completely dedicated Buddhist, and her refusal to marry served as an inspiration to young Dolkar.

Dolkar saw fulfillment in the transformational path of Tibetan Buddhism. To Dolkar, a religious life offered the path to happiness way beyond her lifetime. Many of her teenage girlfriends felt the same way. A girl from a nearby village, Lobsang Samten, a diminutive girl with a spray of freckles, had become a nun to escape an arranged marriage. In time, Dolkar took on an increasingly sober view of the world. She stopped eating meat and ceased dancing at Tibetan New Year. Dolkar's parents were vehemently opposed to her plan to become a nun. "You are my only daughter," her mother implored. "I need you here at home to help me." Her father flew into a rage at any mention of Dolkar's religious life.

According to Tibetan tradition, at least one child in each family should enter monastic life to ensure an accrual of merit for the family. Dolma's brother Rinzin was a monk at the local monastery, but his constant joking and fooling put him in direct conflict with the senior monks. Still, Nyima was proud of him.

Historically, Tibet has had the largest monastic community in the world. Since China's annexation of Tibet, that number has been drastically reduced. The Chinese tightly regulate the number of people officially allowed to follow a religious course, because as members of a monastery, the Tibetans' first loyalty is to their exiled leader, the Dalai Lama, who advocates genuine autonomy for Tibet.*

---

* Implementation of state religious policy in Tibet has been particularly harsh because of the close link between religion and Tibetan identity. Tibetan Buddhism is an integral element of Tibetan identity and Tibetan nationalism and is therefore perceived as a threat to the unity of the People's Republic of China.

The Chinese authorities were relentlessly suspicious of Tibetan nuns and monks. At night, the Juchen villagers talked of the religious devotees they knew who had been arrested and were serving prison terms in Lhasa's Drapchi Prison. Each year, officials would tally up the number of disagreements each monk had had with the authorities. Those with the longest list of offenses were given "patriotic reeducation" sessions—tedious courses in Communist doctrine. A flawed recitation could result in a beating or even prison.

Dolma's brother had returned home from the monastery with awful stories. The well-known lama in the area Shabdrung Rinpoche—the abbot of the monastery—had an assistant with a scar from a huge bullet wound on his back from time spent in a Chinese prison that Dolma's brother would see as he sat behind him during prayers. As her son explained the problems at the monastery, Nyima listened with steely intensity. All monks had to have a Professional Religious Personnel Certificate, issued by the Democratic Management Committee (the "committee" was sometimes a lone Chinese official stationed in the monastery or a significantly larger group). In order to get the certificate, one had to declare love for the Communist state above all competing loyalties, which, of course, went against the love of the Buddha. The document signified their patriotic reeducation and adherence to a non-splittist attitude. To achieve the certificate and to join a monastery within Tibet, it was necessary to denounce the Dalai Lama.

The repression caused unrelenting resentment. Once, heavily armed police and soldiers descended on Driru when monks and nuns unified to protest. A group of monks from Juchen piled into a car to confront the police about the unfairness of their restrictions. They noticed a black cat sitting beneath the front wheel. It refused to budge. Unwilling to run over the cat, the monks abandoned their plan. Ever since, it was rumored that the protector deity from Juchen, *Melong-dho*, had transmuted into the cat to protect the monks.

But ten years later, the suppression of monks and nuns was far worse. Refusing to comply with the Communist Party was to risk jail and torture. It became so draconian and surreal that in August 2007, a decree was passed that prohibited *tulkus* (reincarnated lamas) from reincarnating without prior permission from the Communist Party.

Dolkar wasn't intimidated by the brutality meted out to monks and nuns. During the winter, when her workload lessened, she spent increasing amounts of time at Choeling Monastery on the eastern edge of Driru town. Just south of the main Sichuan-Lhasa highway, the town of 39,000 sits on limestone cliffs on the north bank of the Salween River. Choeling was one of three monasteries in the area. It was hewn out of the side of a mountain. Three stories tall, it housed cavernous halls filled with religious paintings and sculptures. The structure faced south to take advantage of the sun's warming rays. The Salween River lazily uncoiled below.

High up on the mountainside, beneath statues of Buddha and in clouds of musky juniper incense, Dolkar found tranquility. The monks rose at 4 a.m., beginning the day with a mellifluous chanting, their faces lit by yak-butter lamps. At the back of the long temple, Dolkar sat among the monks for hours, quietly chanting along, thumbing her rosary or spinning her prayer wheel. The monks, who served her yak-butter tea, sometimes engaged her in discussions of faith. Finally, Dolkar had found a peaceful refuge from her chaotic home. Although they bristled at the idea of their daughter becoming a nun, Dolkar's parents respected her burgeoning spirituality.

When Dolkar shared with Dolma her plan to take her vows as a nun and asked if she would join, Dolma wavered. Deep down, Dolma liked her independence, the bright beautiful clothes her mother made for her, and her jade jewelry. Try as she might, she couldn't quite imagine herself in a spartan nun's maroon habit. And yet, urged on by her friend, she felt it was probably the right thing to do.

For several weeks, Dolkar's parents fought relentlessly over their daughter's desire to be a nun. Tsedup threatened to disown her if she followed through with her ordination. When she could stand it no longer, Dolkar shot her father one last look of defiance before fleeing next door to Dolma. She implored Dolma to come to the monastery to take their vows. When Dolma's brother overheard, he was adamantly opposed. "She is not going with you," he declared. "Her place is here."

Dolma bowed her head sorrowfully. Dolkar bid her friend goodbye and spun out the door.

Over the course of the year, Dolkar had formed a close bond with Kalsang Labsum, a lama at the local Dephong Monastery. Dolkar wasted no time. At 11 p.m., she went straight to Kalsang's chambers. His attendant, a young monk, disappeared into an inner room to rouse his master. In moments, Kalsang emerged from his room. Kalsang was a thin, stooped octogenarian with a shaven head. His only material possession was the round, steel-wire eyeglasses that perched on the end of his nose.

He had a *geshe* degree, the most advanced academic degree attainable by a monk. Achieving geshe status requires twenty years of intense study and extensive memorization of the five major philosophical treaties of Tibetan Buddhism and texts like *The Perfection of Wisdom*. Academic study is followed by rigorous debates. After the Cultural Revolution, the Chinese banned the geshe degree, widely respected in Tibetan communities and considered a direct threat to Chinese rule. Those determined enough had to escape to India to follow the geshe path.

Dolkar caught her breath and looked at Kalsang. "I'm ready," she announced. The old monk nodded knowingly. Dolkar's life would change dramatically once she accepted the religious calling. But he didn't question Dolkar's devotion. He told her to wait, while he readied the chapel.

Traditionally, when they are ordained, initiates make an offering to the monastery to demonstrate their renunciation of all worldly possessions. In her haste, Dolkar had come empty-handed. She ran quickly from room to room waking up the monks she knew to ask for money. In less than an hour, she managed to collect 500 yuan (around $70).

The geshe beckoned Dolkar into the chapel. A few thick-waisted candles had been lit. On the altar, pictures of the Dalai Lama, normally hidden from the resident Chinese official, were displayed. Dolkar handed Kalsang the notes she'd collected. He bowed in thanks and put them aside. A monk entered with tea and cake for Dolkar, and an offering of barley was made.

As part of her initiation, Dolkar took thirty-six vows. The five core tenets were celibacy, doing no harm (no violence to humans or animals), truthfulness, purity (no intoxicants), and a vow not to steal. In a gesture that symbolized doing away with confusion, hostility, and attachment, the geshe cut off a few strands of Dolkar's hair with scissors. (After the ceremony, Dolkar would shave her head completely.) Dolkar prostrated three times and called on Manjushri, the god of wisdom and awareness.

The final step of the ceremony required that Dolkar choose a new name to symbolize her monastic rebirth. "Kelsang Namtso," Dolkar said. In keeping with tradition, she chose the female version of the geshe's name, Kalsang, in honor of him. It meant good fortune. Namtso means Lake of Jewels.

With that, her rebirth as Kelsang Namtso was complete. A smile broke across her face. No one could undo what had been done.

3

FORGED BY MOUNTAINS

——·—·——

I am sure that the key to understanding climbing is
the coming back. It means if you are really in difficult
places, in dangerous places, if you are in . . . thin air,
and you come back, you feel that you got again a
chance for life. You are reborn. And only in this
moment, you understand deeply that life is the
biggest gift we have.

Reinhold Messner

It felt good to be back. Kathmandu's narrow dusty streets, bustling with
backpackers and street vendors made Luis Benitez grin. He strode past
the cramped climbing and trekking supply stores and Eastern arts and
crafts shops, a cell phone glued to his ear, as he dodged the tourists
and Nepali hustlers selling everything from marijuana to trekking trips
in the Himalayan foothills.

This was Thamel, the hip tourist quarter in the heart of a cramped
filthy city, capital of the beleaguered kingdom of Nepal. It was a
second home to Colorado native Benitez and the epicenter of the
mountaineering community, the starting point for the majority of
Himalayan expeditions. Spending four months of the year here, Benitez
knew everyone from local business owners to waiters in his favorite
restaurants. That morning he'd been pampered at Nadine's, a barbershop
he favored where he'd had a shave and a haircut. Cologne lingered on
his cheeks. Such was his ritual before an expedition.

Compact and spry, with classic aquiline features, thirty-three-year-
old Benitez was already known as one of the world's elite big-mountain
guides. High-profile stories about him had appeared in glossy magazines

and climbing journals. Benitez had his eye on fame. He employed an agent who was maneuvering to get him a book deal, and he jumped at media opportunities when they came his way. From time to time, he employed his own publicist, an unusual step for a mountaineer. His garage in Colorado was jammed full of the latest gear from his sponsors—some one hundred jackets, along with every conceivable piece of equipment.

Even in the mountains, Benitez was a snappy dresser with charm to spare. "No matter how remote we'd be, all of a sudden Benitez would disappear," said Didrik Johnck, a friend of Benitez. "You'd find him in the corner of some bar in a place like Lukla on the way to Everest base camp, chatting to some smoking hot girl." On the backpacking trails around Nepal and India, Everest mountaineers are the equivalent of rock stars. A few months before, Benitez had climbed Everest for the fifth time. It was once a world record for the most consecutive summits of Everest by a non-sherpa.

Benitez made around $100,000 a year as a senior guide with Adventure Consultants (AC), a major guiding company that led the super-wealthy on the "Seven Summit Circuit"—the seven highest mountains on the seven continents around the world. Benitez excelled in thin air at what some climbers call "high-altitude plodding." He was a natural for Everest and other big mountains where climbers trudged up to the top in oxygen-depleted air and where a singular bloody-mindedness was the most important attribute.

At a cost of $65,000 a pop for Everest, big-mountain climbing is largely the preserve of the wealthy. To entertain the rich, Benitez prided himself on the fact that he could both "read the weather on the summit of Everest and order a really excellent bottle of wine in the back country anywhere in the world." And he could do so in several languages: Spanish, German, Russian, Tibetan, and Nepalese.

The job was not without its perks. After Benitez took Canadian entrepreneur Len Stanmore to the top of Everest, he received a Rolex Oyster Explorer II watch worth around $7,000. Grateful clients gave Benitez the keys to their second homes. Benitez vacationed in a multi-million dollar condo in Florida, thanks to a client.

Benitez spent the summer leading clients up mountains in Africa and Russia. Winter brought him to South America on Aconcagua and Vinson Massif in Antarctica. By fall, he was in Nepal and Tibet. He spent so much time in the lea of Himalayan peaks that his registered dentist was Pasag Sherpani, a Nepalese *sherpani* (a female *sherpa*), who had a small surgery in Namche Bazar, the last stop before Everest.

In August 2006, Benitez was back in Nepal to lead an expedition up Cho Oyu, the sixth-highest peak in the world. Seven sherpas would schlepp 5,000 pounds of supplies packed into blue 110-liter plastic barrels over Nepal's border into Tibet and then up the mountain to the base camp. Chongba was the expedition cook. Ang Tshering was the *sirdar* (sherpa leader); Chulidum, the lead climbing sherpa. The other four sherpas helped to lug gear and direct the climb.

Preparing for an expedition was like furnishing a small army for battle. In addition to cookware, a shower, a toilet, medical supplies (including everything from condoms and pregnancy test kits to drips and bandages), and storage tents, there were satellite phones, laptops, a printer, and paper supplies that had to be hauled up the mountain. The weight of the expedition's food—containing luxury foodstuffs from sushi to M&M's—was worked out down to the last gram to determine how many yaks would be needed to carry it up the mountain.

Benitez's first stop in Kathmandu was to see travel agent Ramesh Kumar°, a small, shrewish man in his late forties who operated from an office in an alley. A native Nepali, Kumar was a greaser of wheels— a man who could pay bribes, get visas, or read the demands of a corrupt bureaucracy—who made expeditions like Benitez's possible. AC maintained a storage apartment above his office in which tents, ropes, and other hardware were kept. Kumar, well-versed in the often seedy nature of transactions in the mountains, greeted Benitez while he juggled two ringing cell phones. Afterward, reviewing last-minute details, Kumar handed Benitez $25,000 in cash to take to Tibet to pay the China Tibet Mountaineering Association (CTMA) for the permits needed to climb Cho Oyu. Benitez stuffed the notes into his backpack.

° Ramesh Kumar is a pseudonym.

Benitez had been scrabbling around Kathmandu meeting and greeting his five clients. Each had paid $16,000 for the privilege of being escorted up Cho Oyu. They arrived from all over the world to stay at the musty, midrange Hotel Tibet in Kathmandu. Benitez welcomed his clients enthusiastically, reassuring them about the climb ahead. Each climber had trained for the mountain ascent over several months.

Briton Phil Varcas, a compact, self-contained thirty-one-year-old who helped run the family air-conditioning business in Berkshire, England, was an old friend of Benitez's. He noted Benitez's infectious enthusiasm in mountaineering and the pleasure he derived from "teaching people everything he knew." He had climbed with Benitez on other expeditions and had worked as base camp manager on Everest the year before.

There was Australian Jan Anderson, forty-three, a hospital accountant from Brisbane who had developed a curious passion for mountaineering but was often overcome with fear. Both she and Varcas had climbed with Benitez on Ana Dablam in Nepal the year before, but altitude sickness had forced their retreat. Benitez loved working with clients like Anderson, whom he could imbue with confidence. He regarded Anderson as a "personal project." Despite several attempts, she had never succeeded in reaching the summit of an 8,000-meter peak.

Australian Scott Curtis, thirty-three, a joshing, personal lending manager at a bank in Brisbane, Australia, was backpacking around Asia on a sabbatical and had decided to climb a mountain on a whim. At twenty-four, lanky, fair-skinned Emanuel Smith* was the youngest and most ambitious climber in the group. From the lowlands of Belgium,, Smith was determined to summit Cho Oyu in preparation for Everest.

Kevin Cubitt, a British property developer, was seeking a new direction in life. He felt that a mountaineering expedition would offer some solutions.

With Benitez was assistant guide, Paul Rogers, a Briton who had lived in New Zealand for many years.

---

* Emanuel Smith is a pseudonym.

The day before they left Kathmandu, Benitez sat in the Java House, a Western-style coffee shop above the chaos of the rickshaws and scooters in the streets below, sipping a latte, while he organized final details on a cell phone, fielding regular calls from his boss, Guy Cotter, in New Zealand.

—·—·—

As a child, Benitez had been plagued by chronic asthma and allergies. The son of an Ecuadorian father and American mother, Benitez loathed the onset of summer and its attendant allergens. Benitez looked forward instead to the onset of the cold Missouri winters. The snow and cold brought liberation. For days in the summer, Benitez was confined to his bedroom, during which he scoured old *National Geographic* magazines. In those glossy, color-drenched photos, Benitez discovered a portal to another world. Here were saturated pictures of African chieftains and Amazonian tribes. He was drawn to images of the Himalayan mountain range and the dramatic climbers with their fierce beards and sun-chapped lips.

One issue in particular won Benitez's attention. It featured an extensive spread on the first U.S. Everest expedition led by American Jim Whittaker. When Benitez read that Whittaker had overcome childhood asthma, he tacked a huge Everest poster to his bedroom wall. Benitez decided that he too would explore the celestial reaches of the highest mountains in the world.

Slowly Benitez tested his limits, stealing out of the house surreptitiously to climb the big oak tree in his backyard. High up in the branches, he sat for hours looking out over the roofs of the surrounding houses. Over time, and with a dedicated swimming regimen, Benitez's lungs began to strengthen and his asthma and allergies vanished.

By age eleven, he began to spend a few weeks every summer in Quito, Ecuador, with his aunt. High in the clean mountain air, where he could breathe easily, he felt at home. From his aunt's house, Benitez could see the looming goliath of Cotopaxi, the second-highest peak in the country and the highest active volcano in the world. It arched up from the highland scrub plains, crowned with snow.

When he was sixteen, Benitez decided to climb Cotopaxi, without telling anyone. A half-hour into his climb, Benitez reached the Jose Ribas refuge. He slept until midnight and left on the heels of other summiting teams. Soon, he passed the other groups but was struck by a splitting headache and a wave of nausea that took him to his knees. Overcome by dizziness, he carried on.

At the summit, he circled the volcano, looking down into its volatile depths. At around 5:30 a.m., the dawn broke over the mountain peak. A prism of light haloed the summit. A wave of euphoria rose in Benitez's chest. The mighty Andean cordillera stretched out, partly shielded by black clouds. Below, flashes of lightning and thunderstorms erupted. The raw power of the mountain gave him a sense of self-esteem. The sunlight chafing his skin induced a feeling of invincibility.

—·—

Benitez had been emboldened by Cotopaxi. During spring break from his junior year in college, Benitez declared his intention to go climbing in Europe. His father forbade him to take the trip. Benitez dropped the issue and insinuated that he'd head instead to Colorado.

Benitez was high above the Atlantic enjoying a first-class seat on an American Airlines jet bound for Switzerland by the time his parents discovered his true plans. He had used his father's frequent flyer miles to get the ticket. Benitez climbed every big mountain in the Alps that he could. He climbed the 16,000-foot peak Mont Blanc on the Italian–French border. He hitchhiked to the foot of the notoriously dangerous Eiger and scaled the west side. He crossed the peak to climb the Monk and then the Jungfrau. Climbing solo as he did was highly dangerous.

Benitez's parents' disapproval only furthered his passion. The mountains became a symbol of rebellion from his suburban life. After dropping out of the University of Missouri, he moved to Colorado to work for Outward Bound. Out in the wilderness, Benitez found out that he could be king over powerful company executives. All skinny arms and dressed in tie-dyed T-shirts, he was thrilled to boss around directors of *Fortune* 500 companies on hikes, kayaking trips, and rock-climbing outings in the Rockies. "He went from having no self-esteem, clawing around in the dark, to finding something that he could be passionate about," said Benitez's younger brother David. When he wasn't working for Outward Bound, he lived out of his Honda Civic, staying in campgrounds around the West and climbing.

He progressed up the ranks at Outward Bound, becoming a senior course director. While other instructors had to cut their teeth on smaller mountains in Colorado, Benitez's Spanish won him invitations to guide big mountains in Peru and Ecuador. His father, however, derided him. "You're nothing but a glorified camp counselor," he'd huff.

At twenty-six, Benitez became a guide with Alpine Ascents International, one of the new companies that specialized in leading people up big mountains. Soon enough, he would get the chance to achieve the premier ambition of every climber.

——·—·—

In May 2001, Benitez made his first attempt of Everest leading a blind man, Erik Weihenmayer. Seasoned climbers called the expedition crazy, a foolhardy gimmick that would result in death. Ed Viesturs, the celebrity American mountain climber who reached the summit of Everest six times and who climbed all fourteen of the world's highest peaks, was unequivocal. In an interview with *Men's Journal*, Viesturs said, "More power to him and I support his going but I wouldn't want to take him there myself." He added, "For me the risks are too great. It will be the hardest ever guided ascent of Everest, if they pull it off."[1]

But Benitez saw the expedition as an opportunity to fulfill a dream he had nurtured since childhood. The task at hand: To lead a blind man to the highest point on earth was the ultimate challenge. What better way to prove his credentials as a guide?

Early on in the expedition, it looked as if the naysayers had been right. The first ascent from base camp took thirteen painful and dangerous hours to cross the Khumbu Icefall, a huge, constantly shifting glacier. Crevasses spread open in seconds, sending carefully placed ladders tumbling into the abyss. With such fickle footing, it took no more than the slightest movement to set off a thundering avalanche. In this setting, Weihenmayer could not rely on his advanced sense of touch or hearing to get into a steady climbing rhythm. He had to cross ladders slung across bottomless crevasses. Sometimes his feet would miss the rungs and swing perilously unmoored. Just before they finally reached Camp One, Benitez accidentally cracked Weihenmayer in the face with his ski pole, almost breaking his nose, while helping him cross a crevasse.

Benitez and Weihenmayer were arm in arm when they topped Everest on May 24. On top of the world. Tears rolled down Benitez's face inside his mask. There was a curious sense of oneness. A rebirth. He had the world at his feet.

The yawning sky was deep cerulean. Behind Benitez was Nepal. In front of him, rolling away to the far horizon, embracing the curvature of the earth, was Tibet.

4

ESCAPE

—·—·—

All objects of religious belief and worship in the world—whether in heaven or hell, whether Christian or Buddhist—are the product of people's imagination and do not exist in the reality of practical life.
Official document posted at
Serthar Monastery in Kham

As Dolma jounced down the rutted track, the little pickup's engine groaned. She was startled when she glimpsed Kelsang racing toward her at full speed, waving her arms excitedly. At first light that morning, Dolma had headed out to harvest the family's barley fields with two cousins. Barley was one of the few crops hardy enough to thrive in the arid and rocky topsoil of the plateau. Across the fields, their scythe blades had swung ceaselessly back and forth over the ground.

It was August 2006, the Tibetan year of the Fire Dog. The air was thick with the smell of the loamy earth. As the truck slowed alongside her, Kelsang quivered with excitement. "Come, Dolma!" she cried. "We have to talk. I have something to tell you." She was hopping impatiently from foot to foot.

Dolma bade her cousins farewell and watched as the truck rattled away. Under the vast sky, the two friends were alone. Kelsang's hair was shaved short, and she wore a rosewood rosary on her wrist.

Almost a year had passed since Dolkar's initiation as a nun and her life as Kelsang had begun. After her ordination, Kelsang had fallen asleep in the geshe's antechamber. The following day, the geshe had lectured in the open air. Crowds of people flocked to hear him teach. At 6 p.m., as the shadows lengthened and the crowd dispersed,

Kelsang's parents had appeared with Dolma. When Dolma caught sight of her friend among the cloisters, she ran to her. Kelsang couldn't stop smiling. Dolma choked up, but then caught hold of herself. "You've done it!" Dolma exclaimed.

When Kelsang's parents approached, their eyes fell. Tsedup solemnly asked for the geshe. Kelsang's mother fell in beside him. Kelsang pointed to his quarters, and her father strode off impatiently. Later, Kelsang understood that he had repaid every penny of her borrowed offering.

When he returned, Tsedup cracked a reluctant smile. The geshe had told him that he should be pleased with his daughter's decision. He cast a sidelong glance at Kelsang's mother. "We are both very proud of you," he said. Kelsang dropped her head; the emotion was too much. Her father had pursed his lips and looked at her once more, before turning away to go back to the village.

Now, standing in the road, rivulets of sweat running down her sun-burned face, Kelsang grabbed Dolma's arm. "I have found a way out. We can get to India."

—·—·—

Since her initiation as a Gelugpa novice, Kelsang had grown increasingly frustrated. Only a few nuns were allowed to stay at Dephong Monastery, and the quota was filled. Several years earlier, a group of nuns from Juchen and surrounding villages had built a small, simple nunnery. Chinese authorities had destroyed it and threatened to arrest anyone who attempted to rebuild it. The officials were particularly strict with the Tibetan nuns. The general understanding was that a woman's place was in the home, where she aided productivity. While monks could rely on alms, nuns received no public assistance.

When Kelsang was ten, riots had broken out in Lhasa, when monks and nuns lobbied for Tibetan independence. Scores were beaten, and others were shot dead in the streets. Many later died in prisons. In the Barkhor district of Lhasa, several nuns had been arrested and sentenced to prison terms for peacefully demonstrating for Tibetan independence. Brutally tortured in Drapchi prison, fourteen nuns secretly recorded songs on a smuggled tape recorder in praise of the Dalai Lama to show people outside that their spirits were not broken. After their songs reached Tibetan nongovernmental organizations (NGOs) in the West they were made into CDs. But the nuns were caught and, in 1993, were given extended sentences of five to nine years. In 1998 they refused to sing songs in praise of Chairman Mao on the eve of a visit by EU officials. Five nuns were later found dead after weeks of torture. Some speculated that they may have died due to the severity of their torture while rumors abounded that they had taken their own lives in desperation.

Of the six hundred Tibetan political prisoners at the end of the 1990s, one-quarter to one-third were nuns. In 2008, 62 percent of the 715 Tibetan political prisoners were monks or nuns, although the numbers fluctuated wildly.[1] The International Commission of Jurists stated in a 1997 report that "women, particularly nuns, appear to be subjected to some of the harshest, and gender-specific, torture, including rape using electric cattle prods and ill treatment of breasts."[2]

The same year that Kelsang had taken her vows, 2005, the Chinese authorities launched a crackdown. "Strike Hard" campaigns had been part of recurrent purges on illegality all over China. But in Tibet, they took an antireligious dimension as dragnets specifically targeted the clerical community for infractions of the rules.

Since local officials had taken note of Kelsang's shaven head, she had come under increased scrutiny. Now a potential target of the authorities for the draconian rules that bound those in the clerical life, Kelsang had to practice her faith alone and in secret. Isolated and without a spiritual teacher, Kelsang felt at a loss. She longed to be part of a working nunnery. Increasingly, Kelsang felt that the only way to be truly free was to escape to India where she could study her faith. Beyond the mountains that cut her off from the rest of the world, Kelsang imagined freedom, a long way from the drab Communist system on the arid plateau.

When Dolma had sometimes raised the idea of going to India over the years growing up, her brother scoffed, chiding her for being selfish: She was needed at home. Dolma had stayed out of political discussions much of her life. She lived in one of the most repressive countries in the world, a place where arbitrary arrests, detentions, and horrendous human rights abuses were common. But, for the most part, Dolma had been largely untouched by the oppressive boot of communism. Her life was good. However, with Kelsang's unwavering dedication to the spiritual life and determination to reach India, and Dolma's unwavering loyalty to her friend, she found herself drawn into the plot to run to India.

In daily life Dolma began to notice things that had previously escaped her. Her grandfather, a tall, garrulous man, often went away for extended periods. When he returned, he was withdrawn. As a former tribal chief who had been active in thwarting the Chinese in the early years of the invasion, he was a constant target of the authorities for questioning and detentions as a counterrevolutionary.

— .— —

In 1949, a comet had streaked across the Tibetan sky. The highest lamas interpreted it as a visit from the god Rahul, a serpent that swallows the sun and the moon as he inspires terror. In 1947, the State Oracle had prophesied that the Year of the Iron Tiger, 1950, would bring great trouble to Tibet. On a sunny day in Lhasa, water inexplicably flowed out of a gargoyle on the roof of the central cathedral. Shortly afterward, forty blasts ricocheted from the ground across the sky near Sera Monastery in Lhasa. The fifth-largest earthquake in the history of the world shook 1,200 miles across Tibet. It was felt as far away as Calcutta.

A cataclysmic force was about to invade Tibet. On October 1, 1949, Chairman Mao Zedung, leader of the Red Army, had established the Communist People's Republic of China (PRC) after years of bloody revolution. Next, his sights were trained on Tibet. Mao saw that the key to dominating Asia was annexing Tibet. To cement Tibet to China not only would "close the back door" against Western powers like Britain, the United States, and Russia but would offer a crucial strategic point from which to wage war. Tibet contained an abundance of natural resources. For China, which contained only 7 percent of the world's arable land but 22 percent of the world's population, Tibet offered a rich resource of water, largely untapped minerals, and, most importantly, land.

On the dawn of October 7, 1950, the 52nd, 53rd, and 54th divisions of the 18th army of the Red Army—some 40,000 troops—invaded eastern Tibet to liberate the country from "foreign imperialists." There were, in fact, few foreigners in Tibet at the time: Robert Ford and Reginald Fox, who were working as radio operators in Chamdo; the Austrian mountaineers Heinrich Harrer and Peter Aufschnaiter; and Geoffrey Bull, an English missionary.

Woefully naive, the Tibetans lay like lambs before hungry wolves. As the Dalai Lama later admitted, the Tibetans' religious conviction had disarmed their ability to retaliate against the Chinese threat. As he put it, "Believing the country would be saved without human effort, through prayers alone, resulted from limited knowledge. From this point of view religious sentiment actually became an obstacle."[3]

The Tibetans called for help from the West and India. But centuries of thwarting entry into The Land of Snows and refusing communication with the outside world would cost Tibet its freedom.

As the Chinese quickly took over the country in the subsequent years, the Dalai Lama continued to try to recruit help from the West and India. But the Chinese asserted boldly that Tibet was their problem and not the concern of outside forces. Britain, the United States, and India pretended that they didn't really know that Tibet was an independent country (Britain actually had a treaty recognizing Tibetan sovereignty). The Dalai Lama and his officials lodged appeals to the United Nations in 1959, 1961, and 1965. These were met with resolutions that expressed 'anxiety' or 'grave concern' and even the acknowledgement that Tibet had the right to 'self-determination'; yet, ultimately, the UN did nothing.

In the years following the invasion, Mao eliminated any Tibetans who resisted through violence, brutal suppression, and programs like the Cultural Revolution and the Great Leap Forward. In the village of Doi in Amdo, northeastern Tibet, three hundred landowners were assembled and shot from behind. This, soldiers told the villagers who'd been forced to watch, was the punishment for resisting communism. Tibetans were dragged to death behind horses or thrown to their deaths from airplanes. Children were forced to shoot their parents. Monks and nuns were tortured and crucified. Abbots were ordered to eat their own feces. Sacred texts were used as toilet paper. Some threw themselves into the river to drown themselves rather than denounce the Dalai Lama.

The International Commission of Jurists, a group of lawyers and judges from fifty nations, released a scathing report in 1959, "The Question of Tibet and the Rule of Law," that declared China's treatment of Tibet an uncontestable genocide.

Amdo was turned into a gulag. Hundreds of thousands of Tibetans died of starvation or as a result of the violent occupation of their homeland and the rigors of the Great Leap Forward.

During the Cultural Revolution, the "Four Olds"—old customs, old culture, old habits, and old ideas—were destroyed as the Chinese attempted to eliminate any notion of an independent country. Lamas were publicly mocked, harassed, and executed. Sacred Buddhist paintings were burned to ashes, monasteries were razed, books torched. Afterward, some villagers were forced to watch flickering reels of Chinese propaganda on the "emancipation of Tibet" on movie screens set up in the fields in the village.

Dolma's grandfather had lived through these terrors. A tribal chief, his gold and turquoise had been confiscated and redistributed to others in the village by Chinese officials. He saw neighbor turn on neighbor, barbaric torture unleashed on those the Red Guards deemed "landlords." In the Cultural Revolution, PLA units went door-to-door taking away land and personal possessions in the first tide of "collectivization." Landowners, nobles, and monks were subject to *thamzing* or "struggle sessions." Signs were hung around their necks, and beggars, who had been promoted to "diligent ones" by the Chinese, beat them. In these interrogations, Tibetans were forced to admit to "crimes against the people." Such confessions met with execution. Foreigners were forbidden to enter the region because they might be witnesses to the mass killing and famine taking place. A massive iron curtain was drawn down on Tibet.

Although the Cultural Revolution ended in China by 1976, the brutal religious persecution continues in modern Tibet.

—·—·—

An attempt to escape from Tibet almost fifty years after the Chinese takeover would be perilous. Dolma and Kelsang would have to find an illegal guide, a "snakehead" who could smuggle them out of the country past the ubiquitous Chinese checkpoints into Nepal and then India. To do so, they would have to cross over the Himalaya.

There are seven or eight mountain escape routes of varying difficulty along thirty-four mountain passes or trails between Tibet and Nepal. Getting out of Tibet depends on how successfully the security apparatus of a sophisticated network of informants, undercover PSB officers, and paramilitary and military checkpoints is evaded. Mountain passes are heavily patrolled by the Wujing,[4] who have orders—under Article 322 of the Chinese Criminal Code—to arrest and, if necessary, kill anyone caught "secretly crossing" the national boundary. Punishment is wildly arbitrary but, at minimum, is a few months of imprisonment in a dank border prison.

More likely than capture is death at the hands of Chinese border police. Killings like that of fifteen-year-old Yeshe Dundrub, shot at night in Saga County (Ch: Saga Xian) in November 1999, while fleeing with forty others to Nepal, are covered up when possible. (Dundrub, whose dream was to be a monk, died in a military hospital bed nine hours after he was shot.)

The easiest passage to Nepal is through Dram (Ch: Zhangmu), an industrial hub on the border between Tibet and Nepal. Often refugees obtain fake border-crossing permits or are smuggled out in trucks crossing the border. Other routes lie near the Nepal regions of Mustang or Humla. Beyond are increasingly dangerous high-mountain crossings.

There *is* another passage in the high Himalaya: A natural mountain path of ice at 19,000 feet that empties into Nepal. More unforgiving than some other passes out of Tibet, the Nangpa La has been since the eighth century a fabled passage for traders and anyone wanting in or out of Tibet. In the past century it has become a conduit for both trade and smuggling. Among Tibetans, *Nangpa* means "insider." It refers to Buddhists and Tibetans who consider themselves 'insiders' compared to outsiders, *phyipa*, who are not Buddhists.[5] *La* means "pass." The Nangpa La was, aside from a smuggling route, a glacial superhighway for pilgrimage to holy sites in India and Nepal.

According to legend, the sage Padmasambhava had hidden in several valleys in the Himalaya. The Nangpa La led to one such refuge—one that connected to the Solu Khumbu region in Nepal, a so-called *Beyul*—a sacred sanctuary for Tibetans. It was also a region long inhabited by sherpas from eastern Tibet, who now made their living as porters for Westerners' climbing expeditions. According to Buddhist history, Padmasambhava had also buried scrolls on Cho Oyu, the mountain that overlooked the Nangpa La, to protect the world from chaos.

Tibetan physiology offers enormous advantages in a hostile environment. Chinese soldiers cannot tolerate the Nangpa La's oxygen-poor air. Here, Tibetans can outdo the Chinese military machine with its satellite imaging, cellular communications, and assault rifle-toting police. They do so simply because they are mountain people, capable of coping with conditions that bring lowlander Han Chinese soldiers and Western mountaineers to their knees.*

By the 1970s, the Nangpa La had become the number one escape route.

The only Westerner to have successfully crossed the Nangpa La is Swiss photographer Manuel Bauer, who trekked over the pass with a Tibetan father and his six-year-old daughter. After almost expiring from exhaustion, cold, hunger, and thirst, Bauer reached Nepal, but collapsed after his three-week ordeal, passing grossly bloody urine. The father had tried to amputate his frostbitten toe with a rusty razor blade. "If I attempted it today, I would almost certainly die," Bauer said. "I was very lucky to make it out alive. My brain stopped working on the pass; I became delirious, the air was so thin. It was so cold, it's impossible to describe. Your body starts shutting down. And there's a constant fear you will be caught."

Bauer made his trek in 1995. In the 1990s, China had an unofficial policy of turning a blind eye to escapees, perhaps reasoning that it would be easier to take over the country if many Tibetans left. By 2006, with

---

* Over centuries, Tibetans have developed broader arteries that deliver oxygen to their muscles twice as fast as Westerners' arteries. Their blood vessels are lined with nitric oxide, which causes the arteries to expand and deliver crucial oxygen-freighted blood to the body faster than normal. And their circulations produce antioxidants to cope with the nitric oxide in their bloodstreams. Also, Tibetans literally breathe more, averaging more breaths per minute, than people born at sea level.

the Beijing Olympics looming in 2008, refugees escaping from Chinese-occupied Tibet ruined China's carefully constructed image. Refugees were bad for business. They were to be stopped at all costs.

By 2006, the Nangpa La was more fiercely patrolled than ever before.

— · — · —

Kelsang and Dolma were only to learn of their route out of Tibet at the last moment. If their path was the Nangpa La, they were guaranteed a brutal trip that could take from two to six weeks. During that time, they would encounter freezing snow, minus-forty-degree temperatures, and perilous, snow-disguised crevasses. They would have to cross three countries and two national boundaries, largely undercover.

Once out of Tibet, over the border into Nepal, they would still be in grave danger. In recent years the Chinese assiduously courted Nepal with large sums of money and trained its military in an increasingly close relationship. The Nepalese border security forces, for their part, were corrupt and dangerous, sometimes raping Tibetan refugees when they could. The Chinese paid them bounties for the arrest and return of Tibetan refugees to China. So they too ran networks of informants and hunted refugees when they crossed the border en route to India. And they aided the People's Armed Police (PAP) when the Chinese soldiers crossed the border illegally to capture Tibetans.

Aside from the danger of hostile soldiers and police, crossing the Himalaya into Nepal was the sort of trip an experienced mountaineer, loaded with gear, would think twice about. Twenty-eight refugees had once made a January attempt on the Nangpa La and were buried under avalanches. Three children died before reaching Nepal and were left buried in the snow. Another three or four with blackened, frostbitten limbs required emergency surgery when they got to Kathmandu.

The PAP had standing orders to shoot any refugee discovered trying to cross the Nangpa La. In October 2005, thirty Tibetans had attempted the journey. Where the Himalayas descend into rocky grasslands near Tingri, in Shigatse prefecture, soldiers surrounded the refugees and opened fire. Only three escaped; the rest were captured, imprisoned, and tortured.

Two nuns, Sonam Nyima and Pema Wangdu, had been among the group. Their wrists were crudely tied with rope, and they were bundled into the back of military trucks. They were later beaten, tortured with electric batons, interrogated, photographed, and imprisoned at Shigatse Prison for three months.

Dolma and Kelsang knew the nuns. Kelsang had listened intently as the young women told their story one day, warning how dangerous the journey was. But Kelsang's determination to escape was undiminished. "It won't happen to us," she reassured Dolma.

—·—·—

Escape details were closely guarded secrets. Normally, people simply vanished without a word. Across the mountains, a profitable, highly dangerous escape industry of guides and safe houses existed. Like Western climbers who depended on a network for access to the mountains, Tibetans who wanted to escape relied on their own. Some of those in the underground network were driven by profit. Others were motivated by genuine altruism.

For months, Kelsang had pestered every monk and nun she knew for news of groups leaving Tibet. Those in the religious order inevitably knew someone who was going to Dharamsala to receive a blessing from His Holiness. Initially, Kelsang found a group willing to take her, but not Dolma. She packed in secret. But she got no further than the outskirts of the village when her father caught her and sent her home with a scolding. On another occasion, her cousin offered to take her along when she escaped to India. Weeks after, Kelsang discovered that her cousin had left covertly.

Kelsang was obsessed with the journey. When her friend Thinley Wangmo, a fellow nun who prayed at the same monastery, got as far as Lhasa and then turned back because she felt sick, Kelsang teased her. As they sat cross-legged in the monastery chanting, she slipped her friend notes, "What are you going to do if you can't make it to India?" Kelsang's eyes twinkled mischievously.

One day Kelsang was crossing the Salween to go to Driru when she learned from a group of nuns that a monk was organizing a journey. After searching over the next few days, Kelsang found him in Driru. At first, the monk refused to take her because including too many people would compromise the safety of the group. But Kelsang persisted. Eventually, he agreed. As a safeguard, he told her only on the day he was planning to leave. "You had better find your friend and come to Driru tonight," he said. "This is the only chance you are going to get." Kelsang didn't hear the last sentence before she was dashing off to find Dolma.

—.—.—

Kelsang and Dolma had discussed their escape often, with vague plans to return to Tibet when it was free of Chinese control. They hoped to study Tibetan in India and to meet His Holiness. Dolma reasoned that once she got to India, she might become a nun. But she couldn't match her friend's fervor for the religious life.

When Kelsang told her parents she wanted to leave for India to see the Dalai Lama, they were vehemently opposed, worried for their daughter's safety. But Kelsang, as was her way, pestered them relentlessly. She pointed out that two nuns had left Juchen six weeks earlier. When they made safe passage to India—about four hundred miles as the crow flies—they had called to report their success. Excited villagers had gathered around the telephone to hear the news, as the nuns crowed about seeing His Holiness. Eventually, Kelsang's parents' attitude toward their daughter's plan softened.

—.—.—

The smell of freshly cut barley hung in the air. "We have to go tonight!" Kelsang urged as she scanned her friend's face for an answer. Kelsang waited for Dolma's answer. "Alright," she agreed, a smile blossoming across her face. There was little time. They would need money, clothes, and food.

When they arrived at Dolma's home, her brother Rinzin was outside painting the house. The pressure from the Chinese at the monastery had been too much for him. He had reluctantly returned to secular life.

Nyima was out back tending her herb garden. Her hands were full of freshly plucked radishes when the girls emerged. They stood before her, side-by-side, shoulders touching.

"Come on," entreated Nyima. "What is it?" Kelsang nudged Dolma, who slowly looked up. "I'm going to India," Dolma told her mother. Nyima let Dolma's words hang in the air. She suspected that one day her daughter would ask her this.

"Have you decided this for yourself?" Nyima asked evenly. "If you've decided just because other people are going, then I'm not going to let you go." There was a pause. Dolma stiffened as she returned her mother's gaze. "If you have made the decision yourself, and it is really your choice, then you can go," Nyima reassured. Before she would offer her daughter her final blessing, Nyima told Dolma that she had to get the geshe's approval.

Rinzin stopped painting and peered around the house suspiciously, sensing something was up. Nyima chided him to go back to work when he questioned his mother about what his sister was doing. She flashed Dolma a conspiratorial glance.

The girls had little time. It was noon, and everyone who was going to Driru for the day had left. Kelsang's father was still at home. During the previous weeks, his attitude had softened. Slowly, he had realized that Kelsang was not going to give up on her dream of getting a nun's education in India. He agreed to take the girls to the geshe. All three clambered aboard his red Yamaha motorcycle and jolted their way to Driru.

In town, the girls had to confirm their place with the group, but they could not speak openly about India. They scampered around the market in search of the monk. Finally they spotted him, a compact man loitering near a stall. Kelsang was about to ask him about India but hesitated. They decided to follow him at a safe distance until they could speak safely.

As they bided their time, they ran into a distant relative of Kelsang's, also a monk, with whom she had a passing acquaintance. Kelsang asked him to see if the other monk was leaving for India. When he reported back, he shook his head.

Kelsang and Dolma went to a teahouse where they fell into dejected silence. "Let's ask the geshe!" Kelsang suddenly exclaimed determinedly. She wasn't giving up. "He will know if we are meant to go or not. And if it is so, then we shall."

They hurried to Choeling Monastery. During the summer, the geshe who had initiated Kelsang had gone on a retreat, locking himself away for months, deep in meditation, with little food. He had been back at the monastery only a month. Sagging skin hung from his thin arms, and his face was sunken. Kelsang began to babble excitedly about the impending trip. The geshe closed his eyes and rocked back and forth for a minute or two. He told the girls to chant. From beneath his bed, he withdrew an ornate wooden box. From it, he took two bright-red silk protection cords that were knotted in the middle. "You have to be careful," he warned soberly. "Wear these threads to protect yourselves. Chant the Vajra Guru [a Buddhist verse] any time you are in danger." He beckoned the girls closer and touched each of their foreheads with the cords before laying them in their palms.

"You will be able to go," said the geshe. "This is the right time. You will be safe." The girls got to their feet, bowed, and left. Dolma cast her eyes back over her shoulder to take one last look. The geshe's scrawny legs were folded beneath him, his eyes were half closed, and he was once again lost in meditation.

The girls asked several monks who else might be headed to India. There was another monk who seemed to know more than he would let on. Pema, a short, affable monk, was always surrounded by a small crowd. The girls couldn't raise such a delicate matter in their presence. There was nothing to do but lounge uneasily in the sun. As they waited for the crowd to thin, Tsedup appeared. Kelsang pointed to Pema and explained why they were waiting to talk with him. Her father nodded and strode abruptly over to the monk, taking him aside. After five minutes, Tsedup returned. "It has been agreed," he said. "Someone will take you." He confirmed they would be leaving at midnight and that two jeeps would be waiting behind Dolma's house.

Pema appeared by their side. "When you leave, you must not carry lots of things and you must not dress in clothes which give away where you are going," he hissed to Kelsang. "When your family says goodbye, don't cry." Being seen embracing one's family in a tearful goodbye would mean only one thing to a curious onlooker.

When Dolma returned home with the geshe's blessing, Nyima headed off on her bicycle to call in the debts the family was owed. Dolma went to say a farewell to her grandfather and aunt, and they gave her pictures of themselves to take to relatives in India. Her grandfather tucked 800 yuan ($120) into her hand. "Be careful," he warned as he hugged Dolma goodbye.

Dolma returned home to find her mother counting out money on the kitchen table. She had a thick wad of notes, some 15,000 yuan (around $2,000). She handed out 12,000 for Dolma. In rural Tibet, 12,000 yuan was the result of several years' work.

Next door, Kelsang's mother was desperately trying to hold her emotions in check. She had coped with Kelsang's ordination and her willful pursuit of a religious life, but the thought of a dangerous escape through a threatening landscape was hard to bear. From his pocket, Tsedup produced 800 yuan, which he pressed into his daughter's palm.

The two families walked outside. It was midnight and bitter cold. All scanned the streets nervously, looking for Chinese officials. The girls were dressed simply in what few warm clothes they had. Both were wearing sturdy, black boots and brown Chinese-made down jackets. They had one bag between them.

Slowly, they made their way to two idling jeeps. Dolma walked a few steps behind her mother, emotion welling in her chest.

Pema stood beside a filthy white jeep. Rinzin stood nearby. He awkwardly wiped his hands on his trousers when he saw his sister. He told her to be careful. "Remember me when you meet His Holiness," he said. Dolma nodded silently.

In total, there were ten individuals—from Juchen and nearby villages—escaping. Five local youths, most in their twenties, were waiting nervously. Dolma recognized some of them. There was Dorje, a twenty-seven-year-old who taught Tibetan dancing, and Palden, a nomad, who planned to return home after meeting the Dalai Lama. And Nuba, who was journeying to Sera Monastery° in southern India to continue his religious studies.

Dolma could see her mother's eyes were filled with tears. Kelsang's stalwart father was fighting back his emotions.

"Hurry," Pema urged. As Kelsang and Dolma climbed into the jeep, they were met with the stares of three timid nuns in the backseat. The faces belonged to Thinley Wangmo, a tall, willowy girl in her early twenties who had once tried to escape and turned back; Lobsang Samten, the tiny nun who had taken her vows to escape an arranged marriage; and Tenzin Choetso.

The girls' relatives huddled together, not waving, as the jeeps inched out onto the road. Dolma tried to snatch a last glimpse of her mother through the filthy windows. But the darkness had swallowed everything. All she could see was black.

° Monasteries in exile are named after corresponding monasteries in Tibet. Sera Monastery also existed in Lhasa.

5

FORBIDDEN KINGDOM

—.—.—

To-morrow, when we enter Lhasa, we will have
unveiled the last mystery of the East. There are no
more forbidden cities which men have not mapped
and photographed. Our children will laugh at
modern travellers' tales. They will have to turn again
to Gulliver and Haroun al Easchid. And they will
soon tire of these. For now that there are no real
mysteries, no unknown land of dreams, where there
may still be genii and mahatmas and bottle-imps,
that kind of literature will be tolerated no longer.
Children will be sceptical and matter of fact and dis-
illusioned, and there will be no sale for fairy-stories
any more. But we ourselves are children. Why could
we not have left at least one city out of bounds?
    Edmund Candler, The Unveiling of Lhasa

Luis Benitez settled into the soft seat of an Air China Airbus 319 as
a flight attendant in a starched uniform served him a freshly chilled
Coke. Below, the first snow-capped peaks of the Himalaya were visible.

Mountaineers called this the "million-dollar flight." It was a one-hour
plane ride from the dusty confusion of Kathmandu over the Himalayan
range to Lhasa, the Forbidden City on the edge of the Tibetan plateau.

Benitez was calm as he gazed out of the portside window at the
corrugated sea of Himalayan peaks. There was Cho Oyu, the turquoise
goddess. Next to Cho Oyu, he caught a lingering look at the east face
of Everest. It knifed up into the jet stream more defiant and lawless
than ever.

—.—.—

In the nineteenth century, explorers had raced to reach the North and South Poles. Tibet had comprised a sort of third pole. It had been a piece in the "Great Game," the race between the world's superpowers—Britain and Russia—for territory in Central Asia. After colonizing India, the British Empire had expanded northward. Tsarist Russia spread south. Between them lay miles of unexplored deserts and mountains.

The ancient trade routes of the Silk Road had joined Europe with Asia through Tibet. Traders in long caravans laden with silk, spices, and gold threaded through barren mountain passes crossing the fearsome Altun Shan Mountains in far northern Tibet and the barren Taklamakan desert (now in Xinjinag Uyghur Autonomous Region). If they survived, traders pressed on through the Hindu Kush into Afghanistan, Iran, and Europe. The Kunlun Mountains in northern Tibet were so perilous that even bandits avoided them.

The most alluring part of the Great Game was the discovery of the fabled mountain theocracy of Tibet, "the missing piece of the imperial chessboard." To Victorian explorers, Tibet was a mythical land. Early on, the British undertook a project to map India and Central Asia for the Great Trigonometric Survey of India in 1802. In 1852, they determined that Everest was the world's highest peak. Tibetans, without measuring instruments, already knew the peak's dominant status. They called it simply Qomolangma, goddess mother of the world.

Those that pressed to discover what was beyond Everest rarely came back. The harshness of the terrain and climate along with the tribes and brigands who ruled the mountain passes in Afghanistan, Pakistan, and Tibet could quickly snuff out a life. When Andrew Dagleish, a Scottish explorer and trader with the Central Asia Trading Company, attempted to map the desolate regions of northern Tibet in the late 1880s, he was hacked to death by a towering Afghan on the Karakoram Pass (between China and modern-day Pakistan). In Rudyard Kipling's *Kim*— a novel about a boy who befriends a lama on the path to enlightenment during the Great Game—agent E23 tells the book's hero, "We of the Game are beyond protection. If we die, we die. Our names are blotted from the book. That is all."

But to many, the lure of Tibet offered the unrivalled thrill of the great unknown. It was erotic in its appeal. The English magazine *The Spectator* described Tibet as "the woman's apartment of the world." One Briton compared it to "the modern Brunhilde asleep on her mountain top." A slew of books with titles like *Lhasa and Its Mysteries* or *Tibet, the Mysterious* became bestsellers. According to Sir Henry Cotton, M.P., for many young officers in India in 1903, "the glamour of the Forbidden City was irresistible."

At the turn of the twentieth century, European and Russian explorers disguised themselves to reach Lhasa. Legendary Swedish explorer Sven Hedin, dressed as a lama, his skin darkened with fat and soot, was stopped by a Tibetan militia at Tengri Nor, just five days from Lhasa. Armed with a proclamation from the thirteenth Dalai Lama, the militia was instructed to block any foreigners' entrance into the "kingdom of holy books." Hedin later became close to the Nazi regime and also Mao Zedung, relationships that marred his formidable legacy as an explorer. Tibet though had consumed him. Every attempt to reach Lhasa was thwarted by Tibetans, who shunned contact with the outside world.

Eventually, British officers hit on the idea of entering Tibet with highly trained Indian spies skilled in the use of sextants, compasses, and astronomy. The "pundits," as they became known, trained in making an exact stride of thirty-three inches, whatever the terrain, up or downhill. With such a reliable gait, they were able to calculate on an adapted hundred-bead rosary the measure of a half-mile.

Nain Singh, a schoolmaster from a Himalayan village, took on several disguises as he braved brigands, high passes, and meetings with Tibetan panjandrums before he eventually made it to Lhasa. He recorded its location as 29 degrees and 41 minutes, staggeringly accurate. (Today, Google Earth records it at 29° 39 N91° 07 E.) When he entered the famed city on the roof of the world, he was shocked to find a stygian hellhole.

Scores of men died in the process. Sarat Chandra Das entered Tibet in 1879 and 1881, bringing back political and military intelligence to his English bosses. When the Tibetans learned that the Sengchen Lama of Shigatse, the chief minister, had helped Das, he was denounced as a traitor and publicly flogged. His servants had their hands and feet cut off and their eyes gouged out; his family was imprisoned for life. After his flogging, the lama was sewn alive into a yak-hide sack and thrown in the Tsangpo River.

British spies were successful in mapping one million miles of unknown territory within Tibet. Frustrated at their inability to conquer the country, the British eventually resorted to savage force. Sir Francis Younghusband was a British officer who had once crossed the Gobi Desert and then the mighty Mustagh Pass; at 19,000 feet, the trail demarcated the border between India and China. He had used reins knotted with turbans for ropes and a hefty pickaxe in one of the most daring feats of early mountaineering. He was the man chosen for the job. Younghusband set out at the head of a massive caravan with 1,100 troops, 10,000 porters, thousands of pack animals, and two ten-pounder screw guns, called Bubble and Squeak. Younghusband took enough clothing to fill twenty-nine containers. Eighty-eight porters died of frostbite and exhaustion on the barren journey up to the plateau.

In a valley at Tuna, seventy-five miles south of Gyantse, the Tibetans found that the scraps of paper from the Dalai Lama they wore in charm boxes around their necks were no protection against the 1,400 machine-gun rounds, 50 shrapnel shells, and 14,351 rifle rounds of Young-husband's invading army. Within four minutes, 700 Tibetans were mown down. "I got so sick of the slaughter that I ceased fire, though the General's order was to make as big a bag as possible," Lieutenant Hadow, operator of the Maxim guns, wrote in a letter home. "I hope I shall never have to shoot down men walking away again."[1]

On August 1, 1904, Younghusband marched triumphantly into Lhasa through the west gate of the Forbidden City. After 3,000 deaths, Younghusband saw himself as a liberator of oppressed backward people. He puffed out his chest when he saw Tibetans lining the streets and clapping at the sight of the army. What Young-husband didn't realize was that the clapping was not applause, but the Tibetans' efforts to ward off evil spirits. The Dalai Lama had fled to Mongolia.

Younghusband was profoundly affected by Tibet and the lamas who preached compassion. He later renounced his military life to become a religious mystic. "I gave myself up to the emotions of this eventful time," he wrote after leaving Lhasa the last time. "This exhilaration of the moment grew and grew till it thrilled through me with overpowering intensity. Never again could I think evil or ever be at enmity with any man. All nature and all humanity were bathed in a rosy glowing radiancy. . . . [T]hat single hour on leaving Lhasa was worth all the rest of a lifetime."[2] In 1936, he founded the World Congress of Faiths, an ecumenical organization.

After conquering Tibet, Younghusband was appointed president of the Royal Geographic Society in 1919 and soon after organized the first Everest expeditions in the 1920s. From Khamba Dzong, once a staging point for his invasion of Tibet, he orchestrated the first attempt on Everest summit by George Leigh Mallory.

The Chinese have used the example of Younghusband's invasion of Tibet to warn of "Western imperialism." Today, in the huge fort to the south of Gyantse near the site of the Younghusband massacre is a dingy commemoration, "the Memorial Hall of Anti British." Murals depict British savagery, while a film loop plays *Red River Valley*, a feature film that depicts Tibetans and Chinese resisting the evils of British imperialism.

— · — · —

The race to climb mountains has always had a messy, uneasy relationship with politics. The first reconnaissance missions for Everest under Younghusband were made only after the Dalai Lama gave permission. In exchange, Sir Charles Bell, the first European to be invited to Lhasa, promised the Dalai Lama a cache of weapons. But in 1925, the thirteenth Dalai Lama grew weary of the intrusive Western climbers and banned them from Everest for ten years.

Today, summiting the Himalayan peaks has become mired in controversy and commercialism. In the 1950s, Sir Edmund Hillary and Tenzin Norgay, with dashing exploratory brio, had amazed the world with their ascent of Everest. At the time, conquering Everest was the equivalent of reaching the moon.

A host of Europeans raced to make their mark on the Himalaya. The Germans were obsessed with Nanga Parbat, the Italians and Americans with K2, and the British with Everest. Ardito Desio, who successfully conquered K2, encouraged his team onward with the inspiring reminder, "If you succeed in scaling the peak," he said, "the entire world will hail you as champions of your race."[3]

Having established their authority in Tibet, the Chinese maintained control of all Western mountaineering expeditions and largely forbade access to the Himalaya from the north side. Inspired by a growing relationship with the Soviet Union, which had nurtured an interest in mountaineering at the height of the Cold War, the Chinese turned to the Tibetan peaks. A successful Chinese ascent of Everest would bolster their claims of Tibetan sovereignty. With customary Communist zeal, the Chinese hammered out a two-hundred-mile road from Lhasa to Rongbuk Monastery, which was completed in March 1959. That same month, a bloody uprising broke out in Tibet and the Dalai Lama fled into exile.

In spring 1960, the Chinese trucked in six tons of equipment and enough tents to house an army of 214 climbers at Everest Base Camp to conquer the mountain. They erected huge placards dictating Communist doctrine to remind workers of their duty in these far reaches: "Heroes rise into heaven with a loud laugh at Qomolangma down below" and "Man will triumph over nature." Such sentiments were sacrilegious to Tibetans and shocking to Western climbers. Legend has it that when a team of Chinese climbers made it to the summit on May 25, 1960, they left a bust of Chairman Mao wrapped in the Chinese flag (although the summit claim has often been contested).[4]

After the first Chinese-led climb to the summit of Everest, the Chinese denied most climbers access to the Himalaya by the northern Tibet approach. They wanted no Westerners as potential witnesses to their military offensives. And the paranoia of the Cold War made them jittery.

In the meantime, during the 1950s, Nepal opened its borders to mountaineers. The Nepalese monarchy led by King Tribhuvan feared Communist China's intentions on its borders and sought a way to curry favor with Western powers. Allowing access to Western mountaineers was a way to develop diplomatic ties and bring in revenue.

— · — · —

As more mountaineers attempted to climb the Himalaya, climbing styles and methods evolved. The sixties saw an era of "super expeditions"— teams of eighty to a hundred-fifty climbers. The seventies saw so-called siege climbing replaced by alpine-style climbing, where more focus was placed on solo athletic ability. Advances in clothing and equipment allowed climbers to eschew snaking trains of porters laden with supplies and equipment. Elite climbers like Reinhold Messner, who first climbed Everest without oxygen in 1978, used lightweight gear to move up and down the mountain quickly.

Perhaps the best mountaineer ever, Messner considered reaching the highest peaks as fulfillment of his spiritual quest. As he told *National Geographic* in 2006: "I am sure that the key to understanding climbing is the coming back. It means if you are really in difficult places, in dangerous places, if you are in . . . thin air, and you come back, you feel that you got again a chance for life. You are reborn. And only in this moment, you understand deeply that life is the biggest gift we have."[5]

The first commercial teams attempting Himalayan peaks in the eighties ushered in an age of moneyed, amateur climbers and a new "extreme sports" buzz. In 1985, climbing novice Dick Bass, a super-moneyed, fifty-five-year-old from Texas, was escorted to the top of Everest. He was guided by a controversial, brash young climber, David Breashears, who facilitated an age of egoism and commercialism in the Himalaya. As Rob Buchanan wrote in *Men's Journal* magazine, "With the exception of Edmund Hillary and Jon Krakauer, there may not be anybody who's done more than David Breashears to make Mount Everest into the media phenomenon, and tourist magnet that it is today."[6]

The focus had switched from the quiet nobility of climbers like Sir Edmund Hillary to the individual as superman, conquering the summits. The bloody-minded ruthlessness needed to reach the top of

8,000-meter goliaths imbued a narcissism and rampant egoism among solo climbers that began to overshadow the mountains themselves.

By the early nineties, a slew of commercial outfitters were jostling to take eager clients to the summit of Himalayan peaks if they were willing to pay the price. Increasingly, inexperienced climbers began to attempt mountains like Everest, with deathly consequences. The Nepali government had already realized Everest was a major financial asset, raising climbing permits sevenfold to $70,000 for a party of up to seven and $10,000 for each additional climber.

In May 1996, thirty expeditions crowded around the base of Everest. Most of the climbers were inexperienced neophytes. Manhattan socialite Sandy Hill Pittman, a former New York fashion editor, had sherpas carry a coffee machine that made cappuccinos to base camp along with her more important climbing gear. Texan pathologist Beck Weathers, fifty-six, hadn't told Adventure Consultants expedition leader Rob Hall before the climb that he had recently undergone eye surgery. Around the South Col, a good distance up the mountain, he lost his vision entirely and admitted to Hall that he had undergone an operation and that he urgently needed to descend.

The ropes used for the steepest legs of the climb had not been fixed—an oversight that required everyone to wait an hour while sherpas installed them. Thirty-three climbers were bottlenecked in the death zone, sucking down vital oxygen and fighting the extreme cold as they stood waiting for lines to free. A few climbers managed to stagger on to the summit before turning around and returning to camp. Three hours later, a howling blizzard struck Everest's southwest face. Climbers were stranded, unable to make out the trail back to the safety of the tents at Camp IV as the temperature plummeted and winds kicked up. In such whiteout conditions, it was impossible for anyone to see a hand in front of his face.

Doug Hansen, an American postal worker who labored in two jobs to afford his dream of Everest, died. Andy Harris made a brave attempt at rescue, only to be lost in the void. Hall, unable to traverse the ropes down with badly frostbitten hands and feet, slumped to the ground. His regulator was choked with ice. At 9 a.m., he radioed base camp and asked them to relay his final farewell to his wife Jan in New Zealand, who was pregnant with their first child. He expired shortly after the call was made.

All together, eight people were dead.

The Himalayan commercial guiding business went into overdrive. People were thrilled by the tales of death and derring-do on Everest in the 1996 disaster, and flocked to the range of guiding companies offering climbs to the summits. By 2006, the number of expeditions to Everest more than doubled. In 1996, there were a total of 188 expeditions to the Himalayan range. By 2006, there were 388.

Today, in Everest Base Camp, there are regular reports of theft and prostitution in what has become known as the "highest garbage dump in the world." In May 2008, teams removed ten tons of trash in a single operation. The approach to base camp from Nepal, once thick with juniper bushes, is now barren and rocky as successive expeditions have burned them all for campfires.

Sir Edmund Hillary was disgusted, "Everest, unfortunately, is largely becoming a commercial, money-making opportunity. If you are reasonably fit and have $35,000 you can be conducted to the top of the world."[7] He sniffed, "It's all bullshit on Everest these days." Most of all he reserved scorn for the glory-hunters who sought to "get their name in the paper."[8]

AC was just one of several Himalayan guiding companies that competed for clients in the high reaches of the Himalaya. The tight bonds between guiding outfits that have managed to survive in this inhospitable climate are aptly named "the brotherhood of the rope."

— · — · —

Two days before Benitez flew to Lhasa, he sat in the Hotel Tibet in Kathmandu waiting for a visitor. Below his window in the $35-a-night hotel, rickshaws and scooters thronged the filthy, choked streets as mangy stray dogs poached food from roadside vendors. Strewn over the damask coverlet on his bed was $5,230. An additional $25,000 was stored away in his backpack under the bed. Hearing a tap on the door, Benitez drew the curtains.

A hulking, ruddy-faced figure in a blue-checked shirt and khaki travel pants filled the doorframe. The first thing people notice about Henry Todd is the size of his hands. Benitez always felt that they looked like bunches of bananas. Todd extended a bear-sized paw.

"Everything all right?" Todd asked breezily, in a clipped British accent. At six foot, three inches tall, sixty-one-year-old Todd had a crumpled, lived-in face, drooping eyes, and a head of ashen hair that gave him a dignified air. A longtime Himalayan operator who had seen and done it all, Todd had earned Benitez's deep respect. Guides sometimes told their bosses they didn't want to work with him. But Todd knew the world of mountaineering—and its seedy inroads—better than most. "Pretty good," Benitez offered. "The money is here."

The founder of Ice 8000, Todd is one of the premier Himalayan outfitters and the biggest supplier of oxygen for climbing expeditions in the Himalaya. The money that lay on Benitez's bed was to cover the cost of twenty-one seven-pound bottles of oxygen for the expedition.

Benitez had done business with Todd for years. In the Himalaya, a nexus of commercial guides interwove friendships, favors, and business. Ten climbers were allowed on one $80,000 climbing permit. Rather than paying for empty spaces on permits, AC and Todd split permits. This year, Todd had asked AC to get the permits for Cho Oyu. Ice 8000 and AC also split satellite-phone permit costs.

In the seventies, Todd had run the biggest LSD drug operation ever investigated and prosecuted by the British Police. He had had connections with the Brotherhood of Eternal Love, a U.S. drug distribution network allied with Timothy Leary and the Hell's Angels. Todd, operating under numerous aliases, had been the Brotherhood's European link. When fifteen police officers splintered the front door of his London home in a raid in March 1978, they discovered 3 million units of LSD. According to Detective Dennis Greenslade, "The officers were pulling up the carpets which were so saturated with the drug that they all began to go off on acid trips."[9] After a two-and-a half-year British police investigation known as Operation Julie, Todd was sentenced to thirteen years in prison for his part in masterminding "the biggest acid lab in the world." He was released after seven and a half years.

After his release in 1985, Todd dove headlong into the climbing industry. The lawless frontiers of the Himalaya, where life was cheap and expendable, seemed the perfect place for a man who wanted to escape his past. To Todd, Kathmandu was home. He set up Himalayan guiding companies that offered the cheapest expeditions in the Himalaya: tattered tents, little food, and barebones amenities. He didn't guide clients: He just got them to the mountain and let them get on with it.

Todd ruled his territory fiercely and was known for his unbridled temper. He viciously attacked one client, journalist Finn-Olaf Jones, after Jones offered an unflattering portrait of Todd on a Discovery Channel Website that he was posting as he climbed the mountain. Todd punched Jones in the side of the head and threw him onto a moraine. Jones was guarded by sherpas armed with ice axes before taking a helicopter out of Everest Base Camp.

As news of the assault hit the headlines, even the Nepalis, normally receptive to bribes, couldn't turn a blind eye. Todd's company, Himalayan Guides, was banned from operating in Nepal for two years. But the restriction made little difference; Todd ran his expedition by radio, instructing climbers from the north side of Everest in Tibet using his connections with the Chinese. He returned to Nepal and renamed his outfit Ice 8000. The man who once supplied half the world with LSD now furnished climbers on the south Nepalese side of the Himalaya with bottled oxygen.

Todd counted the money on the bed and slipped the notes into his jacket. "Coming down to Tom and Jerry's for a drink later?" Todd asked as he made for the door. The hot, sweaty bar in Kathmandu's Thamel area was a favorite meeting point for expedition guides.

"Maybe," said Benitez, knowing full well he'd retire to bed early. Todd gave a quick handshake and disappeared.

Men who run businesses guiding clients to the top of the world's most daunting peaks in the toughest conditions on the face of the earth form tight alliances, shun outsiders, and watch out for one another in the lawless frontier governed by the almighty dollar. Benitez always found an ally in Todd. "We only have each other up there," Benitez admitted. "And somehow it's comforting to have a guy like that watching your back."

"Once somebody did you a favor, they owed you," Benitez explained. "We were in bed with Henry Todd, he was the middle man, always was and always will be. If you wanted stuff, he would get it. You just never asked where it came from or how he got it."

6

LHASA

—·—·—

What will happen when China really wakes up, runs
a line from Shanghai to Lhasa . . . and controls her
own gun factories and arsenals?

Rudyard Kipling

The two jeeps lurched over the narrow iron bridge that crossed the
Salween River. Echoing in the canyon below was the sound of steel,
clanking and booming. It was a chill September night. As they traveled
on, farther from Juchen, the mood in the cramped interior of the vehicle
alternated between sadness and tension. In the front, Tenzin Choetso
and the diminutive Lobsang Samten sat next to Pema. In the back,
Kelsang nestled between Dolma and Thinley Wangmo who pressed up
against the door.

The jeeps labored up bumpy sandstone tracks and along roads that
bordered deep, gashing gorges. At 17,000 feet, the high pass westward
was treacherous. As they headed up and down the winding mountain
roads, Kelsang's head spun and her stomach heaved.

Gazing out of the window, lost in her thoughts, Dolma was overcome
with a graying melancholy. As she tried to doze, half-formed memories of
her family came to mind. She wondered if she would see her mother again.
The images of her parting played over and over in her mind: Her mother
bravely holding back the tears. And her last view of her sister Kyizom,
asleep at home. As the jeeps ground west, she wondered about her plan.
Would she be caught? Thrown into jail? Tortured and interrogated?

Dawn unveiled a series of mud-walled encampments along the roadside. Chinese flags flew from the corner of the compounds, an order from
the local PSB that every household must fly a flag or risk punishment.

Nearing Nagchu, an industrial town, the roads evolved from mud tracks to straight asphalt.

Along the road, a checkpoint at an abandoned nomad house that had been requisitioned by the police loomed outside Nagchu. From here on, the journey would be increasingly dangerous. The city was being transformed into a military, transport, and logistics hub and was now home to thousands of soldiers in expanding garrisons.

"If we are stopped, just say that we are going to Lhasa on pilgrimage," Pema instructed. The girls nodded nervously. The absence of a large group of people from Juchen might well have been noted by local officials. The jeep slowed as a PSB officer motioned them to stop.

Dolma and Kelsang pretended to be asleep, but they sneaked a glance at the officer through narrowed eyes. Although they couldn't see his face, they caught a glimpse of a greased assault rifle slung around his chest. Kelsang and Dolma had stashed handfuls of waxy banknotes in their coat linings. The rest, a thick wad to be used to pay illegal guides in Lhasa, was in Dolma's lap. Money, food, and pictures had been stuffed in their bag, clear indication of an escape attempt, were someone to search it. Dolma clutched it tightly.

The policeman gave a bored glance at the driver's license before waving them on. Searches in Tibet were routine. But the brush with a uniformed Chinese official sent a wave of fear over the girls.

Filled with as many as 100,000 unregistered migrants, Nagchu has wide roads lined with Chinese restaurants run by former soldiers. At 15,000 feet, the city is completely devoid of trees. One of the highest, coldest, wind-whipped cities in Tibet, Nagchu barely warms more than one degree all year. A mining hub for copper and gold (worth as much as $722 billion by some estimates), the city is filled with trucks laden with the earth's bounty.

The jeeps pulled into a cheerless gas station on the western edges of town to refuel, but there were too many soldiers and police to risk stopping. As dawn broke, the girls saw nomads out on the vast grasslands. Puffs of smoke drifted from stovepipes jutting out of dark brown yak-hair tents. In the distance, the dun-colored mountains were dwarfed by a low-hanging cobalt sky.

As part of the billion-dollar 1999 Western Development Campaign (or the Great Leap West) to "throw off backwardness" and to exploit and cultivate China's underdeveloped western regions, authorities had attempted since 2000 to resettle Tibetan nomads into gloomy communist housing blocks. The goal, as one official put it, was to "end the nomadic way, of life for all herdsmen by the end of the century."[1]

By 2005, in Quinghai (a Chinese-named region in northeastern Tibet that comprises most of Amdo), 89 percent (roughly 100,000) of the nomadic population had been pushed off the land. China now has administrative control of the land (and its resources) formerly governed by nomads. As roads, railways, hydropower stations, mines, and military garrisons have been built on the land, nomads have found themselves jammed into drab, communal housing blocks called "socialist new villages." Deprived of their customs and right to roam the land, nomad communities are ravaged by alcoholism and unemployment.

In the distance, the girls could make out a fast-moving streak of dark green. There, rising out of the plateau were the huge battleship-gray concrete and steel arches of China's marquee achievement—the world's highest railway line—the $4.3 billion "Sky Train." Running 2,100 miles, the railway connects Beijing to Lhasa. Every mile or so, olive-fatigue-clad soldiers were camped alongside the tracks, protecting the line from attack. The Chinese worried that Tibetans might attempt to blow up the line. The Sky Train is seen by Tibetans as the "second communist invasion." It offers brazen testament to China's ability to enforce its will over Tibet's inhospitable terrain. Hundreds of Tibetan homes had been bulldozed to make way for the railroad. At best, home-owners were paid $100 compensation for the land some families had occupied for generations.

Military hardware, tanks, and missiles had rolled into Tibet by train to fortify the region as a Chinese bulwark against the West and India. The plateau offers an advantage for medium- and long-range nuclear missiles. In 2008, Western analysts found sixty launch pads for DF-21 nuclear missiles in northern Qinghai at Tsaidam, just 100 miles on a fast, straight new road from the new railhead at Golmud.[2]

Thousands of Chinese workers had been shipped in to complete work on the railway line. Near the Yangpachen Gorge, faced with a two-mile-thick hump of mountain, engineers realized that they could not get the huge German drilling machines up to the plateau. So they used human labor, sending in workers with picks and dynamite to hack and explode their way through the mountain. Despite the Chinese government's proud proclamation that not a single railway worker had died on the project, Tibetans regularly saw officials burying the corpses of unlucky workers. It took two years to break through the mountain and an unknown number of lives.

The railroad enabled Chinese colonists to flood Tibet, true to Mao's vision of colonization. Part of the Western Development Strategy, the plan was to overwhelm Tibet economically rather than militarily. The railway forced Tibet's modernization and assimilation.

The Communist Party sells Tibet as a romantic frontier for new settlers, part of the "One China" policy. But in reality, most Chinese don't know anything about the mysterious land in the West that makes up most of their country. Information about Tibet is heavily restricted on the Web. Chinese are fed a steady diet of propaganda about the "jackal" Dalai Lama. Simultaneously, they are sold Tibet as a promised land to settle, far from the toxic Chinese cities (China has sixteen of the twenty most polluted cities in the world, where the World Bank estimates that around 750,000 Chinese die prematurely from pollution-related disease every year).[3] Salaries in Tibet can be twice as high as those in mainland China. And the government offers financial incentives and tax breaks to Han Chinese who relocate to Tibet. When they arrive, they are given preferential treatment for jobs and education.

Looking up at the elevated tracks, Dolma turned to Kelsang. "Do you remember how angry Kalsang Shagya was when he heard about the railway?" she asked. Kalsang Shagya was a militantly nationalistic monk in Driru. He prominently displayed a flag of Tibetan identity that bore the legend, "Son of the Snow Mountains," on the back of his car. It was a brave declaration that got him into constant trouble. When the railway came through Nagchu on its inaugural run, Kalsang had planned to burn Chinese flags in public. Authorities had been watching Kalsang closely. A huge billboard had been placed in the market heralding the "glorious" opening of the railway. Kalsang crept up one night and daubed the poster with paint. After the PSB found cassette tapes of the Dalai Lama's teachings in his room at the monastery, he had fled. His absence, which was quickly noted in Juchen, provoked heightened security in the tiny hillside town.

—·—·—

In Damshung, a city fifty miles north of Lhasa, the jeeps slowed to a stop. For such a large group to be seen in public was risky, but everyone needed to eat. After a simple meal of noodles at a roadside restaurant, they journeyed on.

By late afternoon, they arrived in Lhasa's western suburbs. They passed through areas in which entire Tibetan villages had been bulldozed to make way for new apartment buildings. Where ramshackle Tibetan houses had stood, newly paved, clinically straight roads with meticulous flower beds ran through faceless suburban neighborhoods. As of yet there were no inhabitants or finished buildings, just a crosshatch of perfect urban streets set in open fields. All stood waiting in anticipation of newly arriving colonists from lowland China.

The once forbidden Holy City, which explorers had died trying to reach, was fast becoming a multibillion-dollar megalopolis. The pace of change fueled by the Chinese government was unimaginable; the chatter of road drills and dump trucks departing offered a constant humming soundtrack of progress.

Closer to the city center, a concrete factory with three towering silos displayed massive neon billboards advertising Motorola Razr cell phones, risqué underwear, and Budweiser. Kelsang had never seen luminescent pink and sky-blue lights before. Swish SUVs and sedans pulled up to liveried doormen in front of the fragrant Jardin Secret Hotel, one of a number of new luxury hotels in Lhasa. They drove past the entrance to XZTV, a television station that pumped out Communist propaganda twenty-four hours a day—soap operas that positively portrayed Wujing doctors tending Tibetans overwhelmed with gratitude.

As they journeyed across the city, Dolma and Kelsang snatched just a glimpse of the gleaming roof of the Dalai Lama's former home, the Potala Palace. "Look," Kelsang cried. "There it is!" She had only seen the Potala in pictures. In her family's living room was an inspiring depiction of the sacred palace ringed with a fluffy halo of cumulus clouds.

In Lhasa, where scores of seemingly independent businesses were fronts for the PSB, it was far too dangerous to stay in a teahouse or a hotel. Instead, the group headed to the first stop on an Underground Railroad of safe houses run by sympathizers who helped refugees out of Tibet. As they passed alongside a large field, Dolma and Kelsang watched convicts from the nearby prisons break up rock.

Down a deserted street where the houses were low, two-story limestone affairs, the driver parked the jeeps. They continued on foot for twenty minutes, past a small plaza, before they came to a house. An older man and woman sat outside. After Pema had exchanged a few words with the couple, he beckoned his group. The man, in his sixties, was tall and bald, with a deeply wrinkled face. Inside the house, they were shown a sparse, dormitory-style room. Eight expectant faces greeted them, among them two nuns, who Dolma and Kelsang were later to learn had been shot at and caught escaping before.

As the group dumped their bags on the beds, the owners of the safe house appeared with a thermos of yak-butter tea. The tea eased Dolma's headache a little. Pema warned them to be careful as they headed out for food, advising that they leave in groups of no more than three, and that they refrain from speaking with anyone.

At dusk, Dolma, Kelsang, and Tenzin Choetso left the safe house. As there were no restaurants in the suburb, they had to walk for an hour before they came across a Chinese street vendor. He was hawking lianfang, a common roadside snack that comprised slabs of starch extracted from white flour. Dolma handed over some money for several packets, some biscuits, and soda. Back in their room, the girls collapsed on their beds, exhausted.

—·—·—

The next morning, they were awakened by Pema's cell phone. His face turned somber as he took the call. The nuns looked on plaintively. When he hung up, Pema explained that the police were looking for Kalsang Shagya and were closely monitoring Tibetans traveling from Driru. The police may well have noticed their absence and could have alerted the authorities in Lhasa.

After a pause, Pema reassured the group, suggesting they carry on as planned, with a possible detour over the Friendship Bridge. A heavily policed piece of real estate that connects Nepal with Tibet, the Friendship Bridge requires expensive falsified documents from corrupt officials.

Before leaving Lhasa, Pema advised the refugees to supplement their supplies—extra shoes, warm clothes, and blankets might be needed for the journey ahead.

Dolma and Kelsang set out again with Tenzin Choetso, heading west to Lhasa. They kept their heads bowed low, but every now and then Kelsang caught Dolma's eyes and reassured her with a quiet gaze. The closer to the center, the ritzier the stores: shoe boutiques, lingerie stores, and ubiquitous China Mobile stores chock-full of the latest cell phones. In the middle of Lhasa was the Old Town, the Tibetan Quarter. In the Barkhor market—an open-air affair surrounding the Jokhang temple complex (the holiest site in Tibet), hundreds of tourists snapped photos. Strategically placed cameras bristled in every corner of the square, while undercover police lurked undetected.

In 1989, Lhasa had erupted in the worst riots since the 1959 uprising. On March 5, in the Barkhor, Chinese police battled Tibetans demonstrating for independence as buildings were set alight, and police stations were stormed. Eventually, the PLA overran the Jokhang Temple. Martial law was declared soon after. The death toll has never been confirmed.

A brutal crackdown on Lhasa ensued. The authorities razed houses and displaced the inhabitants of the Barkhor area to build a large square that was easier to survey and control. For escaping refugees, Lhasa was extremely dangerous. Restaurants and hotels were often fronts for the PSB, where the movements of refugees were reported.

Informants lurked everywhere. Even seemingly everyday people could be police posing as beggars, pilgrims, monks, street vendors, or photographers.°

—·—·—

Trying not to betray her excitement, Kelsang slipped through the crowds of tourists in the Barkhor to the grand facade of the Jokhang Temple. Yak butter burned in large urns, and juniper wafted in purplish curtains over prostrating pilgrims. Over hundreds of years, grooves had been worn in the stone steps from devotional prostrations. Cadres of Wujing, seven or eight men strong, marched up and down in combat fatigues. On the rooftops overlooking the square, perched under umbrellas and armed with rifles, officers raked the square with binoculars.

Inside the seventh-century temple, Kelsang swooned with excitement. The world slowed to a soft unhurriedness. The phantasmal shapes of stooped monks moved down darkened corridors casting long shadows in the candlelight. The flagstones were sticky with gobs of yak butter.

To the back of the temple, towering above them, his golden features immobile, was the Wish Fulfilling Jewel, a golden sculpture of the Jowo Shakyamuni, the Buddha. Rumors had it that Jowo Rinpoche had once left the Jokhang Temple and visited a man who had so much faith that he had left his shoes—his most valuable possession—in the lap of the statue. A reflection of Jowo Rinpoche purportedly appeared by a spring near the man's home.

° "The police own many, many hotels, restaurants and shops in Lhasa," says Pasang Migma, a former Lhasa Public Security Bureau officer in the criminal intelligence department (the Zianshi). "I couldn't tell you which hotels or restaurants were owned by the police in Lhasa because the list would be too long. Even us police didn't know sometimes who was police and who wasn't. If we didn't own the business, then we paid people who told us about refugees and other things. That's how we know everything." Corruption was endemic. In 1998, lawyers and police held a meeting in which they discussed their plan to raid brothels and karaoke bars spread over Lhasa, according to Pasang Migma. By the time they raided the properties, every single owner had returned to mainland China, tipped off in advance by corrupt senior PSB officers.

Bending low, Kelsang prayed to Jowo Rinpoche for his protection on the dangerous journey that lay ahead. The likeness of Chairman Mao on the one yuan notes that Kelsang tucked into the encrusted railing were incongruous in this sacred setting.

After visiting the Jokhang Temple, the girls set out for their final necessities. Dolma bought two pairs of boots, a wool hat, red sunglasses, and an insulated jacket. The girls had been told to pick dark colors so that they would not be seen at night. But Kelsang chose a bright magenta jacket, explaining that it was the only color a nun should wear.

At the safe house the next morning, Pema announced that the group of travelers would be divided. They were too many to leave at once. Kelsang looked worriedly at Dolma. There was no way, whatever the circumstances, that Kelsang would be parted from her friend.

Everyone scribbled their names on bits of paper. Dolma's and Kelsang's hands were shaking as they etched their names. There was an awkward silence as Pema tossed the names in a bag and rummaged through the slips of paper. Kelsang's and Dolma's names were drawn. They had made the first group together.

The two nuns who had been caught during their previous escape attempt had been separated in the drawing. As tension built in the safe house with preparations to leave, their will to escape deserted them. In their previous attempt, they had been beaten and forced to sign papers promising that attempting another escape would result in the arrest of their family members. After much discussion, the two women decided to turn back.

A stooped, middle-aged man with a round face arrived later in the morning to collect a fee from the refugees. He called himself Tenzin. "It's 5,000 yuan; 1,400 yuan now, and the rest when you get to Nepal," he muttered. Dolma thought of all the time her mother had spent gathering caterpillar fungus on the high grasslands, living in a yak-hair tent, to give her the money to see His Holiness. Kelsang's parents had given their last coin for their daughter to get the lifetime blessings of the Dalai Lama. Dolma bundled together their notes and delivered the money to Tenzin.

With a day left to kill, Dolma, Kelsang, and Pema visited the Potala Palace. As dusk fell across the Kyichu River, the first neon lights began to flicker on in the buildings on Zhonghe International City or, as Tibetans called it, Sin City—a modern enclave where Chinese officials and top military brass lived. Neon lights announced infamous brothels like the towering three-story Xibu where lines of attractive hostesses greeted officials stepping out of shiny black SUVs.

Before they left the Potala, Kelsang and Dolma opted for one final memento. Local Han Chinese vendors offered Polaroids of tourists in front of the Potala. As the photographer was about to take a picture, Kelsang shouted for him to stop. Her face darkened. "Wait, wait," she cried. She turned. Fluttering from a tall flagpole in front of the Potala, guarded by two Wujing officers standing at attention on a dais, was the red Chinese flag. "I don't want my picture taken with the Chinese flag in the background," Kelsang said defiantly. The photographer nodded, sidestepping a few paces to alter his frame. Dolma stuffed the photographs into her bag. As they melted into the crowds of tourists, Dolma heard Kelsang's prayer to the Dalai Lama. Now, they too were ready to escape the confines of their sacred homeland.

7
Turquoise Goddess

—·—·—

The world seemed to me to be instinct with a hither-
to unknown benevolence and goodness. The barrier
between me and the rest of creation was broken
down. The few phenomena, sky, ice, rock, wind and
I, which now constituted life, were an inseparable
and divine whole. I felt myself—the contradiction is
only apparent—as glorious as God and at the same
time no more than an insignificant grain of sand.
Herbert Tichy on Cho Oyu

There was an apprehensive rustle among the climbers as the plane
dropped out of the clouds into Lhasa. Luis Benitez had been here five
times before on other expeditions, but there was still something about
Tibet that heightened his senses and made him, if not nervous, more
jumpy than usual.

The swank, marbled arrivals hall at Lhasa's Gonggar Airport was
dominated by a huge sign that forbid entrance to anyone with a commu-
nicable disease and, lower down, warned that all satellite communications
devices would be confiscated. Chinese authorities were always worried
about information seeping out of Tibet. Over the years, Benitez had
gotten used to hiding satellite phones in his socks or the bottom of the
kit bags.

In 2003, after an AC client had been searched at airport customs,
$700 had gone missing. Today, Benitez watched the customs officials
nervously. His clients, along with everyone else, were being scrutinized
by plainclothes officers from the PSB and immigration officials.

Outside the drab airport, colors snapped vibrantly. The thin air
and bright, unfiltered sun at 12,000 feet on the plateau drew the world

into sharp focus with startling clarity. But an unmistakable feeling of dread lingered. A state-regulated liaison officer from the China Tibet Mountaineering Association (CTMA) fell in step beside Benitez. Assigned as a "guide," the man's real responsibility was to keep close tabs on the Westerners while they were in Tibet. Some of the people on the expedition tried to say hello, but the man, who called himself Tenzin, remained aloof. Outside, a scrum of honking SUVs idled, as drivers from various expeditions shouted and harangued. Benitez picked out a sign for Adventure Consultants. After bundling bags and supplies onto the roof of a Land Cruiser, the expedition headed off on the sixty-one-mile drive to Lhasa.

To Westerners coming from the choking dust and jammed streets of Kathmandu, Tibet seems remarkably orderly. The Himalaya Hotel on the north bank of the Lhasa River is a modern, cheerless place, but clean and comfortable. Early the next morning, Benitez headed off to the CTMA, where he handed over the $25,000 Kumar had given him to clear debts for permits and other expenses.

After a day's rest, Benitez led his team to survey Lhasa's main attractions, heading first to Drepung Monastery. Built in 1416, the ancient monastery sat in a western suburb of the city at the foot of Mount Gephel. It had once housed 10,000 monks, but that number had dwindled to only a few hundred. Tucked into an office on the main floor was a chapter of the Democratic Management Committee whose job it was to ensure foremost allegiance to China.

After touring Drepung, Benitez led the group to the Potala Palace. To the south of the palace was a square where a thirty-five-meter monument marking the alleged "liberation" of Tibet stood. Around the square, surveillance cameras constantly scanned faces for any sign of trouble. Sometimes there were attempts by Tibetans to vandalize the obelisk. Plainclothes police, with their awkward muscular gaits, did their best to sink undercover.

The group was awed by the Potala Palace, once the home of the Dalai Lama. "Over fourteen stories high, the giant stairs give way to rooms full of ornate murals, icons, statues, and prayer books. This was a spectacular sight to behold," wrote Benitez in his expedition log. The massive palace was replete with 1,000 rooms, 300-foot-long halls filled with floor-to-ceiling statues, a dungeon, and a vast rooftop from which to survey the whole of Lhasa. But even in this sacred hub, security cameras and microphones yawned out of corners.

Noticeably lacking was any reference to the current Dalai Lama. Even in the breathtaking Potala Palace, Benitez's group found it hard to focus. All were amped up for the journey ahead, concerned with getting enough rest and being well hydrated. After visiting the Potala, the group headed east to the Barkhor. They laughed at the makeshift stalls selling felt cowboy-style hats, busts of Mao, batteries, and electric blenders. The touristy nature of the area failed to belie the threat within—many of the rough-skinned, baseball-hat-wearing stall holders were English-speaking undercover police who worked for the department of foreign affairs. Their job was to report back any suspicious or unpatriotic activities. English and American travelers—known sympathizers to the Tibetan cause—were under particular scrutiny.

The ubiquitous security machine lent an uneasy feeling of paranoia. The two Britons found a relief from the stress of it all by uneasily cracking jokes and setting dares—sotto voce—on who would tear down one of the Chinese flags and replace it with a Tibetan one.

Down a side street near the Barkhor was an oasis of Western normalcy in a strange land. "It's just like Starbucks!" exclaimed Kevin Cubitt as Benitez led the group to a Western-style café where they ordered cappuccinos over piped jazz music. Here modernity and tradition collided uneasily. In stark contrast to the Miles Davis playing in the background, the frothing of the cappuccino machine, and the rustle of glossy magazines was the sight of pilgrims heading to the Jokhang Temple. Many had traveled hundreds of miles in a painful journey of prostrations. In filthy aprons made from yak hide, wooden guards crudely tied to their hands, they prostrated outside the café.

Something pricked Benitez's sensibilities as he watched the pilgrims. Benitez had dedicated his life to traveling to the most remote and obscure parts of the world and making sure that his clients were safe from the harsh mountain environments, from the mercies of the tough, Third World cultures. But comforts failed to satisfy him in Tibet. The country's forgotten quality—as though it had simply been passed over for centuries while the rest of the world thundered on—made for a certain degree of guilt as privileged climbers took in the views, coffee in hand.

Through the window, an old woman with a deeply lined face caught Benitez's gaze for a nanosecond. On her forehead was a huge fleur-de-lis–shaped callus, the result of thousands of prostrations. An inexplicable sense of self-loathing overtook Benitez as the woman bent to the ground.

Within the same week that Benitez's team set foot in Lhasa's ancient streets, a battered jeep rolled into the eastern end of the city and passed a street or two from the café where Benitez was sitting. Within were two expectant girls from remotest Tibet.

—·—·—

Fluttering in the arid wind, in an achingly bleak landscape of dust and rocks, a giant latticework of faded prayer flags framed the landscape. Benitez and his team headed west from the milky braided rivers of the Kyichu Valley to Shigatse, the second biggest city in Tibet. From there, they would switch south toward the Himalayan range, ever upward along smaller roads and higher mountain passes. They stopped every few hours at dismal roadside stalls. Climbers on other expeditions passing here over the years had bought Red Bull to stimulate against the growing rigors of altitude. One store owner had piled the cans high in a growing monument to the caffeinated aspirations of passing adventurers.

The cross-support of the sixty-foot-high gateway over the dusty road declared: "You are now entering Qomolangma [Everest] National Nature Preserve." When they stopped to take pictures, Benitez warned his group not to get out of the SUV too suddenly, given the considerable shift in altitude. Festooned with faded and tattered Buddhist prayer flags, the gateway (the highest point on the pass) was regarded as a transition point for spirits from the earthly realm to the heavens. Out here, dirt-laden winds made the climbers cough.

A boy clutching a baby goat emerged from a filthy gray tent. His family lived at the gateway, surviving on the money begged from tourists and climbers who stopped here to take pictures. After Paul Rogers had photographed him looking defiantly into his camera, the boy held out his palm for payment. Nothing here, it seemed, was free; the need was simply too great.

The hours passed, and they pushed on. Suddenly exploding out of the surrounding salt flatlands, the snow-draped peaks of the highest mountain range in the world emerged. Piercing bright in the afternoon light, the mountains' proud faces were altogether striking.

Hours after the first sighting of the Himalaya, the group arrived in Tingri, a hardscrabble, godforsaken frontier outpost that rests in a salt plain and is the last scrap of civilization before the mountains. Once Tingri was the main town for trade between Nepal and Tibet, but with Chinese development, Tibetans had been encouraged to move to Lhasa.

Benitez escorted his team to a teahouse where they were shown to rooms with crude beds. An incessant wind blasted dirt through the cracks of the dry, wooden door.

The next morning, Benitez led the team on an acclimatization walk up a smooth, whale-shaped hill behind the town. At an elevation of 14,000 feet, the climbers struggled to adjust. The higher a person travels, the slower muscles respond, as oxygen levels in the blood fall. For days, Benitez's team members had been battling headaches.

As they plodded up the little hill, the group could see the square below, inside the PAP garrison where soldiers played basketball. It was a gray-walled single-story Chinese garrison that sat ominously at the end of the one-street town. Before they had set out, a wizened old man had told Benitez to be careful hiking in the hills behind the base, as the soldiers disliked being watched but also often fired their weapons up into the hills behind when they got bored.

After a few hours, Benitez and his clients clearly saw the target of their quest for the first time. Soaring beyond the dinner-plate flat plains around them was the ice-clad hulk of Cho Oyu. Unlike the clean pyramidal lines of Everest, Cho Oyu is a tangled collection of peaks forming a massif. Viewed from the north, the profile of the mountain is a long, scalloped ridge leading upward to a broad, flat summit. It looks like an indomitable goliath and instilled both fear and awe among the group.

In 1951, Cho Oyu was attempted as a warm-up for Hillary's 1953 Everest summit. He sent an advance party over the Gyabrang Glacier and through the Nangpa La to scout a route. Hillary and noted climber and author Eric Shipton set up base camp at 18,500 feet, and sherpas went back down over the Nangpa La to find an approach from the northwest, the Tibetan side. But Hillary became increasingly worried about Chinese soldiers from the garrison at Tingri who might catch the climbers "like rats in a trap." The party was eventually stopped by an imposing ice cliff and shortly thereafter ran out of supplies. The man who would famously conquer Everest could not conquer Cho Oyu. He recalled feeling "almost a sense of shame that we'd allowed ourselves to admit defeat so readily."[1]

Cho Oyu was first successfully climbed in 1954 by Austrians led by Herbert Tichy. The climbers had to dodge Chinese patrols to make their ascent by slipping over the Nangpa La illegally to the West. Straddling Tibet and Nepal, Cho Oyu was of strategic military importance to the Chinese, who had started to build military bases there.

Suffering from severe frostbite, Tichy had summitted with an otherworldly moment of clarity, something that all mountaineers aspire to—a feeling of transcendence and revelation and escape from mortal constraints. There was, he wrote, "an indescribable impersonal happiness," and he felt "the barrier between me and the rest of creation was broken down." He described how he had "broken through a metaphysical boundary and reached a new world. . . . I felt myself—the contradiction is only apparent—as glorious as God and at the same time no more insignificant than a grain of sand."[2]

In Buddhist scripture, Cho Oyu has an altogether more auspicious standing. The Turquoise Goddess contained Padmasambhava's instructions for saving the world from chaos.

Sacred mountains are a key part of Tibetan life. Buddhist and Hindu pilgrims regularly flock to Mount Kailash—a mountain on the eastern end of the Himalaya near the Indian border that, according to Buddhist belief, is home to the Buddha of supreme bliss. In the same way Western mountaineers feel that reaching the summit of Everest will unlock something within themselves for a transcendental experience, pilgrims see the opportunity in spiritual pilgrimage for death and rebirth. A key escape route for refugees, Kailash is the only mountain in the Himalaya where climbing is strictly forbidden.

When the first expeditions to Everest took place, Sir Charles Bell observed, "An expedition of white men who did not believe in Tibetan spirits and stood outside the Buddhist brotherhood, would of necessity disturb the spirits of the place."[3] For centuries, Buddhist hermits took refuge in mountain caves where they attained enlightenment, seeing the mountain as a pathway to heaven. The lamas warned against climbing up the mountains into the realm of the deities. One of the first expeditions on Everest in 1924 saw eight sherpas blasted into a crevasse and five killed by an avalanche shortly after. George Mallory and his companion Andrew Irvine simply disappeared in a mysterious cloud, a few hundred feet from the summit. The Rongbuk Lama, Ngawang Tenzin Norbu, organized a ceremony for the dead men to try to rid them of the bad karma they had accrued by entering into the pantheon of mountain deities on Everest. A few years later, other climbers returned to Rongbuk Monastery to find elaborately painted frescoes on the walls depicting a furious mountain deity surrounded by an army of men with spears and angered yetis. Lying at the deity's feet was the naked body of a white man, riddled with spear holes.

Cho Oyu became part of the runaway commercialization of the Himalaya. In 1987, when the Chinese finally opened up the northeast ridge and routes from Tingri, a slew of expeditions arrived on Cho Oyu. The commercialization of the sacred peak began bringing with it violence. In September 1989, bloodshed broke out among two rival expeditions on Cho Oyu (the first time in the Himalaya). A Belgian–French team, led by Alain Hubert and Regis Maincent, was attempting the southeast face, while a South Korean team, led by Lee Ho-Sang, was attempting the southwest ridge. The two teams came into contact at around 23,000 feet and a disagreement ensued over the use of fixed ropes. Rope fixing can be like laying toll roads in the mountains. Climbers jealously protect their ropes and sometimes charge other climbers to use them. A pitched battle took place with ice axes and fists flying. Maincent was captured and tied up before managing to escape with a bleeding head wound. He fled from the mountain with his companions. A week later, Ang Lhakpa, sherpa of the Korean expedition, reached 26,000 feet on his own, only to be swept away by an avalanche, never seen again. The other sherpas saw this as a bad portent—that the deities were angry—and refused to climb higher. The Koreans gave up.

By 2006, there were a record 573 climbers on Cho Oyu. Aside from its daunting ice cliffs, Cho Oyu demands little in the way of technical climbing, a fact that makes it an ideal mountain for novices. With only 28 deaths between 1986 and 2006 (compared to 128 on Everest), it had earned a reputation as one of the safest Himalayan peaks.

For Benitez, Cho Oyu simply brought bad memories. The last time he'd been on the mountain was September 11, 2001. American climbers had stumbled out of their sleeping bags and staggered outside the tea-house to the wind-whipped Tingri streets where they quickly wired up a satellite phone to a laptop. There, as the signal faded in and out, they were able to connect to CNN Online. They gasped at a grainy image of the towers falling. After news of the attacks, the border to Kathmandu was closed. All flights in and out of Lhasa were grounded. Despite the protestations of sherpas who considered it an inauspicious time, Benitez went ahead with his attempted ascent. In May that year, a few months earlier, Benitez had made his triumphant first summit of Everest. But his experience on Cho Oyu had put a damper on his enthusiasm, and for the first time, he climbed a mountain reluctantly. He didn't summit.

Guy Cotter also had dark memories of Cho Oyu. His first night in Lhasa in 1995 before heading to Cho Oyu, he had heard a loud explosion. In the mid-nineties, as China enforced a crackdown, Tibetans struck back with bombs in Lhasa and Sog County, neighboring Driru, and in areas were Tibetan independence was strong. After a fax to his girlfriend, in which Cotter described having heard an explosion in the Potala Palace, a ten-strong PSB detachment arrived at his room at the Holiday Inn and escorted him to a Lhasa prison. Forty-eight hours of interrogation later, Cotter was publicly denounced in the *Tibet Daily* newspaper for rumor mongering and was forced to sign a "written statement of repentance" and to rescind his faxed statement. After house arrest, he was deported to Nepal. He never reached Cho Oyu.

Benitez turned his back on the mountain and led his clients back down to Tingri. For a brash, ego-driven climber like himself, Cho Oyu wasn't going to advance Benitez's career much. The Turquoise Goddess wasn't going to land one of his frequent $1,000-a-shot speaking engagements or garner his book deal on *The Everest Within*. Those were the rewards of the Big E.

—.—.—

On September 6, 2006, Benitez and his clients began their ascent of Cho Oyu. They rumbled past the Chinese garrison, radio antennas jutting out from inside the gray compound wall. A few Chinese soldiers eyed them, sucking on cigarettes, as they eased out of town, heading south to the base of the mountain.

The houses on the edge of Tingri were primitive, low-walled buildings. Grubby children scampered out to see the climbers drive by. It was a four-hour drive to Chinese Base Camp along a roughshod road. A forlorn encampment of Chinese soldiers and representatives of the CTMA sat at the end of the road on bleached flatlands at around 16,000 feet.

The soldiers, dressed in olive-green camouflage uniforms, some in greatcoats, and all with oiled SKS assault rifles hanging from their shoulders, exuded hostility. They wore Nike and Reebok sneakers that looked incongruous with their uniforms. In 2001, a soldier had caught one of Benitez's clients taking pictures and had demanded the camera. Benitez saw it as a thinly veiled attempt to get a camera, rather than a security measure. Soldiers often shook climbers down, claiming improper paperwork. Sometimes they simply peered inside climbers' bags to pick out whatever caught their eye. For a climber who has paid $20,000 to climb Cho Oyu, it's a small price to pay. No one makes a fuss.

Morris Cooper° had been with Jagged Globe, a British expedition. He was a former sniper in the British Army and had been in war zones before. "For some reason, I remember being threatened by them [People's Armed Police] more than anyone I have ever come across," he said. "They were just standing there looking at you, and you had

---

° Morris Cooper is a pseudonym.

that sixth-sense-hairs-standing-up-on-the-back-of-your-neck-type feeling. You weren't quite sure why you felt threatened. I've had weapons pointed at me before, but I felt less threatened by that than just having a Chinese guy like these staring at me." It wasn't just the immaturity of the Chinese soldiers he encountered at the base of Cho Oyu (many were quite young), it was the ruthlessness he witnessed. "It was like they wouldn't care if they shot you, that they wouldn't bat an eyelid. That there was no code."

— · — · —

It is gravely forbidden for PAP officers to talk to Westerners and would likely be an imprisonable or court martial offense to talk to journalists. So Akar, a senior PAP officer was understandably wary when we met at an undisclosed location in an international city.

He was a short, stout man with a military buzz cut flecked with quick-silver gray and a cold, ruminative face. He was dressed in glossy black leather loafers. Armani sunglasses with gold detailing sat on the end of his nose. He extended a weak and bloodless handshake as we repaired to a Chinese restaurant. His job was to fight the "splittist activities of the Dalai Lama," he said.

Akar was proud of his unit, reserving scorn for America's military, an enemy to him. "We are champions at kickboxing and always beat the PLA. We are not like the Americans," he said disdainfully, "who will not fight if the body armor doesn't fit or the Hummer is too small. We fight wherever and we don't mind dying."

Akar had split loyalties though. As he sat drinking green tea, he was proud that he was Tibetan, and despite his job, his allegiance as a Tibetan was secretly to the exiled spiritual leader of his homeland. The price of talking out, were he to get caught, could be unimaginable. "I have to be careful what comes out of my mouth," he admitted, tilting his head back and looking down his nose quizzically. He was intractable and surprisingly tacit—qualities that come from years of working at the very center of the Chinese security machine in Tibet.

In 1989, the same year that protests erupted in Lhasa, Beijing erupted in cataclysmic bloodshed, in what turned out to be the greatest threat to the stranglehold of power held by Chinese Communist Party (CCP) since the founding of the People's Republic, forty years earlier. Thousands of ordinary Chinese gathered in Tiananmen Square to mark the death of a reformist politician, to call for the implementation of promised democratic reforms, and to protest lack of freedom in a totalitarian state.

Communist regimes were fracturing the world over. As the Chinese regime saw it, if China's one billion citizens unified in revolt, they would be unstoppable. It was the match that could light a tinderbox, ripping China apart and bringing about the downfall of the regime.

On June 4, 1989, the CCP took violent and decisive action, sending tanks and shock groups into Tiananmen Square. The true death toll of the massacre remains secret.*

China had shattered its image as the so-called peaceful dragon. The World Bank stopped issuing loans to China. For its part, China banned the foreign press. A vicious purge saw hundreds detained without trial. Many were summarily executed.

The regime realized it had to act quickly to salvage its image on the world stage. Chinese leader Deng Xiaoping had already initiated free-market reforms to transform China into an economic goliath with his famous phrase, "To be rich is glorious." After Tiananmen Square, economic reforms were accelerated. Deng realized that brutal oppression of Chinese citizens was politically unpalatable to foreign trade partners. And the CCP could not control one billion citizens through military might alone. The smartest way to control the population was to offer prosperity in exchange for freedom—a basic appeal to individual greed over human rights.

After Tiananmen, the CCP couldn't risk using its military against its own citizens and outraging Western democracies. Instead, the PAP, a highly secretive, paramilitary unit that blurs the line between military and civil police, was boosted and developed. It is controlled by the

---

* The Chinese Red Cross reported 2,000 to 3,000 deaths, a figure from NATO intelligence ran as high as 7,000. The number given by the CCP in later years was an estimate of between 200 and 300 deaths.

Central Military Commission—the PLA's supreme command—and the State Council through the Ministry of Public Security. The direct link to the State Council gives the PAP enormous power.

The PAP ensures that publicly the "peaceful rise" of China seems true to outsiders, but internally the PAP savagely controls any dissent to the Communist Party. China wants its fifty-six ethnic minorities to be unified under the People's Republic of China. In reality, ensuring that Uighurs, Tibetans, and Mongolians—those who once had their own countries and sovereignty—become a part of a "One China" requires the use of force in some cases. For those who resist prosperity over personal freedom, the PAP are the shock troops to quell dissent. In restive outlying provinces like Tibet, where allegiance is to the Dalai Lama, no matter what wealth or economic progress is made, the Wujing are the "sharp knife" or "fist" to enforce loyalty to the Communist regime.

Torture, interrogation, and execution are some of their main activities. Akar sneers sardonically, "When the People's Liberation Army get you, they kill you," he boasted. "When we get you, we want to control you." A recruit from Nagchu prefecture who joined the PAP in 2004 and was sent to serve in the border security branch (Ch: Bianfangbudui) commented, "Our commander instructed us in many types of punishment." He was taught to hang women upside down naked, to pour freezing water over their bodies, and then beat his charges with a belt. He was instructed in techniques on electrocution and in how to effectively fracture a subject's limbs. The PAP train frequently for raiding monasteries; their planned assaults in time of trouble are specifically targeted to the layout of each religious establishment. As internal control of China is their main responsibility, the PAP is the power base of some Chinese leaders. Communist leader Jiang Zemin cultivated the PAP as his own praetorian guard.

For many years, Akar was a recruiter for the paramilitary unit. He was able to take advantage of the system and extract bribes from young Chinese and Tibetans trying to escape rural poverty by enlisting in the PAP. For some, the PAP is a dream job that offers *guanaxi*—connections in China—and a fast track to money and a certain freedom normal Tibetan citizens don't have. PAP officers earn as much as 1,000 yuan a month ($145), the equivalent of an annual income for a rural Tibetan.

"As a recruiter, people bring me gifts, cars, and money to sign up their sons," he said in his thick mahogany voice, the result of incessant smoking. Becoming a senior PAP officer in Tibet was like being given the keys to the city and a license to print money. He added with a chuckle, "There is corruption everywhere in China. PAP soldiers only want to make money and to be comfortable. That is their ambition."

Like most PAP officers, Akar was heavily involved in business. In a major Chinese city, he was involved in running hotels. "You like girls and dancing?" he grinned wolfishly. "Come to Tibet. I'll show you."

Private enterprise in the PAP is encouraged. Unlike Western armies, which are funded by a central government, the PAP is funded both with government money and by shady front companies. It is involved in gold mining in Tibet where it works with Western companies. PAP business revenue has been growing by 20 percent since the mid-eighties. And corruption in its ranks is rampant. According to Tai Ming Cheung, an analyst at the Institute of Global Conflict and Cooperation, University of California, in his paper, "Guarding China's Domestic Front Line": "Some coastal units in Guandong have gained notoriety for engaging in piracy and smuggling activities themselves, sometimes crossing into the territorial borders of neighboring territories and countries." He adds, "Corruption, smuggling, profiteering and other unhealthy practices are becoming increasingly serious problems in the PAP as many units become engaged in business activities."

The PAP is split into four main units: bodyguard work, guarding buildings, maintaining infrastructure, and border control. It has myriad responsibilities that include road, dam, and communications building; dignitary protection work; coast guard duties; forestry supervision; fire control; and guarding prisons and borders. The PAP is also tasked with executions. A busy line of work, as China executes more citizens than any other country in the world.*

---

* According to Amnesty International, 72 percent of all executions in the world are carried out in China. The true number of executions is a state secret, but Amnesty estimates that 1,718 Chinese citizens were killed by the state in 2008 for 60 crimes ranging from nonviolent crimes like tax fraud and embezzlement to more serious offenses like murder.

These squads (Ch: Fajing) operate in Drapchi and other prisons. Tibetans are not trusted in execution units, which are Han Chinese only. The fear is that Tibetans will waver in their duty in sympathy for their compatriots. According to documents from the now defunct Tibet Information Network, recruits to the execution squad are forcibly conscripted from within the PAP's ranks. One former PAP interviewed in Dharamsala in 1999 said, "People rarely prefer to join that branch of the military force. So a sort of ballot would be conducted." He concluded, "The leaders would call for these ballots and those who lose will be sent into that branch."

PAP execution squads operate within the prisons. Yantun Pasang, a former PSB officer, worked in Drapchi Prison, where executions were common. "One day the Wujing dragged two men from their cells and took them out of the prison to be executed," he recounted. The execution squad took them out very publicly in view of all the other inmates. "It was done to scare other prisoners," he said. He describes prisoners being made to stand outside in subzero weather while water was thrown on them. Other times, new officers came to the prison and were made to watch or to carry out beatings under the supervision of senior officers to test their suitability for the job.

Increasingly, the PAP has turned its attention to Westerners in Tibet who, with pro-Tibet sympathies, may have the potential to foment restiveness. The PAP is highly active in undercover work—particularly in large groups of Westerners like climbers—learning English and how to blend in with Westerners without arousing attention.

In the border regions, the PAP controls who gets in and out of Tibet—another opportunity for bribery and making money. Border units undergo specific training in reading false documents. "You have a friend who wants to get out of China?" Akar asked. "I can get your friend across for 5,000 to 10,000 yuan. It would be no problem. All you need is the right permit, which I can get you."

In Tibet, the Nangpa La, controlled by the PAP, is the last resort for desperate Tibetans who want out of their country, sneered Akar. "The people who have to cross that have no money or connections," he said. They are people without passports or the money to bribe officials for paperwork. It has long been suspected that escapees who are fired upon on the pass have not paid the appropriate bribes to the PAP. Either way shootings are common. Akar fixed an unflinching gaze. He said, "There are about thirty incidents a year when we fire on people in the border areas."

— · — · —

Benitez had around $10,000 to pay the sherpas at the end of the expedition and at least another $1,000 as a slush fund stuffed into the secret compartment of his backpack. On the Excel spreadsheet on Benitez's laptop was an expense euphemistically marked as "Chinese Staff Fee." It was an emergency stash of cash that might be used to pay corrupt officials or soldiers—the only law in the mountains of Tibet and easily bribable—were the expedition to run into problems or be halted along the way. He'd already paid a bribe to a Nepalese airport official who found the $25,000 in his backpack when he flew from Kathmandu to Lhasa. In the 1990s, the PAP had reportedly once demanded a 4,000 yuan bribe from a German expedition, simply to allow them to get on the mountain.

Tenzin, the CTMA liaison officer, had joined Benitez's team at the camp. His official job was to smooth any problems with the soldiers or other issues. In reality, he was a middleman between the climbers and the soldiers (he went only as far as Chinese Base Camp). The CTMA officers sometimes ripped off expeditions when they felt they could, tripling charges for Land Cruisers on a whim or increasing permits suddenly when climbers were in the country, so that they had no choice but to pay. It was a nightmare for outfitters. One expedition ended up being charged an extra $30,000 at the end of its time in Tibet and had difficulty leaving the country.

From Chinese Base Camp, everything that Benitez's expedition needed would be transferred from the SUVs to yaks. (Each yak could carry a hundred-twenty pounds of gear.) During the day, Benitez's team practiced rope-climbing skills on some rocky crags of striated rock. A heavy hailstorm had forced them all to retreat to their tents. After two days, it was a relief to finally strike out up the mountain. The trek to Advance Base Camp (ABC) at 19,000 feet on Cho Oyu's southwest face was a two-day journey.

On their right to the east, sitting in a dusty valley next to a frozen river was the Chinese military base, Gyaplung. One can reach it on foot in around thirty minutes from Chinese Base Camp. At 16,000 feet, it's the highest border patrol station in China, built in 2003 by the engineer corps of the PAP, which also constructed a motor road to Gyaplung. The base overlooks the Nangpa La and is placed specifically as a forward operating station to hunt refugees. The base is only seven to nine miles from the border with Nepal.

The climbers walked for ten hours before the road petered out to a single, twisting dusty lane. Lead sherpa Ang Tshering fell in beside Benitez. Over the years, he had become like a father to Benitez, climbing with him on most of his Everest summits. He was a portly man with a wily, avuncular disposition and a broad face framed by gold-rimmed spectacles. Legendary in mountaineering circles, Ang had received medals from the king of Nepal for his work in the mountains. The son of a mail runner on Sir Edmund Hillary's Everest expeditions, he was president of the Nepal Mountaineering Association, the body that regulates mountaineering expeditions in Nepal. As sirdar, Ang was paid $2,291, about $300 more than the other sherpas on the trip. While the guides tended to the clients, a sirdar's tasks included hiring and directing all the sherpas, base camp budgets, and overall responsibility for equipment. He could make or break a sherpa's career.

Pressing up Cho Oyu, Ang and Benitez discussed the logistics of their climb. A young sherpa, grinning, followed behind. On a previous Everest expedition, Sankay Dorje had been a lowly cook but had impressed everyone with his climbing ability when he was asked to step in briefly to replace a sick sherpa and carry gear up the mountain. He surged up from Camp 2 to the South Col at first light, blasting past other expeditions, and had made it back down again in time to serve his clients lunch. It is every sherpa's dream to be a climbing guide, but while sherpas of a lesser caste are permitted to work as cooks and assistants, they are not allowed to be climbing sherpas. "He blew the old guard right out of the water," Benitez recalls. Ang, after much deliberation, agreed that Sankay should be a climbing sherpa. His life was transformed with his new status. Now Sanjay was following behind, trekking to Cho Oyu's summit.

Around 3,000 sherpas currently live in Nepal's mountainous Khumbu Valley. In the sixteenth century, sherpas (literally "eastern people") emigrated from Kham to set up farms and businesses as guides and drivers on the trade routes between China and India. They trudged over the Nangpa La in the shadow of Cho Oyu to settle in the Solo Khumbu Valley in Nepal around the ankles of Everest. Today, many make their living from mountaineering expeditions.

Physiologically, sherpas are extraordinary for their almost super-human strength at high altitudes, largely from their Tibetan heritage and their adaptation to living at high altitudes for five hundred years. They carry staggeringly heavy loads. A comprehensive study in 1999, which examined 635 porters, revealed that the average weight they carried was 160 pounds. Children as young as twelve carry weights of fifty-five pounds between villages. Periodically, flurries of excited doctors arrive in Nepal to carry out medical experiments on sherpas. A study by Belgian doctors found that the sherpas have incredibly efficient metabolism, twice more efficient than that of a Westerner. Some sherpas laugh privately at their fat, rich, white clients. Even expedition leaders are occasionally seen as feeble.

Benitez had fought hard to make his name, often controversially. In 2003, he had been lounging around in Camp II on Everest before a summit attempt when a sick sherpa, Karma, was dragged into camp. Benitez and a few other climbers left their summit attempts to try to save his life. The climbers radioed up and down the mountain for someone to help, only to have their requests ignored. Argentinean Willie Benegas, who was exhausted after two weeks climbing Nuptse with his twin brother Damian, ran over to help. They constructed a makeshift litter and attempted to get the sherpa down the mountain, but the man died in transit. Afterward, Benitez collapsed in the mess tent at ABC. He had failed to save Karma's life. Once he'd collected himself, Benitez immediately began blogging about the rescue on the mountaineering website MountainZone within hours of getting the body back to basecamp.

The new technology that enabled cybercasts proved controversial. Back in 2001 while on Everest, Benitez had posted news of the team's ascent on the Web. Since then, he had continued to publicize his career from the mountain with frequent dispatches to mountaineering Websites.

Climbing expeditions, which for years had been detached from the outside world, were now made answerable for their actions, as news of expeditions entered the public realm within seconds.

On Everest Benitez's was an emotional dispatch that gave a blow-by-blow account of his own hand in the rescue. He wrote, "All I remember is running. Running at almost 22,000 feet to try and help a man I had never known before this day." Benegas, who also helped in the rescue, was shocked. "There are two different people in the mountains," he said. "Those who want to help because they really want to. And those that really want to help because they want to become famous."

After sending the note, Benitez shot back up the mountain with the sherpas who had to get back to their clients. They didn't expect Benitez to make it in step with the sherpas within thirty-six hours. He proved them wrong. It was unprecedented speed, particularly for a Westerner. "Things changed for me after that with the sherpas," Benitez recalled. "I lockstepped with them all the way down trying to save Karma's life and then all the way up. I got their respect."

Some on the mountain saw it differently. Many were quietly dismayed that Benitez had spread the news of Karma's death so quickly. In April 2006, on Everest again, Benitez blogged news of the deaths of three sherpas who had died in the icefall by posting on the AC website as soon as the story reached basecamp. Cotter says he had expressly forbidden anyone from broadcasting the news. "Luis had written in a very heart-wrenching way that had expressed his love and appreciation for the sherpas and what a tragedy it was, but this did not hide the fact that he had reported the deaths before the next of kin could be notified," says Cotter, who immediately deleted the post. "There is an 'understanding' among teams that this type of information is not reported internationally until the next of kin have been informed. News of tragedies like this will travel more slowly to family members in Nepal than to people on the far side of the globe due to satellite communications."

In 2003, Benitez's choice—to abandon his group while attempting the rescue—didn't endear him to expedition leaders, who regarded him as a temperamental maverick. "He went out of his way to be a hero on that one," said one expedition leader who has worked with Benitez. "It's lucky he's strong and was able to get back to his clients. But he didn't save anyone's life and jeopardized the mission he was paid to be there for. I remember guiding with him was like there wasn't enough oxygen in the tent for both of us. It was like he had to be the star all the time."

— · — · —

Halfway to ABC, Benitez's group stopped at an intermediate camp where the Chinese had set up some tents selling tea and biscuits. Jan Anderson was complaining of feeling weak and woozy. She wasn't able to form sentences properly. Benitez ascribed it immediately to altitude sickness. Paul Rogers felt it was due to heatstroke. The two bickered out of earshot. Benitez returned to give Anderson fluids and an altitude drug.

Rogers, who had been with Adventure Consultants for years but hadn't yet reached the summit of an 8,000-meter peak, was increasingly annoyed that Benitez, with all his successful Everest summits, could swan in as an international guide leader. He disliked the brash American and his white photoflash grin, along with his constant media networking. He called him "Donny Osmond" behind his back.

According to his brother David, Benitez's ego had grown with each summit he made. "He has a sizable ego, but I guess that comes with the territory," David noted. "He is going to have it forever. It's part of who he is."

Benitez had joined Adventure Consultants in 2003. His greatest asset to the company was selling trips in the mountains as part of the growing commercialization of the Himalaya. Among his peers he hadn't solidified his reputation as a mountaineer. "He hadn't climbed new routes, which is what gets you respect as a mountaineer," says British guide Victor Saunders. Instead, Benitez was seen as a capable, public-friendly guide, part of the new breed of young climbers who were loquacious, courted sponsorships and the media assiduously, and sold the mountains with a charismatic charm. "Marketing seemed to be his real strength," said Cotter. "He was very good at motivating and getting people out to take trips."

But this skill was also Benitez's downside. He broke the old taboos that climbers should be laconic and modest about their accomplishments. "Getting publicity and overtly courting the media is not looked upon favorably," said Cotter.

Benitez had honed his spiel. As increasing numbers summitted Everest each year, climbers tried to outdo one another with their hardship stories in order to attain book deals and speaking tours. In addition to blind climber Erik Weihenmayer, there had been a seventy-one-year-old, then a seventy-six-year-old, and attempts by a deaf man, a double amputee, a single amputee, and many others with varying disabilities. For his part, Benitez joined the fray with his own triumph of overcoming childhood allergies and asthma.

Cotter was used to dealing with the ego-driven clashes between guides that were an unavoidable part of running a modern guiding company. "There are always issues between guides whose personalities don't match and don't work well together," he said. "We're in the most extreme and difficult work environment there is. Underpaid and high stress, so there are always issues. In this environment, psychological problems may surface."

When Benitez and Rogers called Cotter with their complaints from Cho Oyu, he instructed them to focus on the expedition at hand. Cotter recognized Benitez's leadership strengths but was well aware of his tendency to get wrapped up in helping other people on the mountain or getting involved in causes that drew media attention, to the detriment of his own clients.

The next day, the team descended onto the Balung Glacier, which flowed from the northwest and merged with the Nangpa La. The team then threaded their way in a southerly direction through a rock-laden path up to ABC. On the right was Jobo Rabzang. The leaden sky darkened suddenly. An ugly wet snowstorm began, and they slogged into a hammering headwind. Even marching with their heads down,

Benitez's team was assaulted by the sideways-driving snow. "Very bad, very bad," one of the other sherpas behind Ang and Benitez observed. Storms were looked on as portentous signs that the mountain deities were angry. (The sherpa had been hired by British property developer Kevin Cubitt. The wealthiest clients can afford an extra $1,500 for a personal sherpa to transport their supplies.)

Several sherpas had been hard at work, clearing rocks and boulders to make platforms for tents at Cho Oyu's Advance Base Camp. Only half the yaks had arrived; the rest were still laboring through the storm. Despite the driving snow, everyone pitched in to raise "Big Green," a twenty-foot-long mess-style dining tent. Inside Big Green, a gas-powered heater fired up. Tea was brewed and climbers stamped their feet to warm up.

Advance Base Camp on Cho Oyu forms a single-level amphitheater, around a mile long, which faces down on the Nangpa La. Every day, yak traders cross the blazing white highway like long lines of ants between Tibet and Nepal. They are laden with counterfeit outdoor clothing, manufactured in mainland China, en route to Nepal's tourist trekking and climbing markets.

At ABC, Ang took a quiet moment to observe the pass. It was the route his people had taken to freedom hundreds of years before. Ang had crossed the pass many times. He told Varcas how he had once been caught by the PAP and locked in a police station for several days.

Many sherpas found that wealth and partnership with Western climbing outfitters often put them in morally difficult situations. They were dependent on Western companies that had questionable moral imperatives. Two Tibetan cooks were laboring in Cho Oyu ABC, getting the camp ready for the Westerners. They had been doing the same job back in September 2003, when they had witnessed a sixteen-year-old girl, a refugee from Lhasa, swallowed by a crevasse on the Nangpa La. Her fifteen-year-old sister and others in the group, having no climbing ropes, attempted to tie their belts together and dangle them to the girl, who was screaming in panic. They could not see or reach her, but they could hear her screams. The icy maw of the crevasse gripped her body, but the more she struggled, the more her body heat melted the ice around her and the deeper into the dark clutches of the chasm she fell. The other escapees were frantic and dropped *tsampa* (roasted barley) down to her, but the situation fast became hopeless.

The two Tibetan cooks had been watching through binoculars and hurried to tell the mountaineers they were with. The climbers had ropes, ladders, and everything that was needed to rescue the girl. Instead, as it was summit day, they had turned, ignored her plight, and carried on up the mountain instead, leaving the girl to die.

Ang looked up at the brooding sky, which was darkening by the hour. A snowstorm was rolling in. The third day in ABC, on September 12, the sherpas held a *puja* requesting permission from the mountain deities to climb Cho Oyu. Over several days, they had erected a five-foot pile of rocks as a makeshift *chorten*, a reliquary where Buddhist relics are stored. From it, they hung the Adventure Consultants expedition banner and prayer flags. The expedition's ice axes were propped around the altar. Candles and various offerings of food covered its surface.

As Ang recited prayers, sherpas hunkered down, hoods up, hands in pockets braced against the wind. Every now and then, sherpas grabbed handfuls of blessed rice and tossed them up over the altar. The clients nursed headaches in the altitude, but sipped bottles of beer. After an hour or so, the ceremony drew to a close. Despite brief respites, the storm raged on.

8

SNAKEHEADS

—.—.—

While many westerners have regarded Tibet as the mysterious hidden sanctuary, Tibetans have looked elsewhere for such a place.

Edwin Bernbaum, The Way to Shambala

In the late evening when the thirteen refugees were ready, the owner of the safe house gave a curt nod to his wife and they set out, pulling their collars up, nervously scanning the street for signs of the PSB. To avoid drawing attention, the group of thirteen separated into a handful of smaller groups. The streets were thronged with cars. It was easy to spot PSB cars with their black-and-white decals and banks of lights, but the PAP didn't necessarily advertise their presence. Senior officers drove around in unmarked Land Rovers and Land Cruisers. Kelsang gripped Dolma's hand as they strode along. Lobsang Samten, the petite nun, walked with them.

Half an hour earlier, Dolma and Kelsang had been scolded for delaying their departure. The girls had lost track of time at the Potala Palace. When they tumbled through the doorway of the safe house, flushed and panting, they had been met with disapproving looks. Dolma had mumbled something about seeing the Potala for the last time.

Before setting out, the safe house owner had told them that they'd be traveling to India through Nepal via the Friendship Bridge. It was a two-day drive from Lhasa.

They walked for what seemed like hours, between houses and through dozens of fields. Dolma thought they were heading west on the outer, northeastern reaches of Lhasa. The entire city was encircled by military installations, but the southeast and southwest were particularly dense. They passed compounds fenced with razor wire and bathed in the sodium glow of orange street lamps—PLA equipment factories, depots, and prisons.

As they journeyed on, the refugees passed numerous construction sites. Outside one site, a crowd of laborers was scrambling to watch a fight between two Chinese construction workers. It was a useful diversion, and the group easily walked past unnoticed.

Rounding a corner, the group came face to face with soldiers carrying assault rifles who were guarding a military installation. Dolma felt the skin on her scalp tighten, a little jolt of adrenaline that gave way to leaden fear. But the soldiers watched them disinterestedly.

Immediately to the south was Drapchi Prison. Once a sprawling military garrison, Drapchi at one time housed 1,000 inmates, many of whom were held on charges of "endangering state security" by mounting peaceful protests in the name of Tibetan freedom.

Soon, the road gave way to a limestone track that ran alongside a foul-smelling ditch. Thickets of poplar trees, planted to stop soil erosion, offered cover. Deserted buildings, half-built new ones, and heavy equipment littered the landscape. An hour and a half after they had left the darkened confines of the safe house, Dolma recognized Sera Monastery in the distance.

Above them on a mountain overlook was Lhasa's biggest sky burial site, Gyaltsen Ri.*

The old man ordered them to stop. They stood, anxious and vulnerable, shifting from foot to foot and barely talking for half an hour as they waited. Finally, a large flatbed truck lumbered toward them, followed by two cars. The truck was an eight-ton Qitong—a low-bed outfit, about twenty-feet long—a common site in Tibet.

Two warmly dressed men clambered down from the cab and greeted the man from the safe house. Dolma recognized their accents—the men were from Kham. Penpa was a tall man with distinctive hollowed cheeks

---

* Sky burial is a centuries-old tradition in Tibet where the bodies of the deceased are fed to vultures.

and a hawkish gaze. Gyaltsen,* a stocky man with a goatee, surveyed the group in the half-light.

Penpa and Gyaltsen were elite mountain guides who escorted individuals along the dangerous flight from Tibet. The only way to find them would have been through the Tibetan underground. Like their Western counterparts who are paid to escort thrill seekers through the mountains, so-called snakeheads are highly sought after and command top fees for their work. Theirs is an incredibly dangerous line of business. When caught, mountain guides are met with increasingly harsh prison sentences, sometimes as long as twenty years.

The mountain guides with the best reputations, of which there are only a dozen, are paid accordingly. One named Dorje is easily identifiable because of the scars of frostbite that stipple his body, a result of having to take off his shirt in a blizzard to tie his ripped shoes together on the Nangpa La. He has led well over five hundred people to freedom.

Those guides with reputations for successfully getting refugees out of the country are in high demand. The most famous guide in the underground network is Namkha, who lives in Amdo and has a reputation as the fastest, most efficient guide in Tibet. (It is said he can get a group out through the Nangpa La in under eight days.) Chinese border guards often set up mobile checkpoints within the Himalaya, but Namkha is adept at reading the land to predict where they will set up.

But even Namkha couldn't protect his charges from the brutality of the Nangpa La. During one ill-fated trip, Namkha's group—twenty-two refugees—was caught in a tremendous snowstorm at the border of Nepal. In all, five refugees died from exposure to the extreme cold. The bodies of two ten-year-old boys and the eleven-year-old sister of one of them were left wrapped in blankets on the pass. One survivor had his legs amputated below the knee when he arrived in Kathmandu, the frostbite was so severe.

The guides have tough, ruthless reputations. They sometimes abandon refugees on the high passes to die when it suits them. Sometimes, the more cutthroat insist on sex with the women in their charge,

---

* Gyaltsen is a pseudonym.

often raping them if they refuse. Out on the high passes in the high Himalaya, there is no law or morality.

— ·— ·—

Illegal guides are hard to find, but in Kathmandu toward the end of 2006, I found a guide willing to talk. Lubum,* a twenty-nine-year-old who has made his living as an illegal guide, had been tortured and thrown into prison for his work. He has a pinched, suspicious face that rarely relaxes. "The Chinese say I am a human trafficker. But I did these things for the Tibetan people. It is the only way to preserve our Tibetan culture and language," he told me. He declined to say whether he still actively leads people himself.

"A generation of Tibetans knows nothing of life before the Chinese," Lubum commented. He only became aware of his own heritage after he had escaped to India himself in the mid-nineties. "I knew nothing about China, but in exile I heard how they were destroying our culture and our language." He decided to return to help others escape so that they too could have the benefits of a Tibetan education.

The fee for escorting a person out of Tibet to Dharamsala, said Lubum, is 2,000 yuan (about $300). Victims of persecution are escorted for free. In unmarked trucks, Lubum has led refugees through military checkpoints to Shigatse. On the Nangpa La, he sometimes wraps the hands of children who cannot afford gloves with rags and plastic bags to protect them from frostbite. "The Chinese were after us all the time," he said of his dangerous work. "Going through villages was dangerous as the villagers were often paid by the Chinese to inform on us, so we always had to go the hard way. Over mountains, through streams, to avoid military checkpoints."

Most of the time, he was successful. Often he led groups of as many as fifty people to freedom. Once, however, a young monk suffering from jaundice was violently ill on the journey. "I carried him, but he died on my back," said Lubum. "We had to leave his body in the snow where the soldiers wouldn't find it."

---

* Lubum is a pseudonym.

In December 2002, Lubum paid dearly for his work. An informer turned his details over to the Chinese authorities. He was interrogated for eight months in Gutsa Prison, a few kilometers from Lhasa center. The prison specialized in "confessions" extorted with wooden sticks and electric cattle prods. Lubum was beaten so badly he couldn't stand. He rolled up his trouser leg to show a savage scar where he was thrown onto the bars of an electric heater in the interrogation room. "They wanted us to accept China and to refute Tibet," he said, his eyes smoldering beneath the brim of his baseball cap. "But we wouldn't accept this."

Lubum was eventually sentenced to four years in jail. After several years, his family scraped together enough money to bribe a prison official to release their son. "They gave all the money they had," he admitted.

— · — · —

Penpa was motivated by hard cash, not altruism. Standing near the truck, he was a brooding presence, testament to his years in the People's Armed Police. Several years earlier, he had been patrolling in the mountains when he lost his pistol. He was duly court-martialed and sent to a military prison. After his release, he was shunned by his former Chinese colleagues and his Tibetan countrymen. Now Penpa made a living leading refugees through the mountains that he once patrolled. He was gruff and paranoid. In recent years, the risks of guiding had increased, as the Chinese authorities tried to crack down in the run-up to the Olympics in 2008. So guides had increased their fees.

Something seemed amiss to Dolma. The owner of the safe house had told the group that they would be traveling by jeep, but they had been met by an enormous flatbed truck, far bigger than necessary to accommodate the group.

A quarter of an hour after the group had arrived, countless figures began to emerge out of the gloom, coming now from all directions, some by bicycle, some by car, others marching on foot. Some had come from as far east as Sichuan and as far north as Amdo. Children had been sent by parents eager that they receive a real Tibetan education in exile. One four-year-old, Jinpa,° traveled with his older brother Jigme Kalden.° All the children had small backpacks carrying food and pictures of their families.

Twenty-four-year-old nun Dechen Pema° was a tall, willowy figure from Chamdo prefecture who now lived in Lhasa. She had been entrusted with Samdhup,° a mentally ill, deaf sixteen-year-old whose parents felt that if only they could get her to India, their daughter would have a chance for a better life. For several days, Dechen had met with a shadowy go-between who had finally finessed a deal with the smugglers. That day she had left with Samdhup after a tearful farewell with her parents. They had been driven in a zigzagging pattern through Lhasa, stopping and changing cars every hour or so. Her go-between was taking no chances. All the while, Dechen had calmed Samdhup, keeping her quiet so that she wouldn't alert the authorities with loud noise or embarrassing questions.

In the preceding days, secret rendezvous had taken place all over Lhasa in anticipation of the journey ahead: covert meetings near the Potala Palace, in restaurants, in the Barkhor area. All had been informed of when to meet the truck in the outskirts of Lhasa.

Eventually, seventy-four people stood around the back of the truck. It was a dangerously large group to smuggle out at once. The guides had pooled their resources to make more money.

Kelsang pushed forward as everyone began to scramble inside the truck. The guides ushered the children in first. The shadows inside swallowed them. Outside, an argument had broken out. Two men were questioning the cost of the journey and the number of people traveling.

"You told us eleven people," a nervous looking man protested angrily, in a hoarse whisper. "What is this?"

One man demanded his money back. The two men had paid 5,000 yuan ($730) each, the highest price tag for the journey.

Penpa, the guide, took them aside and reassured them they'd be all right. "Look. Don't worry," he said quietly. "Not all of these people

° Jinpa, Jigme Kalden, Dechen Pema, and Samdhup are pseudonyms.

are going to make it. They are going to drop, they will fall down." He said, with a dangerous smile, "But you'll be alright."

He held open the tarpaulin to let them into the back of the truck. There was the flash of a face reflecting the moonlight. Children cried in the dark, some sobbing for their parents. Suddenly, there was a boom from the left side of the truck as one of the guides punched it violently from outside, demanding the children be silenced.

The engine fired to life with a jolt.

And just as it began to move off, the truck lurched to a sudden stop. Outside, two figures sprinted up to the guides' car. (The guides drove behind the truck as a safeguard; it was too dangerous for them to travel with their charges.) After a hurried conversation with the guides, the figures jumped into the back of the truck, clambering aboard as it lurched off.

—·—·—

One of the newcomers was Jamyang Samten, a tough fifteen-year-old with a spiky shock of hair. Despite the aching in his arms from hanging onto the struts above him as the truck heaved forward, he was brimming with excitement. He'd waited a long time for this.

Raised in the remote village of Theshur in the Jomda County of Chamdo, deep in the heart of Kham, he had nursed his dislike of the Chinese for years. His family had lived in the emerald gorges and rocky mountain ridges of an area known for its fierce Tibetan nationalism. The family's hardy Tibetan ponies were the pride of the village and the soul of the semi-nomadic village community. But one year, Chinese bureaucrats arrived to partition the family's land. Shortly after, they seized all of the horses from the village, placing them in state-run stables. Jamyang was devastated when officials took away his prized black stallion. When Jamyang broke into the Chinese stables to check on his horse, he was caught, beaten, and detained.

Nomads were now forced to pay for fences that divided up the great steppe and prevented wild gazelles and yaks from roaming. It was to be "a beautiful, new socialist countryside," according to Tibetan Autonomous Region (TAR) party secretary Zhang Qingli. The few water sources were drunk bone-dry. Animals died of thirst and malnutrition.

Shortly after, Jamyang was sent to boarding school, where he found that Tibetans and Chinese were segregated. In a class of thirty-seven, he was one of only seven Tibetans. The Chinese students were treated to better food and accommodations, and the Tibetans subject to beatings when they misbehaved. Each morning, they would exercise in the school's central square. Afterward they were called on to recite quotes from Chairman Mao. In class, pro-Communist rhetoric was drilled home.

After a beating for misbehavior, Jamyang hatched a plot with some friends to run from school for three days in the hope that he would be expelled. It worked. Back at home, Jamyang's loathing of the Chinese grew. When Jamyang spied a pendant of the Dalai Lama on a cook at a nearby monastery, his eyes widened when the man told him of His Holiness's escape and the Chinese invasion of Tibet. It was the first time the boy had heard the true history of Tibet. Jamyang determined that he too would flee to India. When Jamyang's father refused his son's plan to travel to India, Jamyang smoothly changed tack, insisting instead that he would go on a pilgrimage to Lhasa.

In Lhasa, Jamyang tracked down a relative and declared his intent to go to India. There was one condition: Jamyang had to get a prediction from a lama at the Barkhor. When he found the lama, the man offered Jamyang a grave prediction—that it was a bad time to travel to India. But Jamyang was determined. When he returned, the relative asked how the prediction had gone. "The prediction was good," lied Jamyang.

After several days in the city, he was escorted by a monk to a rendezvous on the eastern side of Lhasa. There he met Tsultrim Lhodoe, a boy around his age, who was equally defiant and tough. The two bonded immediately. This was to be the adventure of their lives.

—·—·—

In the darkness, Dolma felt Kelsang's hand grip tighter. When the truck lurched into potholes, children moaned. In the back of the truck, several passengers recited prayers. It was swelteringly hot and claustrophobic. Dolma heard Kelsang's disembodied voice whisper out of the darkness, "We're going to die here. We can't survive this."

Every time the truck stopped, the tension in the airless chamber escalated. At one stop, a man jumped out and ran away into the darkness. As the truck slowed, children were shushed.

Once or twice, Dolma heard children being beaten, screams stifled, angry hoarse whispers, and muffled sobs. Worse than the claustrophobia or discomfort was not knowing what danger lurked outside. After two hours of driving, the truck came to a stop and the tarpaulin was thrown open. The children craned to see. There were a few audibly sharp intakes of breath and then relief when they saw Penpa's face.

Outside, Dolma and Kelsang tried to work out where they were. They could make out tangles of juniper and rhododendron bushes and a steep limestone escarpment. In the hills above were eighty meditation caves and stone cottages. They were at Dra Yerpa, a deep, rocky valley and one of the holiest pilgrimage centers outside Lhasa. They had only traveled around ten miles from Lhasa. And now they were heading away from their destination. It was an attempt by the guides to evade the heavily photographed checkpoints on the eastern side of Lhasa before switching back around the city on roads that weren't as thick with security.

Out in the clean air, the refugees naturally splintered into smaller groups delineated according to hometowns. The group from Driru comprised thirteen young men and women.

After a day in Dra Yerpa, during which refugees posed as pilgrims, everyone reboarded the truck as darkness fell. The road was smooth, and a cold, fresh breeze swept through the tarpaulin. It was the chilled air coming off the Tsangpo River, which roared beside the Friendship Highway. The road bucked and twisted along the river.

In the early hours of the morning, they traveled a ghost highway between Lhasa and Shigatse. It was a heavily militarized city, encircled by checkpoints. The authorities posted fliers over the city offering rewards to anyone who turned in refugees. As they neared the city center, thirty-one-year-old Lobsang Choedon grew increasingly nervous.

He had a wind-lashed face turned copper rouge by the elements and a small pot belly.

Choedon and his wife, Yeshe Dolma, had dreamed of a trip to India to see the Dalai Lama. The couple and their two young children lived in the region of Kardze (Ch: Ganzi) in Sichuan (the Tibetan Kham), a bastion of support for the Dalai Lama and a free Tibet. The Chinese called it the "neck of Tibet"—get your hands around it and you can control the country.

The Kardze man and his wife traded caterpillar fungus and yak leather. For half a kilogram of fungus, he could get as much as 30,000 yuan. He had a thriving wheat farm, but Chinese officials had ordered him to grow trees to prevent soil erosion in his most valuable fields. When he started to refocus on caterpillar fungus, he was heavily taxed.

The farmer supported his elderly father, who had spent his life in and out of prison for demanding Tibetan independence. Choedon had served time at Drapchi Prison for possession of a knife that he used for farm work. There he was beaten until he confessed to being a thief.

Despite the obstacles, Choedon and Yeshe Dolma had put enough away for an overland trip to India. Choedon applied for a passport at the police station. It was an impossible task, a bureaucratic nightmare that had to be authorized by the police, the county, the prefecture, and the TAR administration. Choedon's application was denied because of what they called an upcoming "big show." Choedon had yet to learn that they were referring to the 2008 Beijing Olympics. On the eve of the games, travel out of the country by Tibetans was forbidden: China had no intention of looking bad or receiving poor press from Tibetan refugees as it took the spotlight.

But Choedon and his wife, a raw-boned woman with broad white teeth and a cheery disposition, were determined. Meeting the Dalai Lama would bring untold blessings for this life and would mean a good reincarnation in the next. They left their two young children, son Tenzin Dorje, four, and daughter Lobsang Youdon, two, in the care of his parents. They set out with a lama and a nun. The couple made it to Lhasa and then Shigatse. But after they were stopped at a PSB roadblock at

Tingri, not far from the border, they were brought in for questioning. There the couple was separated; Choedon was beaten and urged to confess to traveling to the Dalai Lama. But Choedon held firm, pursing his lips in stony silence. He knew the punishment would only be so much worse if he admitted it.

After two days, Choedon and Yeshe Dolma were eventually released. No proof of their escape plans had been ascertained. But the detention had terrified Yeshe. She now had anxiety attacks at the sight of a PSB officer. She couldn't go through with a second escape attempt. Choedon, undeterred, decided that he would make one more attempt. After a tearless farewell at a Lhasa bus station, Choedon and Yeshe turned away from one another.

Now Choedon was cruising past the same checkpoint where he had been arrested days earlier.

The truck slowed and stopped. Penpa came round to the back and warned that they would be stopped ahead. Inside the truck, the air was thick and hot. It was hard to breathe. Dolma held her breath; Kelsang stiffened beside her. Outside, Mandarin voices were audible. Chinese soldiers. Someone coughed and was quickly stifled. There were footfalls. No one could make out what the soldiers were saying. Dolma kept looking toward the back, expecting to see the tarpaulin yanked up, muzzles of guns and torches shining in. But after five minutes or so, the truck moved off.

They pushed on into the night before turning off the pavement. When they at last came to a stop, Dolma saw that they were in a desolate ravine. Unlike Shigatse, where large trucks were not unusual, in Lhartse they were more conspicuous. The truck veered off before the main checkpoint into the city. They rested for a day; then come nightfall they set off again.

When at last the tarpaulin was thrown up, Kelsang and Dolma found themselves spilling out of the back of the truck. Dolma gathered her coat around her as the wind sucked and moaned. Grit stung her face, making her squint. Others turned their backs to the roaring gusts. Kelsang drew next to her, shouldering against the wind. "This isn't Dram," she shouted dispiritedly. "We've been cheated!"

A particularly strong gust whipped the hat that Dolma had bought in the Barkhor off her head. It tumbled off into the night. She made to grasp at it as it floated away, cartwheeling over the ground, but she was too slow. As she recovered herself, there in the black night, the landscape roared away from under her feet. Somewhere beyond lay the Nangpa La.

9

City on the Mountain

— . — . —

We were too tired to help. Above 8,000 meters is not
a place where people can afford morality.
Japanese climber Eisuke Shigekawa

The toughness of the endeavor shocked Benitez's clients from the outset. They set out at 7 a.m. for the first climb to Camp One at 21,635 feet, which could take anywhere between four and eight hours. Heading southeast, the team trudged over the glacier and then up the western flank of Cho Oyu. They moved through a hanging gully carved out of the rock walls. About halfway, after two hours, they passed a field of lapis blue penitentes, a swathe of thirty- and forty-foot-high ice formations that angled toward the sun. Afterward they arrived at a steep hill. Climbers had a range of sobriquets for it: "Horrible Hill," "Heart Attack Hill," or "Terrible Hill." It was a sheer trail that zigzagged across a precipitous face with sharp, angled turns. Scree slipped under the climbers' boots as they made the slow ascent up the precarious path.

As the team headed upward, they began the process of acclimatization known as "climbing high and sleeping low." Over the next two weeks, they would climb up to high camps and return to Advance Base Camp to get their bodies accustomed to the altitude before finally making a bid for the top.

Several hundred yards below Camp One, the climb was particularly hazardous. Boulders the size of televisions clung to the mountainside. A swift movement by a climber could easily send the rocks tumbling down. Benitez had seen climbers bowled off their feet.

The previous day, Benitez had constructed a "mountain safe" in ABC next to his tent. As increasing numbers flocked to the mountains, theft was rampant. Base camps were like licentious, frontier towns for the few months that they spread like algal blooms on the sides of mountains. Earlier in the year, the giant battery that the Discovery Channel documentary filmmakers had been using to power their production site on Everest had been stolen. Prostitutes plied their services at Everest Base Camp, and young Tibetans sold marijuana. Benitez weighted down a large blue barrel with rocks. Inside he stashed the money he would turn over to his sherpas at the end of the expedition. He had secured the cylinder with a sturdy padlock.

That night Benitez's team had warmed up in Big Green and watched *The Matrix*. In the morning, the skies had begun to clear, and as they marched up, the views were spectacular. After five hours, the group made it to Camp One, a jutting outcrop of crystal white snow on the western side of the mountain, looking down on the Nangpa La. The powder snow draping the higher buttresses of the mountain shimmered to a soft peach hue in the alpenglow, a setting sun sinking beyond. They snatched a short rest and then turned back the way they had come for the descent to base camp.

Heading down the mountain, nursing headaches, Benitez's team passed several groups making their way up to Camp One. Benitez noticed a particularly outlandish character with a long, red-beard. To Benitez's trained eye, the man was ascending dangerously fast. More dangerous still, he was alone.

Heaving for breath, the man slumped down beside the AC group. In a thick Eastern European accent, he made conversation with Paul Rogers about climbing the South Pacific Alps on New Zealand's south island. He was, he claimed, on Cho Oyu to make a documentary about his climb.

As the man gathered himself together, heading back on the steep trail, Benitez shook his head. He was the first to speak, "What a joker!"

— · — · —

Sergiu Matei, a news cameraman from Romania, had saved up, sold his prized possessions, and worked overtime to achieve his dream: the summit of an 8,000-meter peak in the Himalaya. A forthright and blustery former rugby player with a propensity for plain speaking and salty language, the brawny twenty-nine-year-old liked the extreme demands of mountain climbing.

Matei had been inspired to climb after filming a demonstration by climbers who rappelled off the side of the Romanian PRO TV building in Bucharest. He had cut his teeth on the rocky crags of the Carpathian Mountains in his native Romania where the tallest peak was only 8,000 feet. On one climb, he met Alex Gavan, a twenty-four-year-old who shared his dream of climbing Cho Oyu. A passionate climber whose e-mail signature read, "Climbing mountains outside is climbing mountains inside," Gavan claimed that he wouldn't use sherpas or oxygen for his Cho Oyu attempt. He would take all his own gear up and down the mountain to save money.

Inspired by Gavan, Matei asked to come along. Raising the $15,000 for permits and minor support plus flights would be a struggle, but Matei was determined. He sold his beloved Volkswagen Corrado and two camera lenses and hustled as hard as he could to find sponsors, soliciting any and all. (He convinced a pig farmer to contribute 3,000 euros in exchange for mentioning the man's farm in any media.) Matei and Gavan could afford only the lowest-grade gear. They bought secondhand sleeping bags and used ice axes.

Matei's colleagues at PRO TV thought that he was crazy. He was an award-winning cameraman who had worked in Iraq, Afghanistan, and Kosovo. Matei had grown up in the impoverished shadow of Communism. He lacked years of climbing experience, but he had felt the thrill of the mountains and was keen to see the Himalaya.

Matei arrived in Kathmandu on August 26, 2006, depressed and homesick for his wife. Now that the expedition was underway, he began to question his experience and what it had all cost. He simply wanted to be at home. His mood wasn't helped when he arrived to discover that all his gear had been lost by Austrian Airlines somewhere en route. Matei and Gavan, who had bought in with another self-guided group, had paid only for transport to ABC. Theirs was a threadbare affair. In Kathmandu, they haggled for barrels to transport their equipment. Without the money to fly, Matei and Gavan would take a truck from Nepal to Tibet.

After two days, they arrived amid the excited bustle of Chinese Base Camp. In stark contrast to the well-outfitted climbers around them, Matei and Gavan had only three barrels and their packs. Without sherpas or oxygen, they were easily identified as the most frugal climbers on the mountain. It also made them controversial. Climbers died without proper support, and many saw the Romanians as recklessly endangering themselves. The big outfitters complained about solo climbers whom they were criticized for not rescuing when things got nasty and the outfitters were their last hope.

Two days after leaving base camp, Gavan and Matei arrived at ABC. They staggered into what had become a small city of tents arranged along a mile of jumbled moraine. The terraced camp was burgeoning each day as more climbers arrived; sponsors' flags were hoisted alongside the flags of countries from around the world. Around forty international expeditions jostled for space. Experienced climbers like Slovenian Pavle Kozjek thought it was the biggest base camp he had ever seen in the Himalaya. It was growing evidence of the rampant commercialization of the mountains. It took forty-five minutes just to walk the length of the bustling boomtown.

Most of the climbers at ABC were using Cho Oyu as a warm-up for Everest. For the most part, the international climbers were moneyed professionals: an eighteen-strong team of British doctors studying the effects of altitude, a Russian nuclear scientist, engineers, geologists, an accountant, four policemen, and several businessmen. In the middle of the camp was a huge green tent next to which was the tallest flagpole of all, flying the red Chinese flag. In addition to housing the largest team at ABC, the Chinese camp had a full medical facility. Some of the Chinese were rumored to be in training to take the Olympic torch to the top of Everest two years hence.

Life in ABC was frenetic. There were parties at night, caseloads of wine, the aroma of freshly cooked food seeping out of cook tents, stereos blasting American rock. Some tents were flanked by reclining chairs where climbers could lie with a cold beer, tanning. One night when the pungent whiff of marijuana drifted into Matei's tent, he purchased a joint from a Tibetan family. He drew in lungfuls, the drug swirling in his bloodstream as he marveled at the power of the mountains around him. There was nothing that couldn't be bought here.

At ABC, Cho Oyu Himalayan Experience (Himex) owner Russell Brice, fifty-four, a New Zealander with a mercurial temper, other climbers reported, was like the unofficial mayor. He had silver hair and drawn features pulled tight over a thin face. Sherpas called him Ban Dai, "Big Boss."

Himex (one of the first companies to run expeditions up Cho Oyu) was the biggest outfitter operating in the Himalaya. The company had helped three hundred climbers summit more 8,000-meter peaks in twenty years than any other company. The most illustrious and expensive company to climb with, it boasted an enviable safety record.

Brice was a tough, accomplished climber in his own right. He had summitted Everest twice and had paraglided and skied off the top of Cho Oyu. On the way up, he had set a speed record on the mountain, running from Camp One to the summit and back in eleven hours. His company had been one of the first Western outfits to run expeditions up Cho Oyu, starting in 1996.

From Everest expeditions alone, Brice brought in over a million dollars a year. He liked to boast that he threw the best parties on Everest—lavish affairs with crates of wine, tables overflowing with food, TVs displaying the latest climbing films. Fond of a drink or two and known for a brittle personality, Brice was quick to take offense and took slights personally.

For Brice, 2006 had been a financially successful year. In the summer, he'd wrapped up filming with the Discovery Channel on a documentary covering Himex's Everest Expedition. Viewers in living rooms around the world thrilled to the heroic souls conquering Everest. The show, *Everest: Beyond the Limit,* would make Brice famous beyond the mountaineering community. (Brice had reputedly been paid several million dollars for the filming contract.)

But Brice was gaining a reputation in the mountains as a hard-nosed, controversial operator, according to climbers, some old clients, and reports in the press. In May, British climber David Sharp—soloing up the mountain—had been left to die on Everest's northeast ridge. A team of Himex climbers discovered him—his lips blue, his oxygen mask askew. A total of forty climbers saw Sharp, literally freezing to death in the high altitude, and possibly past saving, and carried on with their summit attempt. Brice allegedly radioed his group to carry on. (Brice has since denied these claims and one accuser has since changed his story.)

A shrewd businessman who had been climbing in Tibet since 1974, Brice maintained good business relationships with the Chinese authorities in Tibet and had a virtual monopoly on the north side of Everest. Brice maintained storage facilities in Tingri and was able to obtain permits for climbing in Tibet when other expedition leaders were refused.

New Zealand climber Marty Schmidt, a kinetic, wiry-limbed mountain guide from California, remembered his first ascent of Everest with Brice from the north face. No one had attempted the route before. Despite a close call with an avalanche, the ascent was a success. Brice knew he had struck gold. "Russell was in Beijing negotiating with the Chinese for a better position on the mountain for next year before I'd even reached the top," Schmidt recalled. "With Russell, it's turned into a business. He's got overheads and he has to make a certain amount each year and he has to produce."

—·—·—

In 2003, Schmidt's attempt at Cho Oyu had been thwarted when his client, sixty-seven-year-old Clifton Maloney, an investment banker, ran out of steam.*

Forty-one-year-old Schmidt, an obsessive mountaineer and former air force para-rescuer, offers no-nonsense, military-style expeditions with an emphasis on self-reliance. He doesn't use sherpas and eschews oxygen for his summit attempts. As he had led Maloney down Cho Oyu, Schmidt had come across a stupa in the middle of the trail. Schmidt was around fifty meters ahead of his client.

One hundred meters below on the Nangpa La, Schmidt saw a gaggle of Tibetan refugees corralled by PAP soldiers at gunpoint. The contents of their backpacks and suitcases—clothes, food, shoes—had

_____
* Schmidt was climbing on a shared permit with Henry Todd.

been spread out on the ground. In moments, a gunshot cracked the air. Several refugees picked up rocks and started stoning the soldiers. One soldier went down in the attack. The others quickly surrendered.

The Tibetans had hurriedly grabbed their bags and made off up over the pass into Nepal, taking some of the soldiers' weapons with them. The PAP recovered and began to fire on the fleeing Tibetans. The refugees returned fire on the soldiers. "We decided we would rather die in the mountains than go back to Tibet," says Dhukar, a tough youth from Amdo who had been with the group. His father had been involved in an underground printing business making illegal prints of the Dalai Lama and his pamphlets of his teachings. Later, he suspected one of the group had been an informant and had given away their position to the PAP.

The Tibetans had fired back at the soldiers several times. Schmidt cautiously descended after the horrifying scene. He found the body of a young Tibetan woman lying on the Nangpa La and assumed she was dead. Terrified, the two bolted the scene—and Tibet—as fast as they could. They made it back to base camp and on to Tingri, where they decided to get out of the country as fast as possible. "I wanted to get out of China. That was the goal. You say nothing. You get out," said Schmidt.

A few hours after the shooting, American climber Dave Morton and a climbing buddy had been fired on by PAP soldiers near the Nangpa La. At 15,000 feet, it was near impossible to run. But the two men had managed to evade their attackers, making their way to Namche Bazar.

At the time, Brice had been running an expedition on Cho Oyu. When the soldiers descended after the mountain shooting, Brice gave them food, shelter, and medical attention. He reported that he had heard shots from his base camp and that a Han Chinese had fired to attract attention. The man was brought into camp, his limbs blackened with frostbite. He'd been left on the pass for several days. Brice treated him before soldiers from his unit took him back to base.

To the chagrin of the Chinese, Morton went public with his story. When, in 2005, he returned to climb Cho Oyu, the PAP stopped him and forbid him from climbing the mountain at Chinese Base Camp.

For his part, Schmidt, unsure of who he would even report it to, kept quiet about the scene he'd witnessed, not wanting to be banned from coming back.* In the Himalaya, few were willing to raise their voices if it meant jeopardizing their ability to climb.

——·—·—

On Cho Oyu, one of Brice's greatest allies was Henry Todd. The British outfitter had married Brice's base camp manager, Sue Harper. They'd watched each other's backs for years and both remembered the shooting incident back in 2002, another example of the wild frontier where the men did business. "Russell and Henry are Alpha males," says a friend to both men, British mountain guide Victor Saunders. "They are Silverbacks."

Here Benitez was seen as the new kid, an up-and-comer in Brice and Todd's world. In Brice's tent at ABC, the three men drank tea and chatted about conditions on the mountain. In September 2006, Todd was on Cho Oyu to offer logistical support to several expeditions.

——·—·—

A night's sleep at 20,000 feet is an uneven affair as the body adjusts to the rigors of oxygen depletion. Because it demands relatively little in the way of technical climbing, Cho Oyu is often underestimated. Benitez and his team struggled up from Advance Base Camp to Camp One. They had been on the mountain for ten days.

Just before Heartbreak Hill, they came across a French Canadian team, L'échappée Belle Cho Oyu 2006, that was attempting to rescue one of their members. The man in question was paralyzed on his right side, and his team leader diagnosed a stroke. Rogers initially felt that the man might be dehydrated. Benitez rushed in, confirmed the diagnosis

---

* Maloney and Schmidt made a second attempt on Cho Oyu in September 2009. After successfully summiting, making Maloney the oldest American at seventy-one to reach the top of an 8,000 meter peak, the two men rested at Camp Two for the night. Maloney turned to Schmidt and said, "I'm the happiest man in the world, I've just summitted a beautiful mountain." The following day, Schmidt discovered that his client had died in his sleep.

of a stroke, and busied himself contacting climbers at ABC, asking for help and a stretcher.

Todd was sitting at ABC scanning radio frequencies. It was the climbers' way of keeping the progress and gossip about the teams on the mountain up to date. Todd sent his sherpas to help. He praised Benitez's quick actions. "This is one of those situations where the quality of people on the hill come into their own," he said. "I'm not worried by this. I know you'll save him." It was the sort of situation Benitez thrived on. Praise from Todd was a sign that Benitez was gaining the respect of the old guard. The French Canadians got their man down, saving his life, although he would suffer the effects for the rest of his life.

Rogers pushed up to Camp One with the clients, while Benitez helped oversee the Canadian's evacuation. When he arrived at the small, snowy shoulder of Camp One, it was laden with orange expedition tents. Granite walls reared up around them, fronds of cloud ringed the angular ramparts of nearby Shishapangma. Unlike the plush comfort of ABC with its hot showers, toilet tents, and the reassuring interior of the mess tent, the penetrating cold and meager amenities of Camp One were a shock to Benitez's team.

From Camp One, the climb upward was icy and slick. After a night of rest, the team trudged through knee-deep snow for two hours before reaching a near-vertical headwall of two-hundred-thirty-foot ice cliffs. The area was congested with climbers waiting to clip in to the two fixed ropes. Just before they reached the ice cliffs, Varcas admitted to the guide, Rogers, that there were issues at home. His mother had called him the previous night to tell him that his cousin had died. It sapped Varcas's will to carry on, and he abandoned the mission.

Benitez kicked his crampons into brittle ice and led the rest of his team upward toward Camp Two. It was a slow plod in deep snow up a sharp glacier-covered shoulder. Straining with forty-pound packs, clutching ice axes and ropes, was daunting work. The ropes creaked, and shards of ice and snow formed cyclonic spindrifts that stung their faces as they made slow progress up the face of the ice cliffs. A sapphire sky flashed above them. Over the top of the ice cliffs, storms had left thick snowdrifts. The glare from the snow was blinding, even through dark lenses. Cubitt reached the top but was completely exhausted. He descended, while Benitez took the three remaining members to Camp Two. On September 21, they arrived at a huddle of tents sitting at the bottom of the northwest face of the mountain at around at 23,000 feet. They marveled as they looked down on a thickening carpet of clouds.

—·—·—

Elsewhere on the mountain, without the measured leadership of a guide, Matei and Gavan had begun to clash. After fighting over how much gear to take on their first ascent to Camp One, they'd gotten a late start and had reached camp late in the afternoon. They returned to ABC in the dark. Matei was getting fed up with the whole endeavor. He lacked the patience required to summit such a large peak, and Gavan was starting to grate on his nerves.

After two days of rest at ABC, the men climbed to Camp One for a night, before trekking onward to Camp Two. As Matei clipped in to tackle the ice cliffs, an American climber sailed past, his feet tangling in the ropes. Matei stopped his ascent to help, pulling the man out of the lines and helping him down. The rescue took Matei's mind off a growing ache in his right lung and a persistent cough that had started early that day. As he put his gloves on again, head down, he started to push to Camp Two and began to hallucinate. The snow suddenly turned bright green. Gavan could see that something was seriously wrong with his partner. "Are you OK?" he shouted. Matei summoned energy to shout back. He was dizzy and needed to descend. Gavan headed up.

Matei struggled back down the ropes and half-walked, half-limped, his brain cartwheeling. His vision turned kaleidoscopic and faded in and out. Matei panicked, reaching Camp One after two and a half hours. A Danish climber recognized the symptoms of high-altitude pulmonary edema (HAPE) and called a doctor. Matei's impatience to bull up the mountain so fast had contributed to the condition.

Matei was given Diamox to ease the fluid in his lungs. The doctor suggested Matei avoid further exertion and stay in camp. To attempt the fixed ropes on the ice cliffs in such shape would be ludicrous.

But Matei could only think of the comfort of ABC and a phone call to his wife. He was gravely shaken. He pulled a sleeping bag from his tent on Camp One, along with a down suit he had stowed there. He half-fell, half-strode down the mountain. After nine grueling hours, in complete darkness, Matei arrived at ABC.

—·—·—

A storm kicked in. Stuck in ABC for several days as rasping winds grated on the rocks around them, partying went into overdrive. Benitez and the other guides were invited to a steak dinner at Brice's camp. Benitez e-mailed home. Throughout his expedition, Benitez had been blogging about the trek for AC's Website. His September 24, 2006, entry was headlined "Bad Weather Fiesta!" He wrote, "The music got louder, the wine came out, and it became an official 'make the bad weather go away party.'" As the wine flowed and climbers got drunk—Emmanuel Smith and Scott Curtis joked about with oxygen masks—others raised toasts, the storm lashed at the tents, and the world went gray.

A snowball fight erupted. At first, the British, Americans, New Zealanders, and Australians were beating the Chinese climbers. A sixtyish Chinese man sat outside their tent directing the Chinese climbers like soldiers, ordering flanking attacks and urging his men to throw harder and faster. Climbers jokingly called him "The General."

The wind rasped on the rocks, and any metal became cold to the touch. Day and night were undifferentiated as the snow fell at the rate of thirty inches a day, silently burying everything and lending a soft, timeless quality to the world.

Sky and mountains joined in a seamless world of dirty gray.

10

THE INSIDER PASS

Danger was cumulative, of course, it crept up step
by step half noticed as your journey took you
deeper, farther. Until you woke up at night in a
place beyond help.
Colin Thubron, Shadow of the Silk Road

The wind gnashed at Dolma's clothes. Dry gusts threw sand in her face
as she and Kelsang jerked the hoods of their coats up, pulled on
face masks like bandits, and marched into the storm, their long brown
chubas—thick woolen coats—billowing around their ankles. Beneath
their feet was an ocean of gravelly hummocks that masked deep pockets.
The first time Dolma went sprawling, she cut her hand on low-growing
thorn bushes. The thorns jabbed into Dolma's hands and spiked her
legs, causing her skin to itch and bleed. Kelsang helped her up and
they pressed on.

Twenty minutes earlier, the truck had come to rest in a sand-blasted
arroyo, surrounded on three sides by the hulking shoulders of smooth-
topped mountains. Dolma's limbs were stiff in the biting cold, after the
cramped confines of the hot, airless truck. She was parched, but there
was no time to stop for water. In the pitch darkness, a few refugees had
flashlights. It was slow going, as they lurched over the uneven ground
rising up over unseen grass-covered hills and then hiked up and down
invisible ascents and descents behind the dim fingers of light.

Penpa reassured the team of refugees that they were only a few days
away from the border. The steepness of the terrain and the exertion took
its toll after a few hours. People started to lighten their packs. A monk
from Kongpo, Thupten Tsering, tossed a heavy sausage out of his bag;

others discarded excess clothing on the side of the path. The Kongpo monk was the only one who had done any physical training for the arduous journey. In Lhasa, he'd bought some knock-off Nikes and a gray Chinese laborer's outfit and jogged every day. It was so unusual to see anyone out running in Tibet's high-altitude capital city that it was suspicious. He led at the front, though, so it was paying off.

Several hours into their trek, the group came to a mountain stream. The water was gritty, but it slaked their thirst. A few escapees filled large Coke bottles with the water. At dawn, they could just make out the towering red-brick walls of Sakya Monastery, which loomed over a small town. In this vast landscape of scrub and denuded hills, stripped bare by centuries of overgrazing, the landmark was uplifting.

After a day and a half, the refugees crested a tall peak and descended into a valley to arrive at a small, abandoned house that was used by nomads for shelter in winter. Most of the water collected from the stream had been consumed, so the guide ordered Jamyang and Tsultrim to scout around for some other sources. They circled the area, eventually finding an old water pump. It creaked but produced nothing. The boys returned empty-handed.

After a head count, it was discovered that one boy was missing. Penpa called back to the truck drivers. The boy, rigid with fear, was discovered crouched in the back of the truck. Forcing him out, the drivers pointed him in the direction of the rest of the group. Gyaltsen set off to find him. The rest of the group slumped to the ground, grateful for the time to rest.

Before Gyaltsen headed back, Lhundrup, a thickset monk with a placid, mature demeanor who had become the unofficial leader of the Driru escapees, had ambled over to the guide, who was sitting on his haunches warming his hands near the gas flame. A few of the group had packed gas stoves, as fires here would alert the security forces to their location. Lhundrup, who had made the passage to India before, recognized their route. He knew they weren't headed to Dram. When the monk confronted Gyaltsen, the guide nodded his head. They would be heading further up, over the Snow Mountains, as he called them, to the Nangpa La. The other routes out were simply too dangerous.

As Lhundrup turned, he saw other groups making themselves comfortable with sleeping bags, pulling out warm clothing they had brought and chewing on healthy supplies of food. Clearly, some were more in the know than others. Dolma and Kelsang nodded stoically when Lhundrup returned and relayed the news. They had only enough food for about four days.

When Gyaltsen returned later that day, he was alone. The first casualty of the journey. Far from help and beyond turning back, the rest had no choice but to go on.

— · — · —

As night started to fall, the group began their trek into the darkness. The terrain gently swept upward as the ground below their marching feet degenerated to a plantless landscape of dust and rocks. After a while, Penpa ordered silence as they started to negotiate a complex labyrinth of mountains and passes. At the crest of one hill, they stopped dead in their tracks. Below they could see the brightly lit confines of the Dakmar PAP base, which was crawling with soldiers.

"No torches," whispered Penpa to the straggly line behind him. The few weak beams of light were quickly extinguished. The trails were well trodden by the thousands of refugees who used them, but in the dark, they were hard to navigate. The PAP had set carefully laid traps around the base: tin cans tied to ropes that they suspended at shin height and, worse, sharpened barbed wire strung at face height.

After an hour or so, the group descended into the comforting fold of a valley. At the bottom was a gurgling stream. Parched with thirst, the desperately thirsty travelers lapped at the water gratefully. The water felt silky and comforting in the darkness, as Dolma sloshed the liquid over her face.

From here, the path led down into the Tingri salt plains, a yawning sun-drenched patchwork of fields. The nearest tree was perhaps seventy miles away. No matter how long they walked, they never seemed to get anywhere in this land without end. Way off in the distance, beyond this vast expanse of nothingness, were brilliant cones of white, as the landscape buckled upward to the mighty barrier of the Himalaya.

The daunting godhead of Cho Oyu stood out thicker and wider than the other peaks that loomed to the east and west. To the west of the mountain was a deep notch, small from this distance, but unmistakable. It was the Nangpa La. The portal to freedom.

To the east was Everest, or Qomolangma, as Tibetans call the mountain: Goddess Mother of the World. Jamyang started singing in praise of Everest. Tibet's mighty mountain was symbolic of the fact that Tibet could never be conquered by the Chinese. He filled his lungs with dusty air and sang, as loud as he could, the songs to the Dalai Lama and Tibet's mighty mountain rippling across a denuded, peopleless landscape way beyond civilization.

Imperceptibly, the pass gained elevation beneath them. A whipping headwind snapped at Dolma's hair as they started on the Laiya La, which crested at 15,500 feet. Unfazed, Kelsang took the opportunity to pester Lhundrup, who had met the Dalai Lama before. "Will it be like meeting the Lama in our village?" she enthused giddily. "Will he touch our heads every time we meet him?" Kelsang, in her imaginings, was naively envisioning daily life with the Dalai Lama. Lhundrup patiently raised his eyebrows. "For new arrivals, you only meet him once," he explained patiently. "You cannot see him over and over." Kelsang nodded silently.

For several days, the group carried on—traveling by night, sleeping by day. Penpa guided under sequined skies, the star-studded dome of the galaxy twinkling above them. They toiled along in the vast landscape feeling insignificant and at the mercy of the elements. On the second day after leaving the truck, the stars were obscured by a thunderstorm. Rain started to fall in sullen gray sheets. Frigid and exhausted, they came upon a low winter house constructed of mani stones, rocks inscribed with prayers to the spirits of the place. The wind howled as they crawled inside. Kelsang shivered in the cold, huddling next to Dolma to stay warm. A few searched outside for fuel. All they found were some discarded torn canvas sneakers left by the nomads and some yak dung. With the tattered old shoes, they made a makeshift fire that filled the room with choking, rubberized smoke. But at least it was warm.

Jamyang and Tsultrim had formed a group of refugees from Amdo with Norbu Palden, a man from Kardze. He had a habit of walking with his hands behind his back, no matter the terrain, like a professor pondering an academic question. He was in his fifties and permanently angry about the Chinese and what they had done to his various businesses. In the hazy light of the fire, he spat with rage as he told of how he had fought them with court cases or defied them in flaming arguments. Jamyang and Tsultrim smirked at the Kardze man's outspokenness, conspiratorially thinking his ardor and chest-puffing a bluff.

Eventually they all drifted off to sleep. None of the children had sleeping bags, so they crawled in with the adults where they could. Kelsang slept fitfully.

The next night they began to walk again. When they roused themselves from their resting places in the rocks, their limbs were stiff, cold, and aching when they started out. In the Driru group, Dolma was drawn to a young girl of nine or ten in a green balaclava and a mauve-armed jacket who shuffled along sobbing. Dolma left Kelsang and slipped alongside, reassuringly grasping the girl's hand gently.

"What's wrong?" Dolma asked. Stuttering, the girl said that her mother had a chronic disease and that her father had died. Life at home was tough, but she had kept the family going by doing laundry for her neighbors, scrubbing sheets in a nearby river. Her mother knew that her days were numbered. She had decided that she could die a little easier knowing that her son and daughter were having a proper Tibetan education in India. She and her brother were packed off shortly after. Her mother had made the arrangements in secret and only told them a few days before. Her brother walked alongside silently. Dolma nodded, not saying much, just holding her hand and listening. Eventually the girl calmed.

Children fell behind, simply dropping on the trail and falling asleep. Choedon, exhausted, slackened his pace and soon found himself walking alone. Without a flashlight, he almost tripped over a black shape in the trail. It looked like a rock. When he nudged it with his foot, a little voice cried out. It was a ten-year-old boy who had gotten lost. The group had nicknamed him Paduk, a type of noodle. Many of the children had been given nicknames derived from the food they missed most as they nursed hunger pangs. Paduk had diarrhea and had lost everyone on one of his enforced toilet stops. Helping Paduk to his feet, Choedon grasped his hand and tugged him along as they tried to catch up to the rest.

Deep gashes appeared in the mountainsides. The carving winds had exposed minerals that had oxidized on contact with the air, turning the expansive banks purplish-brown.

After several hours, they came across shepherds. An old man came toward them. His face was gnarled after years of exposure to the high winds and sun. The guides asked about the location of army patrols. The old shepherd pondered their question. "The men up there on the mountain—the shepherds—are informers," he told them. "They'll report you to the Chinese and get paid 500 yuan [\$75] for each person. Be careful here." It was a considerable amount of money in the hardscrabble existence on Tibet's wild frontiers. Tibetans living in border areas were either sympathizers and helped escapees or they were notoriously venal; many near the border were in the pay of the Chinese. There was no way of knowing. Only snakeheads knew who to trust. Those who worked for the Chinese flaunted their ill-gotten power. When they came across groups, they demanded the clothes on their back, their boots, cell phones, whatever they wanted. The escapees had to hand them over without protest. The Chinese, along with trying to establish a network of informants, were also establishing a border militia—*yulmag*—comprised entirely of local Tibetans who were there to watch for refugees too.

They thanked the shepherd. Before leaving, Penpa and Gyaltsen asked if he would sell them a ration of *tsampa*. A few hours later, the man was back with small bags of the roasted barley flour. As the refugees devoured the gruel, the old man sat on a nearby rock, lost in introspection. The sight of so many Tibetan youngsters, all hopeful for a new life, caused him to reflect. He lamented his passing years and the missed opportunities of his life. The refugees strained to understand his thick accent. "All I've done is look after animals. I won't have a chance of an audience with His Holiness. But you are young. You can still see him." The old man became overwhelmed with melancholy. "When you see him, say a prayer for me." They nodded. "You don't have to be suspicious of me. I won't tell the Chinese anything." He pointed the way to go.

The harsh landscape of razor-sharp rocks and steep ascents stubbed toes, twisted ankles, and sapped energy with every step. One man nursed feet that were so swollen that the inflamed flesh was bursting out of his shoes. Once or twice, Dolma's knees buckled beneath her. The boots Dolma had bought in the Barkhor were coming apart at the seams after only four days on the trek. One of the men traveling in her group gave Dolma a pair of rubber-soled sneakers that were many sizes too big for her. When they rested, Dolma took some cotton from her coat, improvised a needle from a pin, and sewed one end to make them smaller. They still looked like flippers on her petite feet, but they were better than nothing.

———·——·———

Many members of the group had polythene sheets that they used as sleeping bags. On the fifth day of their trek, it rained again, and Dolma lay under her cover, airless, moist, and shivering, droplets battering on the plastic. On they went. Several monks and nuns stoically chanted in low tones while fingering their rosaries, the only sound along with the scrunch of footfalls on the impoverished landscape.

Boredom alternated with terror. Penpa instructed everyone to be careful. "This next village is full of informers, so we need to move through fast," he warned. Day was breaking, a watery light drenching the trail. They sprinted through a dismal collection of low, stone-walled houses pressed into the side of a mountain. Dolma saw little slivers of light from candles leak from cracks under doorways. She tried to limit the sound each footfall made as it scrunched on loose rock and stones. They made it across as the rising amber sun began to turn the village a battleship gray.

Splashing through, an icy brook on the outskirts of the village soaked Dolma's and Kelsang's feet. Frozen to the bone, they slept fitfully in a valley, uncomfortably tossing out rocks beneath them to make the ground at least bearable. The discomfort was made worse by a broiling sun that leaked behind their eyelids.

As night fell, they set out again. A gleaming full moon hung over them, a lambent wash of light casting their phantasmal silhouettes over the landscape and making them easy to spot. The guides chivvied people along, gazing upward reproachfully. A few hours into their trek, they saw five figures moving outside an encampment of houses several hundred yards ahead. Penpa ordered everyone to the ground. They dropped quickly and efficiently in what had now become a well-rehearsed drill. They must get out of the area without being spotted at all costs. They would have to loop the village as quickly as possible.

Running low, the escapees skirted the houses, keeping a nervous eye on any movement. Just beyond, between them and the safety of the vast landscape ahead, was a fast-moving mountain stream flecked with white water. Dolma attempted to leap. Just as she sprung off her rear foot, she lost traction and fell back into the icy river. Someone's hand plunged into the water and grabbed Dolma by her coat.

Back on solid ground, Dolma mustered all of her energy. In moments, her clothes froze solid. Kelsang slid her arm around her friend. There was no time to change into the spare trousers she had in the black bag. With each footfall, there was a cracking noise as the ice hardened and then splintered again with each movement of her body, like a statue coming to life.

Dolma consoled herself, thinking that at least they had evaded the village. A few hours later, as they shuffled through a barley field, their hopes that they had escaped unscathed seemed dashed. Out of the darkness ahead, a dozen flashlights swept the ground in a line. It looked like a line of soldiers combing the landscape for escapees. Someone hissed that the villagers must have told the Chinese soldiers. The group dropped among the stalks of the crop, clinging to the cover. Dolma clenched her teeth, desperately trying to stop them from chattering.

Urgent shapes streamed past the girls. Panicked, people up ahead had seen the lights and turned tail. Quickly the girls vaulted up from the ground and followed, fighting against the barley stalks with each stride. What they feared most were attack dogs, often used by the Wujing. Lhundrup, panting for breath, sprinted alongside the girls. "Here, get down," he strained. "They haven't seen us." They crouched. Lhundrup periscoped above the waving stalks and risked a look. The lights, now a ways back, hadn't changed position. Kelsang turned to Dolma and whispered that the key to their survival was to stick close to Lhundrup.

The only way past the soldiers was to the right, up a mountain pass and then over and behind the military units. They moved along the rim of the valley until they were able to look down on their would-be pursuers. In the bluish predawn light, they could see villagers harvesting barley by headlamps. It had all been a false alarm.

Kelsang dropped to her haunches, stuffing her hands in her pockets. It would be daylight soon, and they needed to find a place to pass the day. One village lay between the refugees and the safety afforded by the mountains' cover. Walking through the village, Dolma was startled when she saw a nomad woman standing stock-still in an alley between two buildings, observing the group wordlessly. After traversing the village, they took refuge in a deep valley.

Dozing fitfully, Dolma was awakened by a commotion. Daylight revealed several figures etched against the sky. A few brave souls crept toward the figures for a better look. Closer, they could see that they were stone scarecrows erected by villagers to frighten wolves away. The daily fear that they would be caught was inducing paranoia.

The next night, beneath a cloudless star-studded sky, clear from the high plateau, they trudged up a godforsaken rocky valley, the stones a forbidding gray. Several PAP tents could be seen dotted around. Soldiers scanned the horizon looking for escapees. Lights swung out like the probing fingers. Dogs barked in the distance.

Slowly, the days began to meld into one. So deep in this vast, unpopulated wilderness was the group that they could now walk in the day, taking advantage of the sun's warming rays. But even in the warmer daylight hours, the particulate dust whipped up by gusts of wind seeped into their lungs, making their eyes water and their throats gravelly. The grueling rigors of the journey were beginning to take their toll—sunburn, blisters, muscles that constantly ached. Worst of all, though, was the constant fear of being caught. When Dolma was frightened, she would chant the mantra of Padmasambhava that the geshe had told them would protect them: *Om Ah Hum. Vajra Guru Padma Siddhi Hum.* Kelsang slipped the rosary on her wrist and fingered the rosewood beads, her face set determinedly as she chanted and pushed forward, each step nearer to her goal.

Even Kelsang, after a while, complained of the gnawing hunger. Others remembered, with stinging regret, how they had tossed out food at the start of the journey. With no sustenance, they were running out of energy, and it was an effort in such a punishing landscape to press forward. Each footfall was clumsy and labored. Dechen Pema, despite her increasing hunger pangs, resisted consuming the blessed barley grains, known as *chakne,* she had in her pack. Hungry as she was, they were sacred.

Three nuns had joined the group of Driru refugees: Tenzin Dolma, Tenzin Wangmo, and Dechen Palmo. They were gaunt women who looked at least ten years older than their twenty-odd years. Prior to the journey, they had made a weeks-long retreat and fast in the mountains around Lhasa. Their bodies depleted, the trek to Nepal was too much. Tenzin Dolma, a small nun with a compassionate streak, began to lag far behind. Each time the group rested, she had sat apart on her own, chanting mantras as a way to overcome her suffering. She'd had stomach problems in Tibet before and was taking medicine, but now the altitude was getting to her as well. The guides called a rest, and the grateful nun sank to her knees dejectedly while Dolma and Kelsang ministered to her.

There was no time to stop. Their steps were a steady rhythm in an expansive gray landscape of rock and dust and huge, rolling hills that were cruelly deceptive. The sense of scale was warped beyond recognition, as if the normal rules of distance and perception didn't apply.

High in the mountains, what looked small from a distance was huge. They'd begin to walk up a fairly benign-looking hill, only to find it took hours of climbing on hands and knees. To take a wrong turn into these labyrinthine valleys, meanwhile, would mean being lost for days, maybe forever. As they tramped higher, the landscape became increasingly pallid, bleached of color. The little figures of the caravan of children laboring up the mountainside seemed to lose color too. The vibrant blues and reds of their anoraks turned to gray in the silvered light.

Granite rock faces reared out of gauzy cloud banks and then retreated. The temperature fluctuated wildly. Without a lick of wind in the valley floors, the temperature surged up into the high seventies, but in the high upper passes, icy gusts of wind chilled the air to zero degrees. They would shiver when they stopped.

Worst, the deadly thirst became all-consuming. The plastic Coke bottles sat in their backpacks bone dry. With each passing hour, they were also heading higher in an increasingly parched landscape, which meant there were a dwindling number of streams to collect water from.

At these altitudes, climbers are instructed to drink at least three to five liters of water a day. Dolma hadn't had a drop of water for several days. They came across some nomads and asked for water, but they refused, claiming that they would be punished for helping refugees. Their thirst was briefly abetted when shepherds, further along the trail, sold the group bags of murky water for 70 yuan (around $10).

As they toiled on, the sky overhead brooded and darkened. Out here, beyond all help, they were hostages to the weather. They began to cast wary eyes upward, terrified at the sight of clouds overhead or the intensity of the whipping winds. By the ninth day, the lack of oxygen in the thin air and steep ascent made for a sluggish pace. The guides advised those refugees wearing belts to tighten them as much as they could bear. The belts would act like tourniquets, they said, keeping the blood up in the upper part of their bodies. At high altitudes—anywhere upwards of 18,000 feet—blood thickens to a tarlike consistency.

Dolma's protesting haunches ached with each stride. Despite the fatigue and the effort of putting one foot in front of the other, they had to be vigilant with every footfall. The trail was rocky and uneven, and snatched at their ankles viciously, twisting them if they were not careful. A twisted ankle out here could mean abandonment and a grim fate. A forty-nine-year-old woman suppressed a scream of pain as she turned her ankle savagely. Hobbling badly, she pressed on, gritting her teeth in pain.

The children were faring worst of all, as exhaustion overtook them. Several had lagged, deliberately trying to get left behind. One fifteen-year-old boy from Kham with long, reddish hair trailed behind constantly. While laboring up a particularly steep incline, he told Jamyang Samten that he was going off to urinate. He disappeared over a rise, checked back to see that no one had noticed him and then simply sprinted away into the dark.

Jamyang had taken five or six children under his wing, helping them along and offering them tidbits of his supply of food, mixing his *tsampa* with sugar to ameliorate the foul taste. It had given them a short burst of energy, but all Jamyang's supplies were quickly consumed.

With hunger gnawing at them, the group began to take greater risks to secure food. In one nameless valley, Penpa proposed buying a sheep from a nomadic tribe. In the face of starvation, the group concluded that to eat meat would be sacrilege. One of the monks, Tsundue, twenty-five, was disgusted. They were going to see the Dalai Lama on pilgrimage, and as His Holiness advocated vegetarianism, this would be an affront to the goals of their painful journey. He wore his clerical status proudly. While other monks and nuns wore jeans to make the journey easier, he insisted on wearing his maroon robes, highly impractical for navigating the tough landscape and very dangerous if caught by the Chinese. He was adamant about not eating meat. To do so would bring bad luck to all of them, he said.

But eventually, hunger won out. They had come to rest in a corral. One of the men slipped out and bought antelope meat from several nomads. He stole back to camp with the meat, arguing that the animal was already dead, so they had done nothing wrong. The meat was a distinctly unappetizing prospect—rancid steaks, gray-blue and foul smelling.

Kelsang and Dolma didn't partake of the meat. The next morning, those who had eaten the antelope were stricken with food poisoning. One monk, Gatsog, was doubled over behind a stone wall. Violently sick from the meat, Penpa was in no shape to lead. As night fell, the group divided up. It was too dangerous to travel in such a large group at the pace of the slowest, so it was safer to break the group into two. Penpa would lead the injured. The more able-bodied would walk with Gyaltsen. Dolma and Kelsang, the nuns from Driru, Jamyang, and Choedon were in this first group. One of the youths from Driru distributed stones behind them, indicating the path to the second group.

Close to the Tibetan border and the start of the Nangpa La, the final leg of their journey was also the most dangerous. The Chinese military loomed nearby.

After a few hours, the refugees heard a truck downshifting high in the mountains. They scrambled down shale walls to a stream, where deep pockmarked holes offered sanctuary. The roar of the truck was swallowed in the mountains. They dusted themselves off and began to walk again. One seven-year-old girl was so tired that she fell asleep as she walked, stumbled, and woke again.

Others, completely exhausted, just fell asleep in their tracks. Choedon realized another child was missing. Throughout the trek, he had taken care of some of the children and was constantly risking his own safety to help. A child they had nicknamed Bagthuk (meaning dough soup) had fallen between the two groups. At 5 a.m., just as dawn was coming up over the mountains, Choedon found him, a small inert bump, curled up fast asleep in the fetal position in the middle of the road that led up to the army base. He was wearing a red baseball cap, a thick scarf knotted around his neck. Fastened around his shoulders was a big pack. When Choedon checked inside, it was completely empty, as the boy had slowly tossed out all his extra clothes and food to save weight. Choedon hurriedly picked him up and half-carried him, half-supported him as he raced to get him back to the other group.

After a night's walking, the first group reached another shepherd's cottage, where they spent the day. Waves of nausea broke over Dolma as hunger intensified. Starving and cold, she shivered, teeth chattering, as she struggled to stay warm. With her body starved of food, her system had no energy to generate heat, which meant she froze at night and was more susceptible to frostbite. The lacerations that the thorns had made on her legs and hands at the start of the trek itched and refused to heal.

On the trail, the glistening Himalayan peaks loomed. To Dolma, the colossal mountains gave off an eerie, powerful radiance at night. The winds picked up out of the darkness with menacing intent. An infeasibly bright moon was reflected on the snowy peaks, which lit the panorama in a monochrome brightness. Higher than the rest was

Cho Oyu. Dolma cast her eyes to the summit and thought about the deities that resided there. The mountain exuded a silent, profound presence.

Along the trail, they encountered a nomad, calmly sitting in the moonlight on a rock, who warned that eight people had been arrested in the area the day before. They thanked him and carried on, more vigilant than ever before. For one man though, sick as he was, the thought of the 19,000-foot pass and the soldiers waiting there was too much. He simply turned on his heel and headed back home to Tibet.

The mountains were chocolate brown cones of wind-spun sand. The powerful winds on the edge of the plateau swallowed up fine sand at the bottom of dry river beds and blasted it up on the mountainsides. The sand sucked every footfall, as if they were walking in molasses. With her hood up and her face mask on, it became an effort for Dolma to draw breath. She pulled her face mask down to breathe. Each time she inhaled heavily, her teeth would become coated with gritty particles of sand. It stung her eyes and matted her hair. When she stopped, the blood pulsed in Dolma's eardrums.

Three-quarters of the way up one mountain, Gyaltsen ordered everyone to stop. Below, clearly illuminated by the moon, was the Gyaplung PAP base. Perched in the middle of glacial hills of gray dust, it looked incongruous. The base was a large H-shaped building with a red roof and whitewashed walls surrounded by a twelve-foot gray wall. In the rear of the compound was a kennel filled with barking dogs. A single, forest-green watchtower sat to the northeast of the base, where soldiers armed with infrared imaging, night vision goggles, and binoculars scoured the landscape for signs of escapees. They could see soldiers walking across an asphalt parade ground, trucks pulling in and emptying soldiers, and a few lazily patrolling the perimeter.

Gyaltsen instructed everyone to take cover behind some boulders and made quick work of dividing the group. It was too dangerous for all to go at once. They inched up nearer for a better look. The base blocked the way to the Nangpa La. The gleaming full moon and dense spray of stars might as well have been a rocketing flare, making it easier for the Chinese to spot them. Gyaltsen divided his group in two (Penpa and his group had still not arrived). He would take one group down before signaling to the others to follow. Dolma, Kelsang, the nuns from Driru, and Choedon were among the first to make their way down.

Dolma slipped and tumbled down a sheer gravelly face. From above, boulders were dislodged by the scrambling of feet further up, which began to crash out of the darkness down the mountain past her. The only warning was a few clumps of rock on rock a millisecond before they almost knocked her off her feet. One whisked past Dolma's head as she lunged to get out of the way. She lost her footing, teetered, and then recovered.

Several hours on, the first group with Gyaltsen reached the shore of the glacial *tso* (meaning lake) Tangyura. Rocks glazed with ice shone in the moonlight.

The escapees snatched fearful glances upward at their marooned companions. Some attempted to signal to them with a flashlight. The people on the ridge mistakenly thought the winking light below was stars reflected in the lake. The shouting from the group on the ridge intensified. They turned flashlights on, sweeping them over the rocks to look for a way down. Terrified that the PAP would see the light and investigate, those down below scurried for cover. The girl Dolma had comforted near Tingri became hysterical. She had become separated from her brother. She shouted for him. A few tried to silence her. The shouting from the top of the ridge started again.

Gyaltsen concluded that the only way to silence the lost group on the ridge above was to cut up the slope again. Dolma, Kelsang, and Choedon along with a remaining group of about twenty were left without a guide.

Above, the stranded group searched to find a route down. But in the thin, cold air, their will to push on evaporated. Exhausted they slumped to the ground.

Below the PAP base was coming to life. News of refugees trying to cross the pass had traveled up the Wujing command.

—·—·—

In the absence of Gyaltsen, Lhundrup took the lead of the refugees huddled at the lake's shore. The only way beyond the military base, a mile or so away, was over the slippery rocks and then to a small, rickety bridge. In the dark, Dolma teetered on the smooth, icy surface of the half-submerged rocks. Some of the exhausted children couldn't summon the energy to scramble over the rocks, so the few adults with any remaining strength scooped them up and carried them on their backs. Dolma and Kelsang lagged behind.

The stress and risk of capture was too much for Tshering, one of the monks. He started to beat a child who he felt was not making pace. He scolded the terrified child, who tried to stifle sobs. The adults had all been assigned children to watch, but the monk had berated the child the whole journey, beating him with a stick, which caused swelling to his face when he didn't move fast enough. Choedon snapped. He stormed back to Tshering and confronted him angrily. The farmer wound up for a punch, before he was pacified by some of the other monks.

Eventually, the group of thirty arrived at a small cave under the mountain, where they took shelter. For the preceding twelve days, Kelsang had pushed on relentlessly, never complaining. Now, for the first time, she had lost her will. "I just want to stay here and rest," she told Dolma wearily. Her face was gaunt and emaciated. Her once-full lips were cracked and sore. The veins stood out on the backs of her hands. Dolma folded to the ground beside her friend, completely expended.

Yet Kelsang's will was like iron; she snapped out of her self-pity within a couple of hours. Kelsang was going to see the Dalai Lama, and nothing was going to stop her. She climbed to her feet. Others rose to their feet behind her. Mustering all their energy, they set out again at around 7 p.m.

They hadn't gotten far when a child's scream echoed in the canyon around them. The group was so fatigued and worried about their own safety that they ignored it. Someone insisted that it was too dangerous to go back.

But Choedon would not back down. An hour and a half later, after skirting the lake's shore, he found a twelve-year-old girl sitting on a rock by the lake's edge, a little silhouette in the night. She was weeping gently. Choedon grabbed the child's hand and tugged her along. Further along the way, a huddled figure waited for them. Tenzin Wangmo, one of the nuns from Driru, had gone back to help. Together, the three quickened their steps to catch up with the rest of the group.

By the time Choedon reached the group, Gyaltsen had returned. His search had been fruitless. He had not found the stranded group and assumed that they had been arrested. He paused, then tried to be optimistic. The pass was nearby. They would be there by morning if they kept walking.

Brown scree gave way to mottled patches of white snow and then just windswept ice and snow. The temperatures dropped sharply the higher they went. They were now also exposed to windchill. The temperatures were at least minus four degrees centigrade, but on the exposed mountainsides, it dropped to minus sixteen degrees. Dolma stopped and tied her shoelaces tighter in a bid to fight off the cold. Starving and dehydrated, the refugees struggled on.

Corrugated granite walls soared around them. Hanging glaciers, pitted and crumpled, hung in valley clefts. The group trudged on a moraine field alongside a hundred-foot-wide glacier that resembled flowing meringue. It was a few hundred feet wide, an ooze of hardened ice with eight-foot-tall crystal teeth like a shark's recurve incisors.

The landscape became increasingly hostile. Dolma and Kelsang, their heads down in the freezing cold, heaving with the exertion, almost collided into each other when Gyaltsen halted. By early morning, the group had reached the Nangpa La.

Choedon, a child holding fast to each of his hands, stopped to drink in the view. His feet were bursting out of his torn shoes. After twelve days, the refugees had arrived at the entrance of the Nangpa La, the keyhole pass between two 8,000-meter peaks. The size of their original group had diminished to around forty.

At 19,000 feet, they found themselves in a blazing white dreamscape. A glacial tongue dipped down to them, which they followed up to a saddle of ice. All was dazzling; on either side were the hulking shoulders of mountains that supported an astral ice field. There was no color anywhere. The mountains and the sky had become one as the crystal horizon dipped away. Iridescent curtains of ice crystals reflected snatches of sunlight.

Below, covered by snow and ice bridges, huge fissures had opened that snaked as much as a thousand feet into the ice. The glacier was alive, moving as much as a meter a day. With a fresh layer of snow, it was impossible to tell where the ice bridges over dangerous crevasses were. Unseen, beneath their feet, frozen chasms dropped into the earth. Traders who used the Nangpa La all had stories of yaks that had suddenly vanished without a trace on this dangerous ground.

Bitter winds had carved the snow into pendulous cornices that hung from the mountains, poised to fall any minute. The slightest sound or sudden movement could cause the massive overhangs to slip anchors and plunge down the mountain.

Escapees who had survived the trail recalled the sight of corpses along the pass, half-buried in the snow, tattered clothing flapping out of the ice. The Tibetans called this blinding landscape "the White." All was deathly still and quiet.

It was dangerous to cross in broad daylight with the PAP lurking nearby. The refugees were visible from miles around. Given the commotion the previous night, Gyaltsen suspected that the PAP had been alerted to their presence, and they needed to get to the border, fast.

In the near distance, scores of tents loomed, strung along the side of the mountain.

When several figures in long garments approached, Dolma brightened. They looked like monks.

11

MURDER OF RAVENS

— · — · —

Kill one, frighten ten thousand.
Sun Tzu, The Art of War

Benitez ambled to the cook tent, his spirits up. The storm had broken, and the summit was peeking out of the clouds where it cleaved the jet stream at almost 30,000 feet. From Advance Base Camp, Benitez would lead his team to Camp One for one night, followed by a night in Camp Two before the final summit. Benitez and his clients had spent the early morning excitedly packing food, warm clothes, and other necessities.

Chulidum, lead climbing sherpa, who had been studying the weather reports, informed Benitez that a gale would sweep the mountain in three days. The previous day, billowing cloud banks had veiled the Nangpa La and then burned off in the sun's glaring haze. Added to the sense of urgency was the fact that many expeditions' permits would shortly expire. The mountain was a hive of activity, as people scrambled to get to the summit before the weather turned sour.

As was customary before summit pushes, *pujas* had been conducted in the early morning. The scent of juniper wafted in among the canopies of tents, as sherpas chanted mantras in guttural monotones to the Buddhist deities for their safe passage to the summit. Prayer flags in long, curved lines snapped in the chill breeze, sending scriptures heavenward. To Benitez, the smell of juniper was the aroma of a summit attempt about to begin. He grew excited.

As Benitez crossed camp at around 8 a.m., he caught sight of some shabbily dressed Tibetans shuffling through camp. The oldest could not have been older than twelve. Focused on his climb, he ignored them.

The climbers were long used to Tibetans arriving in camp selling wares. He went to the cook tent and poured himself hot coffee.

The first gunshot went largely unnoticed by the climbers. Most were still in their tents. The sun had risen, but it hadn't been up long enough to blunt the knifing cold. But the subsequent percussive pops split the thin mountain air. Climbers had blearily unzipped their tents, craning to see the commotion. The smell of cordite from spent rounds of ammunition overtook the scents of juniper.

Slovenian climber Pavle Kozjek, rousing himself at the north end of camp, noticed a murder of ravens take flight in a small pitch-black explosion of wings.

Ang Tshering, the normally cool sirdar, arrived in the mess tent in a panic. "Chinese soldiers are coming," he shouted. "Very bad."

Benitez ducked outside. About a quarter of a mile away, between the amphitheater of ABC and the Nangpa La below, knots of PAP soldiers were fanning out through camp and setting up strategic firing positions in the moraine fall. The glacier had bulldozed gravel and other detritus into a hummocky landscape comprising sixty- to seventy-foot-high cones of rocks and dust sprinkled with snow. The hills and an interweaving network of trails led down to the glacier about one and a half to two miles away.

Benitez could see a half-dozen PAP lined up behind an outcrop of boulders on top of the moraine fall. In the distance, the soldiers were firing on a line of people snaking through the snow below them. More soldiers poured into camp and started blazing away. Some leaned their guns on rocks to still their aim. Some sniped with deliberate calm. Benitez saw puffs of smoke jet from the end of their barrels. They were shooting Type 81 assault rifles, a Chinese knockoff of the Kalashnikov, which wasn't all that accurate at sniping. But you can flip the switch to single-shot fire, and a marksman of steady hand, if he holds his breath, can hit a target several hundred yards away. A few of the soldiers were wearing knockoff Gucci or Armani sunglasses that prevented snow blindness. Quite a few weren't, and, blinded by the dazzling whiteness, they had difficulty focusing down their gun sights. Some pumped a couple of rounds into rocks they thought might be people, advanced, saw their mistake, and carried on firing onto the pass.

Scores of climbers had picked their way to the edge of the horse-shoe-shaped ridge that offered a vantage point down on the Nangpa La to the west. Among them was Sergiu Matei, armed with his video camera. When several climbers lifted their cameras, they were quickly reprimanded by a soldier who flew up, arms waving for them to stop.

Matei was not so easily swayed. As Matei was setting up his tripod, a machine-gun-toting soldier approached, raised his gun, and trained it on the Romanian. He flexed his finger on the trigger. Matei, with customary bluster, ignored him and started to film. The soldier was called away by a senior officer. "The climbers did nothing. They just watched as if it was a live show," Matei later fumed. Below, a snaking line of Tibetans, like ants in the distance from where Matei stood, were being fired at by five or six soldiers. "They are shooting them like dogs," he gasped in disbelief, wrestling with the focus controls as his camera began to record the scene.

—·—·—

Hours earlier, the Nangpa La had funneled the escapees south between sharply serrated peaks. The pass wound below the camp and curled in a southwesterly direction. The group of around forty Tibetans with Gyaltsen neared the camp. The majority headed up through the tents. Wild with hunger, they risked approaching the tents for food. A handful carried on along the Nangpa La.

Kelsang led, helping the exhausted nun, Tenzin Dolma, with four other nuns. The figures with the long coats now waving at them might be monks who would help them. Perhaps it was the group they had lost the previous night?

Dolma and Kelsang and four other nuns approached the snapping orange tents. They picked out a trail alongside the camp. Dolma started to feel dizzy, her legs felt unsteady beneath her. Kelsang rubbed her head in pain, the altitude was causing her a blinding headache.

The northernmost tents in ABC belonged to a Filipino team. To Dr. Ted Esguerra, the expedition's doctor, the Tibetans looked like they had escaped a war zone. Wild with hunger, several devoured soap and candles as they pilfered for food. A handful of them convinced sherpas to sell them noodles and a flask of tea at a hefty price.

Gyaltsen distractedly watched the refugees sipping hot water from the Filipino team. He kept gazing behind and hurrying on, ignoring pleas for directions from escapees. Suddenly he broke into a sprint. A few camo-clad figures appeared in the distance, shouting and shouldering their weapons.

Kelsang was shouting, asking Lhundrup the way. He shrugged. She asked the monk if she should beg for some food. A few climbers stopped what they were doing and stared at them awkwardly. Lhundrup caught up with her. "How can I ask for food if I don't speak their language?" he questioned.

And then, out of nowhere, muffled rifle reports rolled up from the pass below them. The cracks grew in regularity and volume. It was just Western tourists with firecrackers, insisted Kelsang, who hadn't caught sight of the green uniforms in the distance. She was supporting Tenzin Dolma. Kelsang studiously ignored the rifle reports, instead turning to help her sick friend.

The nuns were a terrible sight. Tenzin Dolma was unable to walk alone, and Kelsang and the others were taking turns supporting her, a tough feat in the snow and thin air. Weakened by the altitude and unable to support the nun, Kelsang dropped to the ground hopelessly. Dolma stopped, struggling to help Kelsang to her feet. She tried to pull her friend up, but she too flailed hopelessly, eventually falling over her own weakened legs.

Soldiers appeared, drawing over the lip of a ridge beyond from the north in the direction of the PAP base. Lhundrup shouted, "We have to run now! Go run!" He headed south toward Nepal. The group would have to cross back over the moraine field and over the Nangpa La again. Across the pass was a steep, north-facing mountain up and beyond which lay the Nepal border, just twenty minutes away.

Tenzin Dolma, exhausted and paralyzed with fear, collapsed in the snow. Kelsang tried desperately to drag the petrified nun to her feet. The soldiers were now bearing down on them. The nuns stopped and calmly pulled something out of their backpacks. "This will save us," one of the nuns reassured, producing pills that had been blessed by the Dalai Lama. Tenzin Dolma tried to swallow the tablets but her throat was too dry and she gagged. Kelsang, determinedly, struggled again to drag the nun to her feet. It was impossible.

"Go faster, run," Dolma urged Kelsang. She tried to help her friend, but Kelsang refused, instead telling Dolma to run on ahead while she helped with Tenzin. Dolma refused to leave her side. Lhundrup, just behind, asserted himself. He told Dolma, over the crack and whine of bullets, that Kelsang would manage and she must run.

For the first time on their trek, Dolma left Kelsang's side.

Some escapees were making their way up the imposing sheer mountain to the north. Samdhup, the mentally ill and deaf child, tried to run in the snow, hefting her backpack. Dechen Pema, who had been entrusted to look after the child, pleaded with her to cast it off. She refused as bullets zinged past her ears. "How can I do that when I will have no clothes to change into!" she shouted over the noise of the machine guns. Others overtook her. Dechen tried to tear the bag from the child's shoulders, fighting to pull it off. Eventually she tossed it, and they pressed upward in the deep snow. Dechen pushed the child, who was now bawling, from behind.

Nun Sonam Choetso had been begging food when a sherpa had warned her of the approaching PAP. She threw off her backpack, attempted to sprint, but then sunk into knee-deep snow. The bullets whined past her ear and ripped into the ground near her feet. Lhundrup, striding forward, shouted over to her. He told the nun to lie flat so that she wouldn't be hit. She lay in the snow and remembered that she had a picture of the Dalai Lama hanging around her neck. Hurriedly, she took it off and tied it to the back of her jacket as a means of warding off the bullets. And then she climbed to her feet, gathered her resolve, and pressed forward, ignoring the cries from soldiers to stop.

Another boy, seventeen-year-old Nawang Kona, started to run, but his battered shoes ripped at the first running stride. He knelt down, pulling a string from his pocket to tie his shoe, while a soldier ran up toward him. Securing it as best he could in the few short seconds he had available, he set off as fast as he could, tossing his bag behind him. With deep strides, he ran past Dolma. "Throw your bag too," he shouted.

Tsultrim Lhodoe, Jamyang's friend, attempted to tug along a ten-year-old girl. Tsultrim dragged her through the snow as the soldiers closed in. He snatched the huge bag she was carrying on her shoulders and threw it away, tugging her arm. But still she refused to run. With one final backward glance, he turned and fled.

Many of the children, munching on food from the climbers, just gave up, grateful to be captured and their nightmare trek to come to an end at last. They ravished the food, ignoring the encroaching soldiers threading their way through the tents. One PAP officer had a child under each arm. "Where is the guide?" barked one of the soldiers. Slowly, one of the children pointed in the direction that Gyaltsen had taken, which veered away from camp and up to a ridge. The guide, hiding in the snow, looked down as soldiers tried to spot him. A few PAP set out to crest the ridge. The incline was so steep that the soldiers were reduced to crawling up on their hands and knees. Gyaltsen gave one last look down and then shot off, running as fast as he could. The soldiers eventually gave up and returned to camp.

Choedon had attempted to keep the two children he had rescued by his side as they begged for food. When a soldier yelled for him to stop, Choedon dumped his backpack and set off in a manic zigzag. The children surrendered to the soldiers after only a few steps.

Choedon was being funneled up a gully by the soldiers, where he could be cornered. He knew the risks of being caught again. Mustering every drop of energy, he ran a dogleg, circled back, and headed straight up a steep escarpment where some climbers were standing. Once over the ledge, he pulled himself upright. He slipped among the climbers, jerking up his hood to hide his wind-chapped face. Shortly after, a soldier patrolled among them scanning for refugees. Choedon dropped his face and looked to the ground. His black leather loafers were torn and ripped. Choedon kicked and burrowed his feet into the snow and hunched his shoulders. The soldier walked past.

—·—

Among the cadre of PAP were several Tibetans. As their Han Chinese colleagues opened fire, the Tibetans shouted at the refugees to stop. When they did raise their guns to their shoulders, the Tibetan soldiers feigned problems with their weapons. In reality, they couldn't bring themselves to open fire on their fleeing compatriots. For once, compassion overruled military orders.

On Cho Oyu, the deep ethnic divisions in the Chinese military were exposed.° The Han Chinese officers blazed with abandon. One, from Sichuan, was fitter and more serious than his colleagues. He ran as hard as he could, shooting and firing, chasing the nuns as they ran up the slope. Every ten steps or so, he stopped and fired.

Catching sight of Tenzin Wangmo, he shouted, "Where are you going, bitch?" The nun felt something warm rip past her shinbone. A bullet tore a hole in her trousers, millimeters from her leg. But she pressed on feverishly.

From the top of the pass, Thupten Tsering had seen around five figures. At first he assumed them to be monks, but when they got nearer, he realized with horror that they were military. Now they were only thirty steps behind him, quickly gaining ground.

He heard soldiers shouting more obscenities to the nuns, *"Thama de!"* [Fuck your mother.]

The soldiers were now just fifty paces behind Dolma and the nuns.

Norbu Palden knew that the nuns would be killed or captured unless he did something. He turned and stood squarely in the path of the encroaching soldiers. Jamyang and Tsultrim had smirked at the Kardze man when he had boasted of his fights with the Chinese and how he had

---

° Tibetan PAP are sometimes forcibly conscripted to give the illusion that the Chinese military comprises the different ethnicities of modern China. Yet the reality is different. The training for a Tibetan PAP officer is discriminatory and much harder than for an ethnic Han. According to one source, they are beaten if they don't learn Chinese and are made to do upside-down pull-ups over broken glass for minor infractions. Sometimes they are made to lie on ice as punishment for not making up the bed on time. Most PAP serve two to three years after which they are awarded a certificate that offers them preferential treatment in the outside world, for jobs and housing. This is why Tibetans often serve. Yet, after military service, Tibetan PAP are often deemed pariahs within their own communities.

always fought them when he had the chance. The boys had disbelieved him, thinking it hollow machismo. But Palden wasn't lying; he was lion-hearted. He had to slow the soldiers or they would catch the nuns. The soldiers were closing in on them.

Norbu Palden realized he could block the soldiers by throwing stones, while taking cover behind a boulder on a path between two pitted depressions, which indicated ice chasms underneath. Gathering handfuls of rocks from the trail, he windmilled them at the approaching soldiers in a furious barrage. Behind him, Dolma and the nuns were making slow but steady progress on their hands and knees up the incline. The soldier slowed, and Dolma picked up the pace. Norbu had given the nuns vital time to escape.

The soldiers took cover behind a cluster of boulders. Most were Han Chinese and were clearly struggling in the altitude. After a moment, one of the soldiers slipped to the side of a rock and fired a single shot. It cracked in the melee. The bullet had found its mark.

Norbu Palden dropped to the ground. His right ankle had been hit. Blood leaked onto the snow. His flight to freedom was over. He had little choice but to wait for the PAP to arrest him.

But he had given the nuns a head start on a near-vertical face in waist-deep snow. They struggled up to a ridge where the mountain beyond would offer protection from the bullets. They trooped forward in single file, sinking in the snow, gasping in the thin air, but pressing on. Dolma willed her body to run, but it wouldn't respond. Bullets slapped into the blanket of snow around her, throwing up three-foot fountains of snow. It was as though she were in a nightmare, trapped in her sluggish body, which couldn't function with the lessened oxygen in the air. Her limbs only responded in slow motion, unwilling to react to the panicked signals her brain was sending of immediate danger.

She snatched a backward glance down at Kelsang laboring upward. "Run," Dolma screamed. She saw the soldier close the distance, bearing down on Kelsang. Struggling onward, Dolma and Lhundrup crested a small rocky outcrop. Dolma dropped behind a boulder. After catching her breath, she risked peering over the top. Below she saw Kelsang fighting to get up with Tenzin Dolma. As she watched, a bullet streaked over her scalp with a hot lick of air. Lhundrup dragged her down. Catching her breath, she began to run again. Among the rifle cracks, she heard a cry of pain from below.

Kelsang, with the exhausted nun in tow, was desperately trying to catch up to Dolma. In a split second, a bullet tore into Kelsang's back. She staggered forward, slumping on her right side. The remaining nuns tried to drag her to her feet, but Kelsang was limp and lifeless. The bright snow mushroomed into a brilliant red stain around her body. She was minutes from the border.

12

BARDO: THE IN-BETWEEN STATE

—··—

For those who gain immortal peace,
The demon, death, no longer stirs
Quotation from Uttaratantra Shastra

Benitez stood slack-jawed, watching the scene below. A hundred people were witnessing a murder as unarmed women and children were shot at in broad daylight.

Matei filmed relentlessly, determined to capture the atrocity. In the distance, a small figure was jerked forward and suddenly folded in half at the waist. Matei turned his camera off. "I didn't want to film anyone dying," he later admitted.

Minutes after the commotion, the climbers returned to preparing for the summit, some demanding hot coffee from their sherpas. As the gunshots died, black forms returned, dropping out of the sky. A single raven alighted on a boulder, a predatory, spectral presence behind a soldier shouldering his weapon. The raven blinked and waited. It is said that ravens bring messages from the dead.

—··—

When Lhundrup caught up with Dolma, three nuns followed.

"Where's Kelsang?" Dolma demanded. Lhundrup, his head down, urged her forward.

They clung to the Nangpa La. The icy trail threaded through the ice and granite landscape, the shoulders of mountains enfolding them. Shortly, they reached the windswept top of the pass where a pile of stones formed a pillar. At last they had reached the border of Nepal. The pillar was festooned with fluttering white *kata* scarves and prayer flags, offerings to the deities, which had been left by other refugees. Dolma was at last free. But she was here without her best friend. One foot over the border and she lost control, breaking down in wracking sobs.

—·-·—

The atmosphere in base camp was menacing. PAP were combing the grounds in search of refugees. They stuck gun muzzles between tents, barking at each other in Mandarin. Some snatched up climbers' equipment and hurled it to the ground again after examination. Others lollygagged in the sunshine, smoking cigarettes, a reward for a hard morning's work.

Clusters of climbers spoke conspiratorially about what had happened, but none dared confront the Chinese. Steve Lawes, a British policeman, reasoned: "What could we have done? We had ice axes, while they had Kalashnikovs." Sherpas with the Filipino team and others urged their climbers not to talk about what they had seen. Climbers were shocked to see the Chinese, whom they had had a snowball fight with during the storm, emerge from their green tent in PAP uniforms. The common PAP technique of infiltrating large groups of foreigners was plain for all to see. The sixtyish Chinese climber who had directed the others in the snowball fight—whom they had jokingly called 'The General'—emerged from the big green tent dressed in fatigues with gold epaulettes denoting high rank in the PAP.

In the bright, late-morning sunlight, Norbu Palden struggled into camp with a walking stick, escorted by soldiers. He trailed a path of blood in the snow and over the rocks before he unceremoniously dropped to the ground. One of the soldiers later demanded Norbu's jacket, which he slipped on over his camouflage uniform, admiring himself. It was bounty from the day's hunt.

A Dutch climber, Frank Berkhout, was disgusted at how the Chinese failed to administer any medical treatment to the Tibetan. Bleeding wounds at high altitude lose blood much faster than at sea level because the heart is pumping much harder to oxygenate the body, and more blood is circulated. Norbu was turning ashen. The Dutchman marched up to the camp and demanded Norbu be given proper medical care. As he remonstrated with the Chinese, he eyed a pile of machine guns, still warm, lying on a chair inside their tent. The Chinese eventually treated Norbu with the attention the gunshot wound merited. Around fifteen children and Norbu were now held outside the big green Chinese tent. The children looked terrified, as climbers eyed them and lackadaisical soldiers lit cigarettes.

Choedon meanwhile seized his opportunity in the melee. In a small, snowy gully, he spied a toilet tent. Gratefully he bolted inside and covered himself as best he could with a large white bag. As he lay there, the stench became overpowering. The bag was full of used toilet paper. Terrified, he ignored the smell. Through a narrow slit in the tent, he could see soldiers congregating twenty-five yards away, talking on their radios. "We got one of them," a tinny voice announced on the radio. "One of them is dead." A fortyish soldier with a thin face listened intently, scanning the landscape from behind wraparound shades. Choedon's years trading leather and caterpillar fungus had given him a rudimentary understanding of Chinese. He recognized the Sichuan accent.

The soldiers were livid that they couldn't find the Tibetan who had witnessed the shooting. "He's here somewhere," barked a Chinese soldier. Choedon froze as he watched the man. He recognized him as the same man who had chased him earlier in the day. The same man who had fired the fatal shot that had killed Kelsang.

"I saw him run among the Westerners. We have to find him," the soldier pressed. He was a muscular man in his late twenties, with a healthy, round face and a light, nutty complexion. He had a military buzz cut and wore a gray T-shirt under his camouflage. Striking red epaulettes sat on his shoulders. Handcuffs dangled from his belt. Slung over his left shoulder was an Type 81 assault rifle. He was out of breath and sweaty after chasing the nuns up the mountain. He added, "The one who got among the Westerners must be the guide. We must find him."

More soldiers arrived, leading captured children at gunpoint, just six feet from climbers. An American climber, Jim Finley,* recognized two

---

* Jim Finley is a pseudonym.

children he had given socks to earlier, before the shooting started. They wore them on their hands like gloves. Captured, they marched past escorted by soldiers, and caught his gaze, but betrayed no recognition as they locked eye contact with the American. Finley looked back awkwardly, breaking off.

The two children Choedon had saved on the journey were among those captured now being led to the Chinese tent. The Sichuan soldier recognized them as the children who were with Choedon when he broke from the group.

"Where was the brother you were with?" the soldier cajoled. "Is he here among us?" The children remained silent.

The soldier persisted. "Come now, we know he is here. Where is he?"

Slowly the children nodded, pointing to several tents.

With so many Westerners around, a witness to the murder of a Tibetan by PAP soldiers was in a precarious situation. Calling Tibetan sherpas over, the PAP demanded they gather their bosses for a meeting. The Sichuan soldier was more forceful in his demands, certain that the climbers knew where refugees were hiding and eager to arrest the man who had seen him fire the killing shots. But the sherpas returned empty-handed. Even in the aftermath of a brutal murder, the climbers were focused on their summit attempts and ignored the requests.

Nevertheless, the soldiers convened outside their tent expecting the climbers to do the same. A PAP officer stood with erect, military bearing in the middle of the camp, flanked by fawning acolytes. He paced with his hands behind his back expectantly. But none of the climbers showed up. Eventually the soldiers realized it was useless. They made a further few weak attempts to bait the climbers. The soldiers withdrew, although not that the climbers realized. The children and those captured were dragged off to idling trucks. The soldiers wanted to pose for pictures with their trophies. They made Norbu Palden lie in the snow in front of the children while the soldiers took trophy snapshots.

—·—·—

Sergiu Matei had a half-hour of footage that would shock the world—if only he could get it out of the country. He burned a crater in the plastic casing of his videotape to mark it before stuffing it deep within his bag. Soon after, he sent a text to a colleague at Romanian PRO TV in which he relayed that he'd just filmed a group of Chinese soldiers firing on unarmed Tibetans. Used to Matei's disarming humor, his colleague ignored the message.

Matei was determined to capture footage of the body that lay slumped in the snow. The soldiers had wrapped Kelsang's body in a red blanket, leaving it on the ice. Matei discussed his plan with Danish doctor Pierre Mania. The physician was cautious. "It's too dangerous," he said nervously, as soldiers walked past the pair. When Matei approached the base camp manager, he was warned that such a stunt would likely end with his own death.

Morris Cooper, a British climber, was shaken by the murder and in a terrible dilemma. He was with a team of British doctors. "Was I going to risk my own life to look at a body that is dead or might be dead?" he recalled. "I felt like I should have gone down there. But in the end I didn't. Part of me felt like a coward for wimping out and not going down there."

Steve Lawes had a telescope trained on Kelsang's body. At 2 p.m., a detachment of what appeared to be senior PAP soldiers made their way to Kelsang's frozen corpse. Some were wearing long black trench coats with *Police* stenciled below two Chinese characters on their backs. Some wore white masks to obscure their identities. They kicked the body twice. After photographing the scene, several posed for pictures next to Kelsang's body like hunters beside a prize buck. When the soldiers arrived back in camp after inspecting the body, they angrily confiscated the telescope from Lawes.

Meanwhile, at the Chinese tent, Russell Brice encountered some soldiers who had snow blindness after the morning's hunt. He ministered to them, giving medical attention and eye drops for their condition.

Later in the day, the soldiers had a presentation ceremony outside the Chinese tent in the middle of ABC. According to climber Lawes, it had looked like an awards ceremony for good behavior. There was a speech and a few were handed something. At the end of the formalities, the stiff-backed soldiers were dismissed, and they snapped to the right.

Two soldiers wearing cotton blindfolds for snow blindness turned to the left, crashing into their colleagues. Some climbers smirked uneasily at the slapstick scene.

At around 11:30 a.m., a young sherpa came to the mess tent, announcing that a man was hiding in the toilet tent. Matei jumped up for his camera and headed out. With a violent rip, Matei opened the toilet tent.

"He looked like a hunted animal," recalls Matei. The memory of the man's eyes, wide with terror, would haunt him for years to come. The Tibetan begged the climber for sunglasses; his eyes were in pain due to snow blindness.

Matei struggled to communicate with the stunned Choedon. Frustrated at his inability to connect and, noting Choedon's weakened state, Matei ran back to the mess tent where he tried to convince the base camp manager to help the terrified refugee. He refused. "The Chinese will shoot us if we are caught," Matei reports that he reasoned. "It is much too dangerous."

With the base camp manager and kitchen boys looking on in horror, Matei returned to the toilet tent with food. He used hand signals, mimicking a man holding a rifle to indicate that soldiers were still around. He uttered two words he was sure that they both knew—"Dalai Lama."

Choedon put his hands together in veneration. They understood each other.

Matei filmed the encounter, later saying he did so to gather proof of the Tibetan's existence in camp were he to be captured or shot. Matei also took still images with his camera.

Carefully, Matei coaxed the farmer from the toilet. As they walked to the mess tent, several soldiers approached. Matei slung his arm around Choedon's shoulders and laughed like the two were old friends. The soldiers didn't give them a second look. In the mess tent, Matei gave Choedon hot tea and cereal. He hid the Tibetan in the mess tent for around thirteen hours.

By 2:30 a.m., Choedon, donning fleece pants and socks from Matei, was ready to leave. The coast looked clear. The pass below them glistened in the moonlight. Matei clapped the Tibetan on his back, indicated the shortest way across the glacier, and wished him good luck.

Choedon set out across the frosted landscape, running low and fast toward the Nangpa La. But the PAP had flooded the climbers' camp with soldiers and also set up ad hoc camps out in the snow beyond to stop the Tibetan they knew was hiding. Six or seven soldiers had been patrolling ABC during the day. By nightfall, twenty soldiers had arrived.

A few hundred feet out, Choedon ducked behind a rock. There was no way to get through. He removed his filthy blue anorak, took off his shoes, and wrapped his coat around his feet to prevent frostbite. The fleece pants and thick woolen socks Matei had given him probably saved his life in the freezing cold. At first light, he could see soldiers moving everywhere. It was much too dangerous to travel. He struggled back to the camp and hid in a tent, aided by some climbers.

For eighteen hours, a terrified Choedon crouched in a small tent. At midnight, he again decided to make a break for it. Watchful of soldiers, he followed footprints down to the Nangpa La. Once on the glacial superhighway, he headed south as fast as he could in the direction of the border. He reached a post festooned with prayer flags, left by other grateful Tibetans. With constellations of stars overhead, Orion above him, he shouted in triumph. He wasted no time as he tumbled and rolled down the steep, snowy glacier into Nepal.

13

A DARK SECRET

—·—·—

Have we vanquished the enemy? None but ourselves. Have we gained success? That word means
nothing here.

George Leigh Mallory

Robbed of the desire to climb after the shooting, Benitez, normally an effervescent cheerleader for his clients, lapsed into silence as they trudged out of camp. This time, there was no tingling in Benitez's chest.

The group walked past soldiers scouring the mountains looking for Tibetans who may have escaped. A small form—Kelsang's body—lay on the ice beyond.

Benitez's feet were heavy. The fight to summit the mountain had deserted him. The violence was frightening and he wanted to get every-one out for their own safety. Mountain climbing now felt trivial, that it wasn't worth fighting for in comparison to what they had just seen. The American questioned whether, had he just been there with his buddies, he would have gone down and tried to stop it? Later he would tell people that it just wasn't the type of situation where he could have done a 'Rambo move'—the soldiers were impossibly far away and bullets were flying everywhere. As he kicked his feet into the mountainside, crushed under the horror of what he had witnessed and his inability to stop it, he asked himself if he was just making excuses. "Was I not brave enough?" he asked himself.

Benitez's team was diminished. Only Jan Anderson, Scott Curtis, and Emmanuel Smith remained. (Paul Rogers had left a day early to prepare for the summit.) They plodded upward, each lost in their own thoughts. Six hours later, they arrived at Camp One and collapsed in their tents.

The next morning, Benitez sent Anderson down to ABC: her head-aches were proving too intense for the climb.

With the two remaining clients, Benitez and Rogers began the notoriously long trek to Camp Two. Thick snow dangerously obscured crevasses. Icy air bit into their lungs. Benitez was sapped of any desire to summit. Each step was an effort as he again thought about what he had witnessed the day before and his own inaction in the face of a cold-blooded murder. By the time he arrived at Camp Two, Benitez was spitting with rage at what the Chinese had done. Rogers sensed that the trip leader had completely lost any interest in the climb. Rogers called base camp to ask details about the shooting and got Henry Todd on the radio. Todd, according to Rogers, told him that the issue was 'sensitive' and not to make mention of it over the airwaves.

After a rough night spent in Camp Two, Scott Curtis called off his ascent. And in a sense, Benitez, for the first time in his career, did too. All he wanted to do was break down base camp and head home. Benitez offered Rogers the summit. The assistant guide jumped at the chance. This would be his first 8,000-meter peak and would help ensure his ability to lead larger expeditions.

Rogers and Smith would need to start out early to reach the summit. Benitez helped Smith into his crampons and made sure his oxygen was functioning before bidding the two men good luck. They left at 6 a.m. on October 2, their headlamps lighting the walls of snow. As day broke, swirls of cumulus clouds turned a cobalt blue sky to marble. From the summit, a long, tangled streamer of snow unfurled in the jet stream.

They slogged up through the death zone and Smith beat Rogers to the summit of Cho Oyu by thirty minutes. Smith, his face chapped and reddish, pulled down his blood-red oxygen mask and looked at the cotton-wool clouds beneath his feet. He saw Everest to the west. He had a curious sense of elation.

By late afternoon, Benitez arrived back at ABC with Curtis. On the way down to ABC, Benitez had paused to ask an Italian Team, Il Nodo Infinito, if the media had arrived. There was an awkward silence. They shook their heads. From what Benitez could ascertain, nothing had been reported in the media three days after the incident.

Matei had given a full interview to PRO TV radio via satellite telephone. But the story had not yet been picked up by the international media. Nor had the interview that Dr. Ted Esguerra had given to a Philippine newspaper. But while Matei and Esguerra acted decisively in the immediate aftermath of the shooting, the climbers had squabbled vociferously over what should be done.

Bobby Jackson*, an American who called himself an "adventurer and philanthropist" said the climbers were divided:

> I saw people running scared out of their minds. But what could we have done? There was a lot of heated debate. There were some people who said, "God, don't say anything because if the Chinese military wants to come here and close this mountain or arrest everyone, or detain everyone, they could do that in the blink of an eye. So God, Christ almighty, don't post anything until we leave." Then there was another group of people who said we have to go and tell the world what happened. A couple of those were like, "Let's be famous and see who can post this first." And others still who were like: "If we need to start World War Three over this, we will."

Although a number of expeditions posted daily blogs, often in tedious detail, about their climbs, no mention of the shooting was made to the outside world from the hundred or so witnesses from the satellite hook-ups most expeditions had.

On October 1, the climbers had watched as a detachment of soldiers hiked to the body, covered it in a red blanket, and hauled Kelsang's corpse away. The climbers feared for their own safety. A rumor circulated around camp that seven Tibetans had been taken out behind the glacier and summarily executed, their bodies thrown into a crevasse. As Steve Lawes later explained, "There were still a lot of people up the mountain, and we didn't want to endanger them by making a fuss. We wanted to wait until we were all out of there and back in Kathmandu."

---

* Bobby Jackson is a pseudonym.

Benitez was old friends with Tom and Tina Sjogren, who ran the obsessively read climbing Website, ExplorersWeb (ExWeb). Increasingly, ExWeb had usurped the mainstream media as a portal of breaking news on climbing expeditions. The Sjogrens dismiss mainstream adventure magazines as cheerleaders to the outsize egos of modern mountaineers and their moneyed sponsors. (ExWeb consistently targets expedition leaders and their businesses for exploiting the mountains and putting lives at risk.) In 1996, when the Everest disaster claimed eleven lives, the Sjogrens were on the mountain as members of an expedition run by Henry Todd. Disgusted with what they felt was Todd's poor organization, the Sjogrens eventually broke away and tried to summit on their own. But they needed another oxygen mask. When one of Todd's sherpas arrived with oxygen and an extra mask, the equipment was covered in dried blood. They understood it had been recovered from a climber who had been injured. "Just clean it out with some snow," Todd told the Sjogrens on the radio. Shortly thereafter, the couple abandoned their climb.

Since the Everest incident, the Sjogrens had attempted to unmask Todd, starting the Website in response to what they felt was a lack of objective reporting on the dark side of mountaineering. Their ExWeb special "Oxygen on Everest—The Highest Death Lab in the World" was a scathingly emotional exposé that began: "Imagine you were to dive into the deepest ocean on earth. Would you have your scuba tanks filled and managed by a convicted drug dealer?" The Sjogrens were also at war with Russell Brice. A few months earlier, they had lambasted Brice for not doing more to save the life of David Sharp on Everest. It was the first salvo in a growing feud.

In Colorado, Benitez and the Sjogrens were neighbors. The publicity-hungry young climber, who cultivated relationships with magazine editors and media outlets, had found friendship and a joint goal with the owners of the Website. The Sjogrens set up HumanEdgeTech—through which they sold laptops and satellite phones. They wanted to pioneer split-second breaking news from the mountains on their Website, using the latest technology. Benitez field-tested their equipment and sent them up-to-the-minute dispatches. Sometimes he sent tips on breaking news; other times he wrote full-blown pieces. But many climbers disliked the glowing portrayal of Benitez on ExWeb and his reports, often self-aggrandizing stories about himself.

Back at ABC, Benitez called the Sjogrens on the satellite phone and was shocked to learn that they hadn't yet heard of the shooting. Afterward he fired off an e-mail with news of the incident. The headline of his e-mail read: "Story not being told here in Tibet." He wrote:

> There is a story that happened here on the 30th and 1st that is not being told. It's tragic, it is haunting and it is apparently all too real for Tibetans. On the AM of the 30th, I walked out of our dining tent to gaze over towards the Nangpa La (this is the pass between Tibet and Nepal, commonly used for trading, also used for people trying to escape). As I looked across the broad expanse of the pass, we saw a line of Tibetans heading over towards the start of the pass, a common sight, as the trade routes are open this time of year. Then, without warning, shots rang out. Over and over and over. Then the line of people started to run. Uphill. At 19,000 ft. Apparently the Chinese army was tipped off about their attempted escape, and had showed up with guns. Watching the line snake off thru the snow, as the shots rang out, we saw two shapes fall. The binoculars confirmed it, 2 people were down, and they weren't getting up. Then more Chinese army swarmed thru Basecamp. I figured the safest place for my people at this point was up the hill, so in the midst of this, I made the choice to move my people up for our summit push. The story just gets worse. From Tibetans I know here in camp, apparently 7, yes, 7 [a rumour later de-bunked] people were shot, then shoved into a crevasse, just below where a huge international presence, namely Basecamp, sat and listened.

Benitez indicated he wanted to write a longer story about the incident and the Nangpa La. He asked that the Sjogrens hold off from posting his name in connection with the incident until he was safely out of Tibet. He also sent the e-mail to *National Geographic Adventure* magazine.

Tina was checking her e-mail in the ExWeb offices in Manhattan when she opened Benitez's note. As fast as she could, she ran a story titled, "Cho Oyu Swarmed by Chinese Army—Tibetans Shot at Nangpa La?". Almost immediately, news outlets began to publish small stories about the shooting.

— ·— ·—

Rogers and a triumphant Smith returned to camp. But the euphoria of the successful summit was clouded by the fact that they were return- ing to a murder scene. Other expeditions returned, but the revelry was quickly quashed by the somber mood in base camp and the patrolling soldiers. It was ghostly; climbers were subdued and fearful. The AC team did their best to celebrate the summit success with sushi—a full on dinner of salmon and tuna, in sticky rice, all washed down with Everest beer.

The following morning, shortly after breakfast, Rogers reported to Benitez. The American was loading yaks with the first of the gear to be sent down. As the two men shared a perfunctory conversation about logistics, the subject of the shooting came up. Benitez confided in his assistant guide that he had alerted his friends at ExplorersWeb of the incident. In a flash, Rogers was off, straight to Brice and Todd.

There were rumors flying around camp that Brice and Todd, among others, were informing climbers that the best policy was not to talk about the killing. Pavle Kozjek was disgusted by the conspiracy of silence in the camp when he returned. "For many people in the base camp, the most important thing was to be able to come back again. They decided not to tell what happened because of this."

News of the incident surfacing to the outside world could wreck business relationships. In Tibet, silence, no matter what, was the order of business. Other climbers had heard of the adopted code of silence. The American climber, Jim Finley, who had given socks to some Tibetan children during the shooting, said, "It was like we were all told, 'Oh yeah, you didn't see anything.' But I know what I saw: dark forms, bodies falling on the ice. The word around base camp was that Western guides were trying to convince people that nothing had happened, I think for commercial reasons."

Hearing that Benitez had posted news of the shooting and the perpetrators, Brice and Todd were furious. When Brice, shadowed by Rogers, arrived at Benitez's tent at 3 p.m., he was demanding to know why Benitez had sent an e-mail outside that could land everyone in trouble with the Chinese.

"Paul told me that you sent an e-mail to ExplorersWeb?" Brice accused Benitez. "Are you fucking crazy?" He questioned the number of dead that Benitez had suggested (seven) as inaccurate and said that this was likely to land everyone in the camp in trouble with the Chinese. He harangued the American, saying that he had been shot at himself in the mountains by the Chinese and that Benitez was putting everyone at risk. "If you wanted to send that e-mail, why didn't you wait until we got out?" demanded Brice.

Rogers jumped in with accusations that Benitez merely sought the media spotlight with his e-mail. He slammed the free Tibet cause, arguing that China had modernized the region. And, according to Benitez, he cited American hypocrisy in the wars in Iraq and Afghanistan, saying that the Chinese should not be singled out for violating human rights. He asked Benitez how he could be certain that those fired upon were not traffickers, part of a girl-smuggling ring to Mumbai. He concluded that Benitez's actions were totally irresponsible and would lead to AC being banned from Tibet, never able to return.

Clients of Benitez, shocked, looked on. Indignant, Benitez countered with growing disgust that Brice had treated murderers for snow blindness, the story circulating around camp.

"Do you think it's right, Russ?" Benitez persisted, referring to the shooting. "Do you think it's right?"

"No, I don't think it's right!" Brice responded, as he left the scene.

After the confrontation, Benitez took refuge in his tent. Angrily, he pulled out his crampons and began to sharpen them. Forty-five minutes later, Todd appeared. "You should be fucking hung out to dry for what you have done," he told him angrily.

Todd was furious that Benitez had named the Chinese military in his Web post, which, he reasoned, had made everyone on the expeditions targets of the Chinese, who scanned all communications out of China. Todd told Benitez that he thought his name had been given to the Chinese and told him that he was going to be thrown into jail at the border. And, he advised Benitez to leave ahead of his clients or he would get them all in trouble.

Benitez stormed back. "Henry, I gave a factual account of what happened. I wanted to remain anonymous so if the Chinese have my name, there only is one person they could have gotten it from and that's you. In fact, it's three: you, Russell, or Paul." Todd got to his feet angrily and left. In the following hours, a rumor started to fly around camp that Benitez's name had been given to the Chinese authorities.

For his part, Todd was e-mailing his own press contacts off the mountain to offer his version of the event, one that depicted the shooting as an unexceptional event involving, not unarmed refugees or those of the religious order, but traffickers escorting women bound for prostitution. Publicizing it wouldn't help human rights activists with anti-Chinese agendas, he said.

Todd's supposition of what might have happened was spreading around camp. He'd told climbers that the victims of the shooting might be traffickers involved in the sex trade.

Rogers stormed into Big Green where Anderson and Smith were sitting. "He's got his facts wrong," he raged. "He doesn't even know what he's talking about; they're people-smugglers." He decried Benitez's e-mail saying it was jeopardizing everyone's safety.

Some climbers felt that expedition leaders were spreading the story because it was in their financial interest to do so. Victor Saunders recalls: "There were rumors straight away that they [the victims] were religious; a monk or a nun, had been killed. But then these rumors were pretty much counteracted, also straight away, by other rumors that the Chinese were chasing them because of whatever the Chinese had accused them of doing. There was a rumor that they weren't nuns, that there were traffickers involved. It's the sort of thing put out by people—the leaders of the big groups—who didn't want the Chinese to come in and interfere.

It's not in their interest to get everyone excited." He added: "It's worth hundreds of thousands of dollars if you have a team of fifteen people." The climber concluded: "People believed what they wanted to."

Recalled another expedition leader, "I think people saw through what was going on. We all tend to rationalize our motives." He added: "But there was a human rights thing going on. A murder had taken place right under our noses."

The shooting and the confrontation had induced paranoia into the expeditions. "We all felt that we had to get our people out of there as soon as we could because this could get uglier," said one expedition leader. "The feeling was that we were being watched, and now that people were talking about it in base camp, it was very uncomfortable.

Tibetans lived with the uneasy knowledge that informers were in their midst. Now Westerners questioned which expedition leaders were working with the Chinese and who might turn them in, were they to get news of the murder to the outside world. Climbers descended into conspiratorial whispers and then silence when sherpas or Tibetans came close. Those who had once shared beers with the Chinese at their camp now avoided them entirely.

Benitez, panicked about his role in spreading information and the ramifications of his e-mail, contemplated how he would exit the country. Deeply unsettled by the confrontation with Todd and Brice, he called Cotter in New Zealand. "He was talking about leaving and making a run for the border," Cotter recalled. "I felt that his responsibility was to the group and his clients and that was the main thing he should be focused on." Cotter, of course, had experience of arrest, detention, and interrogation with the PAP in Tibet, and he felt his guide needed to get a grip. "He was unnecessarily in a flap over the situation, as far as I could ascertain. He hadn't been questioned. Part of his personality is to over-react at times. This came out at that point. I just didn't want him freaking out and running away, which is what he had in mind."

Some of Benitez's clients were shocked at the attacks on their guide. In ABC, the AC teams were suddenly pariahs. No one would be seen talking to them, in case the Chinese swooped in. "They are teaching the new kid a lesson," Benitez complained to Andersen. Benitez's clients rallied to his side, offering support. "I felt really bad for Luis," recalls Scott Curtis, "He was more or less being harassed by others on the mountain who were trying to build this into something that it wasn't."

Deep down, Benitez knew why the leaders were so angry with him. "Climbers have always operated under their own code of ethics," said Benitez. "Climbers tend to operate out of the normal paradigm of what you and I find normal. It's an unspoken thing. It's a brotherhood. Everything stays in-house."

Increasingly anxious of the consequences of his actions, Benitez wrote ExWeb two days after his initial e-mail, asking the Sjogrens to rescind their headline-grabbing article about the shooting. "I am getting reports that the shooting had to do with preventing people-smuggling, and until I get the facts, better to pull off, as making companies here jittery," Benitez wrote, "and putting me in a world of shit."

But the Sjogrens were not backing down. Tom wrote back to Benitez saying that he regarded the information about seven bodies as unconfirmed, but that the information about shots fired and people falling, was true. He reassured Benitez saying that his name had not been used and that others were contacting ExWeb to confirm the story. At any rate, as he saw it, the word was out. He ended: "Too late to pull anything now."

By publishing an account of a Chinese human rights atrocity on the Web, the Sjogrens had unwittingly entered the frontline of the twenty-first century cyberwar between China and the West.* In a flash, the climbing enthusiasts had become targets of sophisticated Chinese cyberhackers.

Since breaking news of the shooting, the Sjogrens' Website had been attacked twenty-four hours a day. Later, stories they posted about China would vanish off their Website overnight. In the mornings, their inboxes overflowed with spam containing viruses that crept into their computer

---

* In 2008, the Dalai Lama's office was so concerned with repeated cyberattacks to their computer networks and all their e-mail constantly read, they commissioned investigators at Information Warfare Monitor. They found that a shadowy network called Ghostnet had infected 1,295 computers in 103 countries around the world. Three of the four control servers that controlled infected computers were in Hainan, Guangdong, and Sichuan in China. The fourth was located in the U.S.

networks and sent information back to networks in China. The Sjogrens weren't coming up on Google searches. Someone had attacked their site so that it wasn't registering on search engines.

As news of the story on ExWeb leaked out, pro-Tibet groups gathered force. They took umbrage at the fact that so few climbers would bear witness. Students for a Free Tibet later planned to shame the climbers into talking by naming all of them on a Website.

ExWeb continued its call for more information, witnesses, and photographs. Later, on October 11, Pavle Kozjek responded by e-mailing pictures of the PAP soldiers and the Tibetan children they had captured, as well as a shot of Kelsang's body in the snow. News agencies scrambled for the images. Kozjek knew that attaching his name to such sensitive material might end his climbing career in the Himalaya.

—·—·—

In base camp, all was eerily quiet as people desperately tried to get home.

The days dragged by with painful slowness, but Benitez's post to ExWeb was galvanizing Free Tibet groups around the globe. An e-mail arrived from the International Campaign for Tibet asking Benitez to confirm that a shooting had taken place and if he would talk about what had happened. He refused, deferring until perhaps he was in Kathmandu.

Brice and Todd had told Ang Tshering that Benitez was going to get everybody, particularly the sherpas, into trouble. Ang and Benitez had discussed a strategy for getting out unscathed. Ang proposed that he do all the talking, were they to get stopped. The elder sherpa knew the best language to employ when dealing with the Chinese authorities. Rogers and Benitez deleted all evidence of the e-mails to ExWeb about the shooting from their computers.

After several long days in camp, Benitez's group left ABC, one of the last groups to go. Their gear was carried down by twenty-two yaks. The previous night, Benitez had taken a last lingering look at Cho Oyu, the mountain he would later call his 'nemesis.'

At Chinese Base Camp, they were scrutinized by soldiers but not delayed. The Filipino expedition was not so lucky. All members were interrogated, and their truck was searched before they were allowed to leave.

Benitez's team arrived in Tingri at 8 p.m. after leaving ABC early in the morning. The next morning, they piled into Land Cruisers and lit out over the bumpy mountain roads to Zangmu. At the border, they switched from the Land Cruiser to a jeep. Benitez was visibly nervous as they transferred gear from one vehicle to the next. Shortly afterward, they crossed the two-hundred-foot Friendship Bridge, built in 1985, which marked a cultural divide between the chaotic, unregulated mountain kingdom of Nepal and the repressive, authoritarian, twenty-first-century superpower, China. With everything in China on Beijing time, there is a two-and-a-half-hour time difference between one end of the bridge and the other.

When they crossed the Friendship Bridge into Nepal, Benitez breathed a sigh of relief. At last he felt at a safe distance from the Chinese. But a crude red rope had been strung across the road at Ghorepani, a lush, wooded valley. The jeep was swarmed by Maoist guerillas wearing bandit-style red masks and toting submachine guns and antiquated rifles. The previous year, Maoist guerillas had injured Russian outfitter Alex Abramov and his guide when they tossed hand grenades at their truck. The civil war, which had claimed more than 13,000 lives, began in 1996 when Maoist rebels led an insurgency to overthrow Nepal's monarchy.

The guerillas demanded 5,000 rupees ($62). Ang argued them down to 50 yuan, and eventually the group was waved through.

In Kathmandu, sinister rumors swirled that the Chinese embassy was looking for climbers who had witnessed the mountain shooting to ensure their silence. Benitez's e-mail had been picked up by news organizations all over the world. Local stringers were combing the place for climbers. A headline in the British newspaper *The Independent* read: "China tries to gag climbers who saw Tibet killings." The climbers grew increasingly frightened. Filipino Dr. Ted Esguerra was warned by his expedition leader not to say a word about what he had seen or done. The doctor hid in the Seventh-Day Adventist church in Kathmandu, praying that he would not be taken in.

Benitez safely stowed his clients in the Hotel Tibet before checking into the Radisson to evade anyone he felt might be following him. He called Cotter again and asked him to call ExWeb. Cotter telephoned the Sjogrens and asked them to take down the reference to an "American guide" in the story Benitez had sent.

Benitez was terrified and overcome with paranoia, even in Nepal. Alone in the hotel, wracked with dread and self-disgust, he replayed the scene over and over in his mind. Was Todd right? Was the group in fact a train of traffickers en route to Mumbai?

Benitez closed the thin curtains of his hotel room and closed his eyes. The phone began to ring. He hadn't told a soul where he'd checked in.

14

CAPTURED BY THE WUJING

— · — · —

Firmly crush the savage aggression of the
Dalai clique, defeat separatism, and wage
war to maintain stability.

Tibet Daily

The pilgrims began to stir on the mountaintop. Jamyang snapped awake, uncoiling his frigid limbs. Around him were the huddled figures of other sleeping bodies. The fifteen-year-old climbed to his feet. Taking a few steps to the edge of the precipitous ledge, he froze. Just below was the Gyaplung PAP base. Dogs were barking in their kennels. Quickly he ducked down out of sight.

The group of around twenty sat discussing what to do, split evenly on staying put to wait for the guides or advancing without them. In the distance, gunfire crackled. Two green PAP vehicles sped past below. After several hours, some of the refugees, led by a surly nineteen-year-old, headed off to try to find their way. "I'm not going to die here," he declared. For twenty-four hours, the remaining ragtag group waited in hiding above the PAP base. They were parched. Below, tantalizingly, was the glistening surface of the lake. But they didn't dare go down for water lest the soldiers see them.

A day later, two escapees, a man in his late 30s and a woman in her early 40s, who had splintered off with Penpa, appeared. Penpa, they told the group, had vanished after setting out in search of water and had abandoned them.

The group had to make a decision; they had no food or water and would not survive much longer. After, Sangya, a monk, did a divination ritual with some relics he tossed into the dust. It was decided to head straight down the rocky trail.

At dusk, as the group rested in the lea of a mountain burnished orange by the setting sun and dotted with tents, they heard a figure shout, *"Wei! Wei!"* (Mandarin for hello). And then, *"Shang la ya!"* ("Come up!") Could it be one of the guides, they wondered? Relieved at the prospect of being led to safety, they trudged toward the figure. As they did, the man fired two warning shots in the air. A soldier on a bullhorn ordered them to stop.

The monks shouted first, "Run!" One monk vaulted to his feet and began to run but tripped and fell, crying in pain. Jamyang, fitter than the rest, ran ahead to the river, helping two children along as shots rang out in the air. Affording a look back over his shoulder, Jamyang caught sight of two soldiers firing. Jamyang stopped in his tracks. "Raise your hands in the air!" shouted the soldier. The PAP drew closer. "Throw your backpack on the ground!" they barked. "Kneel down."

In a sharp whisper, the monk who had done the divination ritual declared, "There's only two of them. We can run!" Jamyang crouched in a lunge, ready to leap forward. But a slow-moving dragnet of PAP, a moving green-camouflage wall of eighty or so soldiers, had closed its net around the group: They were surrounded.

The butt of a rifle cracked Jamyang in the back of the neck. The PAP tore off backpacks, aggressively hurling their contents in the snow, and yanked sunglasses off the refugees, putting them on themselves. They turned their attention to Sangya, a clear target in his maroon robes. "Why don't we just kill them?" spat one soldier. "The monk is the ringleader." They kicked and beat the monk angrily. He held up his manacled hands and begged them to stop.

The soldiers hauled the refugees to their feet and marched them to a truck on a nearby road. There, Jamyang was reunited with Norbu Palden. Leaning against the side of the truck, he was swathed in a green army blanket, the gunshot wound on his left ankle angrily inflamed.

Norbu, his face pale, explained how he had been shot. Worse, he relayed to Jamyang, a nun had been killed. At Gyaplung base, spotlights blinded the refugees and a gaggle of jeering soldiers greeted them. Some had German shepherds at their sides.

"It took me a whole day to get you motherfuckers," one soldier spat angrily. The group was forced to pose for a photograph and was videotaped as they waited anxiously for the next move. One of the soldiers ventured that perhaps there were still more in hiding, as he cast an eye beyond the base to the marrow-chilling cold beyond.

They were ushered to some cells in a whitewashed H-shaped building and locked in a refectory-type room. Two doctors arrived to examine them, measuring their height, shoulder width, and weight. Before leaving the room, the doctors distributed pills to the refugees, purportedly to treat "poor eyesight."

Interrogators arrived, firing volleys of questions at the captives. They asked Jamyang's name. "Karma," he lied. Next they fired volleys of questions: Who advised you to flee Tibet? Where did you stay in Lhasa? Were you in a house or a hotel in Lhasa? What type and color vehicles were you traveling in from Lhasa? What is the name of the guide and how much did you pay him? How did you meet the guides? What are their names and where were they born? Do you know the Dalai Lama? Do you have relatives in India?

Jamyang was led back to the cell. After a few minutes, from next door, Chinese disco music started up, and a thumping beat reverberated through the room. Flashing lights shone under the door, and there was a sound of raised voices. The soldiers were partying to celebrate the capture.

Later that same night, the refugees were packed into a truck and driven on to yet another location. After another journey swaying over mountain roads, the refugees were divided by sex and age, and marched into a sterile barracks building. Thrust through the door, Jamyang saw that one or two other prisoners were already slumped on the cell's floor. One was a boy who had earlier fled the group in terror. He smiled when he saw Jamyang. The cell had a raised concrete platform at the end with a thin red mat. A bright security light shone in from outside, making sleep impossible.

Several hours later, a twenty-eight-year-old man from Lhoka was pushed into the cell. He was bleeding from a gunshot wound to his leg.

He too had been with the group. He said a bullet had ricocheted from a rock and struck his lower leg.

In the early hours of the morning, interrogations began. First out was Tsundue, the monk who had refused to trade his monk's habit for lay clothes. After two hours, a pair of soldiers dragged him back to the cell and dumped him on the floor. Battered to a pulp, his face was unrecognizable.

Jamyang was next. He was led down darkened hallways before being ushered into a small room. At the end, sitting behind a desk, was a broad-shouldered Chinese man with hennaed hair, who was wearing a dark suit. Standing next to him was a short, scowling PAP officer. After five minutes of perfunctory questions about Jamyang's hometown, occupation, and other personal details, the officer changed tack. "What do you know about the Dalai Lama," he demanded. "Nothing," Jamyang, replied coolly. The interrogator nodded. "So you like to lie?" he teased. "Then why were you up in the mountains near the border?" He got up and walked around his desk. In his hand, as he advanced on Jamyang, was an electric cattle prod.

—·—·—

The first jolt from the electroshock baton made Jamyang faint. He was bound to a wooden chair by leather straps. When he came to, the questioning about the Dalai Lama began again. When he refused to speak, he was jolted again.

"I know you were going to India!" the officer shouted. "You were going to see the splittists, weren't you? What is the relationship between the Dalai Lama and the Tibetan people?" A white hot pain shot up from Jamyang's bruised bleeding shins. His tormentor produced a long, leather belt. Violently, he beat Jamyang's bare arms. The stinging pain was intolerable. Then he switched to the narrow edges so that when he came down with the belt, it tore crescent-shaped divots out of the boy's arm. Jamyang screamed in pain. But he refused to admit he had been headed to India. The officer grabbed a rubber paddle and began his attack on Jamyang's legs. Then they put steel clamps on his fingers and jerked his hands behind his head.

The torture lasted a full day. Jamyang was dragged back to his cell with fresh welts on his arms. As he laid against the wall, a prisoner approached him. "That looks bad," he said. "You must have done something to deserve that. What did you do?" Jamyang knew the Chinese planted spies among the prisoners. Post-interrogation detainees, vulnerable and eager for a sympathetic shoulder after their torture, were easy targets. Jamyang slumped against the wall, ignoring him.

At the end of the interrogation sessions, many of the escapees were forced to sign a legal document that they had not witnessed the murder of Kelsang Namtso. Those who didn't know how to read and write were made to sign with thumb prints. A few times, soldiers came into the cells with a mobile phone that had a picture of Kelsang's body on it. They demanded to know who the girl was and where she was from. Everyone played dumb.

One day following his interrogation session, Jamyang was ordered to clean the toilets. When he responded, his jailers realized he understood Mandarin. A day later, Jamyang was approached by a tall, thin man in a black suit and white-rimmed, round glasses. "If you saw the body of a dead person, what would you think?" the man asked. It was a strange question. The man persisted. "Would you be scared?" Jamyang answered, without thinking, in Chinese. "No, of course not." The man nodded, warming to the knowledge that Jamyang spoke and understood Chinese. "OK, come with me," he said.

Jamyang was led out of the garrison, handcuffed, and driven south. He bumped over roads for about an hour before arriving at a large house in the middle of nowhere. Jamyang stood in the courtyard while the man who had stopped him the day before went inside. A few sallow-looking soldiers stood around smoking. A figure emerged from the house, escorted by soldiers. It was Norbu Palden. He looked terrified. As he approached, Jamyang asked him what had happened. "No," he mouthed simply, with a dazed expression. As Jamyang looked on, he was loaded into a jeep and driven off.

An old man was escorted past. Again, Jamyang tried to elicit information. "I don't know, I don't know," the man muttered before disappearing. Eventually, the man in the black suit appeared.

He handed Jamyang a white handkerchief to block his mouth and nose. The man nodded. "Follow me," he instructed. Pushing open a door, they stepped into the building's gloomy confines. They stood in a large, windowless room. In the middle of the floor, beneath a white plastic covering, was a body. A black bag lay nearby with its contents spread out over the floor: A few handfuls of *tsampa*, some pictures of a Tibetan family, a woolen hat, and a fawn-colored scarf striped with white and silver.

The man pulled the sheet back. Underneath, stripped naked, was Kelsang Namtso. An angry hole as large as a small plate glared from her chest. Jamyang fought the urge to react.

"Now you understand why I bought you here," the man in the suit offered.

"No," said Jamyang. "I don't understand."

"Well, you speak Chinese very well and we need your help. Look at that nun. Do you know her name and where she is from?"

Jamyang shook his head dumbly. "I don't know anything."

"Come now," said the man. "Are you sure?"

Jamyang was silent.

"Stay here," the man instructed, as he left the room.

Alone, Jamyang shivered. After what seemed like an eternity, the man returned with five soldiers, who carried the body into an anteroom.

As they drove back toward Tingri, the man's cell phone rang. The person on the other end was shouting loudly enough for Jamyang to hear.

"What shall we do with the body?" the voice demanded.

"You have to find out where she's from and deliver the body back to her family," the man instructed.

As they drew nearer to the prison, the man spoke. "This is your first time trying to escape, so we might release you soon," he said. "But if it happens a second time, we'll kill you in a worse way than the nun." They rumbled through the gates of the Tingri garrison.

15

THE RESPONSIBILITY
OF ENLIGHTENMENT

— · — · —

The sage does not wash away sins with water,
Nor wipe away the pain of beings with his hands.
His realization he does not transfer to others,
He frees by showing them the peace of ultimate
reality.

The Buddha

Dolma waited, hoping to see Kelsang crest the rise into Nepal. But all was silent and unmoving in the blazing white. When the nuns told her that Kelsang had been shot in the leg, she didn't believe them. She needed to go back. Her loyalty to Kelsang was overwhelming.

Lhundrup knew Dolma would be shot or captured if she attempted it. Not only that, to go back would put them all at risk of torture and incarceration. Lhundrup half-dragged and half-stumbled, pulling at the distraught girl's arm as they sought refuge in Nepal. She must think about all of them, he said, not just herself.

As they struggled through the snow, the hard base layer underneath gave way, and Dolma slipped up to her thighs. The potentially fatal threat of avalanches or crevasses lurked with every step.

The glacier headed steeply downward. The constant downward movement of the flowing ice had pushed car-sized chunks of lapis blue ice to the edge of the pass. At the edge of the glacier were five- and six-foot-tall penitentes—ghostly, icy sculptures.

Loose rocks lay over the glacier. There was no trail here. Crevasses lurked beneath them. It was a constantly shifting landscape, with danger at every step. Hairline cracks, about around one to two inches apart, latticed the ice. The only sound was the Styrofoam squeak of their footsteps in the crystalline snow. On the horizon beyond was the peak of Nangpa Gysum, the guardian of the Nangpa La, looming in the marbled sky like a flint arrowhead, snow clinging to knife-edge rims that connected it to lower peaks squatting on either side.

After an hour or two, the group met a line of traders driving yaks up and over the Nangpa La. Lhundrup stopped to talk to them. He waited until Dolma was out of earshot. "A nun has been shot back there," he told them. He asked how much it would cost to check on Kelsang and, if she were alive, to take her back to Driru. After some haggling, the men agreed to 200 yuan ($30). Lhundrup gave them the money on the condition that they return her body to Driru if she was dead.

Two hours later, the traders attempted to reach the body. But after seeing the mountains dotted with PAP, they carried on, not daring to stop.

As the group descended into Nepal, they faced another grave danger: The Nepalese police were often just as threatening as their Chinese counterparts. Paid to turn refugees over to China, they were notorious for rape, robbery, and on occasion murder. Tibetan refugees were worth bounties paid by the PAP units on the border, so the Nepalese hunted Tibetans for cash.

The pristine blanket of snow covering the frosted glacier dipped down into a jagged icefall with hanging ledges and towering seracs. The flat, rocky area before the icefall—called Dzasampa—had long been used by nomads, traders, and refugees. Squat stone walls had been erected to give shelter from the whistling winds. Exhausted beyond measure and squinting with snow blindness, the forlorn group of Tibetans collapsed on the ground. Most of them had tossed their bags during the shooting. Few had blankets, food, or spare clothes. The children were shivering uncontrollably. A few had burning frostbite in their fingers and toes. Dolma, who had resolutely kept her belongings, shared her blanket with two children.

Despite her total exhaustion, Dolma slept fitfully. When she awoke, a searing pain burned her eyes. She'd sacrificed her sunglasses to Lhundrup when she had seen him in pain with snow blindness as they entered the climbers' camp. He had protested, but she had insisted, saying she had long hair that she could pull over her eyes. The monk gratefully accepted, but the altruism had cost Dolma. When she tried to open her eyes, they swarmed with tears.

A few hours later, Dechen Pema, Samdhup, and another nun appeared out of the white. They arrived looking bedraggled and lost. They had had a narrow escape. After a bullet had pierced Dechen's pant leg, she had taken Samdhup and, with another nun, hidden in the snow. After an hour and a half, the gunfire receded to just an occasional single shot. And then nothing. They had crouched in a fold in the mountain, just above the climbers' camp. As the sun rose, the snow melted around them, and their clothes became a damp, soggy mess. After five hours, at about 3 p.m., they had dared to peek over the bank. They saw some figures moving around in the climbers' camp beneath the tents. On the opposite mountainside, they saw a few soldiers laboring up an incline.

The nuns decided to make a break for it. In a crouching run, they looped around and found the footprints of the others. A few minutes later, they found Kelsang's crumpled body lying in the road. Dechen stopped, crept closer, and knelt. Kelsang was lying on her side; her eyes had turned glassy and lifeless. Gingerly, Dechen pulled up her right arm. Blood seeped out of a chest wound, staining her *chuba* and pooling around her body, congealing in the snow, frozen. Dechen had laid Kelsang's arm back gently.

Across the pass, they could see that the soldiers might have spotted them. They were now turning back and heading toward them. Without wasting a second, the exhausted girls turned and lunged toward the border. They were mentally and physically broken, distraught, lost, and starving. Finally, Dechen pulled the blessed barley from her pack and shared it among them. They munched the waterless grains with dry mouths, eventually falling on their hands and knees and eating snow to wash the barley down. The tiny sustenance energized them. They traveled overnight, following Dolma's and Lhundrup's tracks in the snow lit by the moon.

When Lhundrup waved to them, the nuns approached. Out of earshot, Lhundrup warned the nuns not to tell Dolma what had happened to Kelsang. When Dolma pressed them for information on her friend, the nuns relayed that she had been shot in the leg and arrested by the PAP. Dolma frowned, again determined to go back, thinking perhaps she could liberate Kelsang. Again, Lhundrup talked her out of it.

It was time to go. The group was a sorry sight as they staggered over the boulder fields and massive expanses of rubble, those snow-blind clutching to their fellows. Yak carcasses and giant boulders as big as houses littered the landscape like the discarded playthings of giants.

After several hours, they entered Bhote Koshi Valley, a vast flat-bottomed plain in a U-shaped valley of sand, rock, and sparse desert scrub. Here the air was richer. They felt their consciousness returning to normal as if a magic switch had been turned on and their brains were operational again. Out of the bright white landscape, Dolma's eyes began to readjust. The sloped mountains on either side were thick with heather and stunted alpine vegetation. They tramped across a rudimentary wooden bridge spanning a small river.

A few craggy peaks, with icy veins, jutted up beyond. On the right was a stone cottage hedged by a pen of sheep. Just beyond was a glacial brook. A yellow sign hanging from a corner declared, "Welcome to Arya Guesthouse." The two-room stone dwelling had a corrugated steel roof and a blue-painted stovepipe that leaked wisps of smoke.

This was the first safe house in Nepal after the Nangpa La. They scrunched over an alluvium field to reach a cracked wooden door. It was sweaty and hot inside. The walls were draped with red, white, and blue plastic sheets, deployed as crude insulation. Flames licked at soot-stained kettles and saucepans bubbling on a blackened stove, which sat propped on a pile of flat stones. Grime-encrusted kitchen utensils hung above a makeshift sink and kitchen counter. Shelves were stacked to the ceiling with boxes of noodles. One narrow doorway led to a richly stocked storeroom in the back; another to a room lined with cots.

Kalden*, a sixtyish man wearing a dusty baseball hat and a filthy once-cream-colored anorak, ushered them to benches and pulled some makeshift menus from a low table. Then he replaced them with dog-eared pieces of paper. The first menu was for mountain climbers and

---

* Kalden is a pseudonym.

traders; this second set, with cheaper prices, was for Tibetans. In neat Tibetan script, the prices for food and accommodation were displayed: one night's stay—50 RS; one bag of boiled potatoes—120 RS; firewood per person—20 RS; one cup Tibetan beer or wine—15 RS; one jug of the same—100 RS.

Kalden cracked a smile. He'd lived in this valley at 12,000 feet since 1959, when he and his family had fled the fighting in Tibet. Thousands of Tibetans had passed through here. He knew most of the Tibetan guides by name but had grown cynical about their mission in recent years. He regarded them as businessmen hungry for a profit and unconcerned with the true fate of their charges. Often, unescorted escapees caused problems. Starving, terrified refugees would break down the door or smash the windows to get in for food. Other refugees cheated him, refusing to pay for their food when leaving. Another time he was on the hillside overlooking the house when some refugees ambushed him. They tied his arms beneath his legs and stole his watch and the dzi stone around his neck.

Kalden had seen people in every condition imaginable: women with babies in rucksacks arrived every month. Once or twice he'd delivered babies in his backroom. One time a woman had crossed the Nangpa La to give birth in Nepal because of the Chinese one-child-per-family policy. Outside were graves, some more recent than others, of those who had paid the ultimate price for attempting the Nangpa La. One year, during a massive, weeklong snowstorm, Kalden had had to bring all twenty of his yaks into his house. Out of the blizzard, forty escapees arrived and crowded in with the yaks, desperate for warmth.

Today, the group of Tibetans gratefully drank their fill of yak-butter tea before collapsing in bed.

Two days later, Gyaltsen appeared at the safe house. He had had a narrow escape. The refugees at ABC had split when they saw soldiers hastening toward them in the snow, and Gyaltsen had ducked into a tent in the Filipino camp. The team's doctor, Dr. Ted Esguerra, and the cook hid him among their packs and luggage. The rest of the team was angry that the doctor had put them all in danger. He ignored them. A few minutes later, a disheveled band of PAP had arrived at the tent begging for coffee and clearly suffering from the altitude; their chests puffed like bellows as they rested on their rifles. The team shook their heads and said they had little to offer. Inside the tent, Gyaltsen had burrowed deeper into the packs. That night the sherpas took a white meal sack and cut out armholes, a slit in the top and tugged it over the guide's head. It acted as camouflage vest in the snow. In the moonlight, Gyaltsen had stolen out of camp undetected.

The group, set off again. The mile-wide, tawny valley was a ubiquitous moonscape of alluvial riverbeds and frozen boulder fields. The trail, dust and sand, was just a faint steak demarcated by yak droppings and discarded sneakers. Hastening winds chased down the valley and threw up small pearl-colored clouds. A rusty yellow sign announced: "Way to Nangpa La." For the first time, Dolma saw sherpas with baskets strapped to their backs. Nepal, on first blush, felt strange and unwelcoming. In the middle of desolate valleys were *chortens*, which they took care to circumnavigate. Piles of mani stones had been worn smooth by the wind.

Thame, one of the first villages they arrived at after the safe house, was a windswept settlement perched on the side of a massive canyon at 12,500 feet. The village stood in relief against the 21,000-foot hulk of Thamserku, wreathed in a scarf of mist. Gyaltsen warned them to be wary of Nepalese police dressed as tourists. These days, the Wujing were also far more aggressive, even crossing the border, violating international sovereignty, and coming as far as this village to look for escapees.

Beyond the village, the trail narrowed to a steep, single-file track that doglegged around the circumference of mountains and then over a crude metal bridge above a deep gorge. Below, the Bhote Koshi river of churning glacial melt roared downstream in a furious, milky-white torrent that carved deep gullies out of the rock. Halfway across the bridge, a blast of icy air ripped down the ravines with the cascading water.

On the other side of the bridge, in bright warming sunlight, rock faces were daubed with intricate murals of Padmasambhava. They were now in the Khumbu Valley: the *peyul* or sacred valley that Padmasambhava had predicted Tibetans would retreat to in times of conflict.

Hundreds of feet down the mountainside, Dolma saw emerald forests of juniper and pine. High above, she glimpsed a couple of eagles soaring in mountain thermals. Once again, the world seemed to have come to life. From the Nangpa La, they had descended 7,000 feet. Dolma's sense of smell returned, and the aroma of fecund forests drifted up from the valley.

Along the trail, a man in a bright red North Face jacket hastened toward them. He was tall, with copper-colored skin and slate-gray hair neatly parted. Jampa° was a linchpin for many of the safe houses of Nepal. Jampa led the group to a safe house. There, he produced a large, butter-stained notebook that listed some of the escapees that he had helped. Carefully, he added the name of each refugee to his ledger, noting their age and provenance. Afterward, he would call the United Nations facility in Kathmandhu to alert them to the number of people coming through.

The refugees' shoes, particularly thin-soled sneakers, were by now shredded to ribbons. A few begged Jampa for new footwear. Jampa sent word to a friend who returned with dozens of cheap shoes. It would be Dolma's third pair on the two-week trip.

That night, an exhausted figure ambled into the village. Limping, sunburned, barefoot, and exhausted, it was Choedon. As he entered the safe house, a sudden silence fell. Everyone stared in shock. They had felt sure that the kind-hearted farmer had been shot dead. Choedon broke into a smile. When he sat down on a proffered chair, they saw that his feet were cracked, sore, and bleeding. Someone had stolen his shoes while he dozed near the trail. For two days, he had walked Nepal's trekking trails barefoot.

With relief, he told them of his escape. He gratefully took the hot tea that was pressed into his cupped hands.

At 5 a.m. the next morning, the group headed off to Namche Bazar, the sherpa capital. Along the trail, Penpa appeared. Somehow, he maintained, he had managed to escape the dragnet of soldiers but had abandoned his group to do so. There was a bullet hole through

---

° Jampa is a pseudonym.

the front of his black trousers. He passed a few cursory words with Lhundrup and fell in beside them as they walked. Later, his story aroused suspicion. Many thought that his group had been sold off to informers. How could such a large detachment of soldiers know precisely where to intercept the group? The fact that all who had been shot (with the exception of Kelsang) had been hit in the leg might have indicated that some soldiers had attempted to maim rather than kill their targets.

After several hours of trekking, Namche's blue-roofed guesthouses appeared on a distant mountainside. The town sits on terraced cliffs in a concave semicircle. Beyond is the ochre peak of Kwangde. Hundreds of feet below in a canyon, the river gains force heading south. The narrow, cobbled streets are filled with cramped stores selling last-minute mountaineering supplies and sherpa-made arts and crafts. The traders from Tibet set up their wares in the middle of town—pink rock salt, counterfeit jackets, and cheap electronics. The town is also a Nepali garrison. Menacing Nepali soldiers in their distinctive sky-blue uniforms had withdrawn to the town from outlying bases after consistent attack by the Maoists.

The group wasted no time there, it was too dangerous. On the trail on the other side of town Jampa bade them farewell, warning them about checkpoints and giving locations as far as he knew. As they descended the mountain trails, gaggles of tourists labored up in expensive hiking gear. One or two were being carried down on the backs of sherpas; the altitude was too much for them.

Along the way, Lhundrup was able to find a working telephone. He called Kelsang's uncle, a monk at Sera Monastery, in the Tibetan exile settlements at Bylakuppe in southern India. Lhundrup relayed the news of the shooting. Kalsang Chonjour took the news badly. He'd known his niece was on her way and that her parents were nervous about their only daughter traveling to India. As he hung up the phone, he couldn't bring himself to call them to break the news. He agonized for days, chanting mantras in the temple and burning incense in offering.

Continuing on the trail, the sweet foliage mingled with the homely scent of freshly sawn wood. The refugees neared the mountainside village of Lukla. It has a single, 2,000-foot airstrip that angles up into the sky off the side of the mountain. Given its strategic importance, it is heavily guarded by the Nepali military, and plainclothes police mingle with tourists in the village's cobbled streets, looking for Maoist insurgents. It is a dangerous place for Tibetans, not only due to its Nepali military presence, but because of its general lawlessness.*

Gyaltsen pulled them off the trail, down a steep ravine before the village, in an attempt to circle it. A few miles along, they entered deep thickets of bamboo. Unlike the arid air on the Tibetan plateau, the air was moist under a green canopy of forest. Dolma's face swelled from heat and exertion. The nuns untied their heavy *chubas* and knotted the arms around their waists as they began to drip with sweat.

A few hours later, the group cut back up to the trail, beyond the sandbagged machine gun emplacements and checkpoints surrounding Lukla. They were near the main highway from Kathmandu to Dram. Thirteen checkpoints lined the route, and the area was thick with Nepalese security.

From the roadside, the group boarded a bus and headed south to a Tibetan settlement near Phablu. From there, they walked to Kotari, a main transport hub for the remote region and a dangerous stop so close to the border of China. It was a squalid frontier station of fieldstone buildings and muddy, narrow, pitted streets. Chinese paid Nepalese soldiers bounties for Tibetan refugees that they returned. Sometimes they were spotted leading handcuffed Tibetans to the border into the waiting arms of the PAP. They returned carrying cases of potent Chinese beer that they lugged back to the police station.

In the town, they were led to a small, two-story private house in the village—the last safe house on their route. They were greeted by a portly man and his wife who ushered them into backrooms, urging them not to talk to foreigners.

---

* A few months earlier, a Tibetan woman and her husband had been escaping Tibet and took refuge in a house in an unknown village in the border. Local men forced their way into her room and dragged her husband out and locked him in a nearby house. They then raped her repeatedly over a period of sixteen days before letting them both go.

Shortly after arriving, they went out for food. In streets thick with diesel fumes, Lhundrup advised all of them to change their money from Chinese yuan into Nepalese currency. Being caught with yuan was a dead giveaway. As Dolma was stitching up her money in her coat, Penpa appeared at her side.

"Which nun was shot to death?" Penpa asked casually. He'd been oblivious to the attempts to shield Dolma from the truth. Dolma had managed to suspend disbelief, clinging to the hope that the rumor of Kelsang's death wasn't true. She broke down in deep, wracking sobs. Lhundrup helped her to her feet and escorted her back to the hotel room.

"Was Kelsang really killed in the mountains?" Dolma asked Choedon back at the hotel. Choedon nodded slowly and gave a brief, unemotional account of what he had seen. Five days after the shooting, Dolma lay face down on the bed and pulled at her hair as she sobbed convulsively. Lhundrup enquired for further details and teased out the full story for Dolma to hear. Kelsang was gone.

—·—

A few hours later, the Tibetans clambered aboard a coach that had been sent to take them to Kathmandu. As they climbed into the plush gray seats with white cotton headrests, the air conditioning thrumming, they couldn't resist grinning. An official from the UNHCR Tibetan Refugee Reception Center, JangChup Rabjor, a thirty-eight-year-old former Indian army officer, traveled with them, successfully fending off several bids for bribes by Nepali police. Sometimes the UNHCR paid "fines" to the Nepalese police for imprisoned Tibetans, outbidding the Chinese.

It took twelve hours to travel the bumpy seventy miles of heavily patrolled and checkpointed road to Kathmandu. Cows blocked the road, and chickens ran squawking from under the wheels of the bus as they threaded their way through the motor rickshaws and honking dusty traffic to the first real place of sanctuary on the eastern edge of the city. Eventually, the coach stopped before some heavy brown-painted steel gates at the end of a winding back street. Its presence wasn't advertised with signposts.

A security guard swung the gates open as the bus arrived in the court-yard of the Tibetan Refugee Reception Center in the early afternoon. Hundreds of escapees watched the new arrivals. Nuns and monks, having crossed the Nangpa La, were wearing their maroon robes once more. Children played. Families lay in the balmy haze of the midday sun. As they clambered out of the bus, the refugees experienced the first calm in twenty-two days. Together they had crossed grasslands, tundra, glaciers, crevasses, and the highest mountain range in the world. Only three children were still with them.

The center was a cavernous, pale yellow, two-story building with south-facing sunlit terraces. Dolma was shown to a gloomy dormitory with steel cots lining the walls and advised not to leave the compound. The Chinese embassy in Kathmandu was trying to suppress news of the shooting incident, so to leave the center would be dangerous.

A few hours later, Dolma was led to the center's medical clinic. Outside, Dolma saw a woman who had had both feet amputated due to frostbite. Another had lost all her toes. Inside one of the administration rooms was a wall covered with gruesome pictures of frostbite victims: blackened toes and faces, amputated feet, and frozen eyes leading to permanent blindness.

Despite serious malnutrition, Dolma was in good physical health. Others were not so lucky. A number of refugees suffered from frost-bite. Others had horribly swollen and lacerated feet that were infected from the trek over rocks, ice, and snow in inadequate shoes.

— . — . —

The phone continued to ring in Benitez's hotel room. Reluctantly he answered. "Is this Luis Benitez?" a female voice inquired. A lump formed in Benitez's throat. "Who are you?" he barked anxiously. "How did you get his number? How do you know where I am?"

"Please don't hang up," she said. Benitez questioned how she had managed to track him down.

The woman had been in touch with Elizabeth Hawley, a redoubtable former journalist in her eighties, who is a legend in mountaineering circles. Each year, she logs every expedition for the Himalayan Database, the most comprehensive account of mountaineering expeditions in the Himalaya. She's known for her rigorous attention to detail and her sharp tongue. Over the years, with her surgical fact checking, she has exposed climbers who have falsely claimed to have bagged summits. She first arrived in Kathmandu in the 1960s as a reporter for *Time* magazine, sending political dispatches back from the little mountain kingdom. But she quickly found her niche reporting on the exploding mountaineering scene following Hillary's successful conquest of Everest. Nothing happened in Kathmandu that she didn't know about; her contacts were second to none. Over the years, Benitez had developed a close friendship with Hawley. Of all people, she would know his whereabouts.

The woman on the other end of the telephone was Kate Saunders, the communications director of the International Campaign for Tibet (ICT), the largest of the pro-Tibet groups. She had called Hawley for information on climbers who might talk to her, and Hawley had volunteered Benitez's whereabouts. Behind her steel glasses and long brunette hair, Saunders, forty-two, is a fierce, uncompromising Tibet advocate. From its Washington, D.C., headquarters, ICT runs an extensive information network to retrieve information from Tibet with which to lobby Western governments.

Working from the group's townhouse in Washington, Saunders and her team had been galvanized by the news of the shooting. It is virtually impossible to get independent witnesses, let alone Americans, to testify to Chinese rights abuses inside Tibet. The shooting marked the first time outsiders had witnessed a murder by a member of the Chinese military machine since the 1950 invasion. Researcher Chris Ratke and Saunders were hot on the trail to break the story to the world. Saunders had spent four sleepless days desperately trying to get the climbers who witnessed the murder to attest to what they saw. As they called and e-mailed guides on the mountain and the offices of guiding companies, many confessed ignorance.

On October 4, Ratke called the International Mountain Guides main office in Ashford, Washington. Owner Eric Simonson said he had talked to his expedition leader, Mike Hamill, the previous day but he didn't mention anything about a possible shooting. Yet Philip Desjardins of the team said that it was the main topic of conversation in base camp when he returned from the summit on October 3. Simonson called Ratke the following day and left a message saying that the team did confirm a shooting had taken place; one person had been shot, but there were possibly seven or eight others also shot. He said that he didn't want news of the shooting released to the media until his team and clients were safely out of the country.

Many Western climbers simply turned their backs on what they had seen, refusing to bear witness. There was nothing to be gained by speaking up about Kelsang's murder except banishment from the world's most glorious mountain range. "It was incredibly difficult to get people to talk," said Saunders. "They just wanted to hide away. When they got to Kathmandu, they just got on the plane and went home." One exception was the British policeman Steve Lawes, who became the first climber who didn't insist on a pseudonym. His story made the British press and was later picked up by other news organizations. Other climbers started to talk.

Benitez refused her request to talk to the media using his name. But, Saunders calculated, if she could get him to meet face to face with the refugees, his conscience might be pricked and he might bear witness. Benitez agreed to meet the survivors of the shooting. If nothing else, at least he'd find out whether the group had indeed been traffickers.

Meanwhile, the story was beginning to break. At the Refugee Center, ICT's doughty researcher, Kunchok Chodak, was trying to interview the Tibetans to uncover details. Most of the forty or so he approached were hesitant and afraid, but Dolma Palkyi was an exception. She was angry about what had happened to Kelsang and was intent on speaking out about the atrocity that had occurred on the Nangpa La. Chodak reported back to ICT headquarters that the murdered Tibetan had been a seventeen-year-old nun named Kelsang Namtso.

Benitez waited anxiously in the lobby of his hotel, a blue baseball cap pulled down low over his eyes. By chance, Russell Brice emerged from the hotel restaurant with a business colleague and caught sight of him. Brice grinned and shook his hand as if nothing had happened.

Kunchok Chodak hustled Benitez out of the hotel before any journalists could spot him. At the refugee center, director Kalsang Chung greeted Benitez. After a few pleasantries, Benitez was escorted to the medical center. As he trailed the director, he cast his eyes around to see children playing, nuns and monks scooping rice from steel bowls, and others limping around the compound on crutches.

The director showed him a room in the clinic where they used only traditional Tibetan herbal remedies. Many of the escapees that they treated recoiled in horror at the sight of syringes, antibiotics, and the other implements of Western medicine.

Upstairs on an open-air balcony, Benitez was led to a group of shell-shocked Tibetans. Ragged and wind burned, they looked exhausted. Standing at the back of a group was a young woman with a long black ponytail, sobbing uncontrollably. A couple of girls were doing their best to console her.

For the past three weeks, Benitez and Dolma had shadowed each others' trails across two countries and the biggest mountain range on the planet. At last, they were face to face. The director explained that the nun who'd been shot was Dolma's best friend.

The director ordered everyone into his office. Benitez hesitated. Through the door, he felt sure that something was going to happen that would change his life forever. He hovered outside, fighting the urge to bolt the other way. With a heavy heart, Benitez eventually trooped into the room and squatted down next to the director's desk. The director told the girls what a brave, heroic thing the American had done. Benitez felt an overwhelming sense of embarrassment. He was being hailed as a hero, when in fact he had turned and led his clients up the mountain. "I felt that I didn't deserve the accolades that he was giving me," Benitez later admitted. "I just had this intense feeling of embarrassment because I felt I hadn't done anything."

As Dolma looked over at Benitez, she saw tears welling in his eyes. Why, she wondered, was the American crying?

Benitez was overcome. He cried for himself and his own pathetic response on the mountain, and he cried for Kelsang Namtso, a seventeen-year-old nun he had never met. He vowed to tell the story of what had happened whenever he had the opportunity.

As he was led outside, Kunchok Chodak asked if he would mind talking to some local journalists who were waiting.

"You know that you might not be allowed back into Tibet if you do that," he told the climber. "The Chinese could ban you from ever coming back." Benitez felt as though he had been "ambushed."

He was, though, willing to talk.

16

A LIE UNCOVERED

—.—.—

The greatest achievement is selflessness.
The greatest worth is self-mastery.
The greatest quality is seeking to serve others.
The greatest precept is continual awareness.
The greatest medicine is the emptiness of everything.
The greatest action is not conforming with the world's ways.
The greatest magic is transmuting the passions.
The greatest generosity is non-attachment.
The greatest goodness is a peaceful mind.
The greatest patience is humility.
The greatest effort is not concerned with results.
The greatest meditation is a mind that lets go.
The greatest wisdom is seeing through appearances.

Buddhist Teacher Atisha

As news of Kelsang's murder broke to the world's media, China quickly attempted a cover-up. On October 12, spokesperson Liu Jianchao held a press conference at China's Foreign Ministry in Beijing. In a crisply pressed suit, he told the assembled journalists, "If the reports are true, then the relevant Chinese departments will conduct an investigation. It is the responsibility of the Chinese border police to maintain the peace and security of the Chinese border."

The same day, Xinhua, the Chinese news agency, issued a more detailed statement. Xinhua is a powerful tool that the CCP has used to rewrite history and promote its image and agenda. The 10,000-strong news agency is controlled by the publicity department of the Communist Party. Its primary role is to promote the image of China as a peaceful, harmonious, rising world power. According to Reporters Without Borders, "Xinhua remains at the heart of the censorship and disinformation system established by the Chinese Communist Party."

In its press release, Xinhua declared:

> Nearly 70 people attempted to illegally cross the border between China and Nepal in the Tibet Autonomous Region on the early morning of Sept. 30 and one died during a conflict with border control guards, said an official of the related department of the region Thursday. A small squad of Chinese frontier soldiers found the stowaways and tried to persuade them to go back to their home. But the stowaways refused and attacked the soldiers. Under the circumstances, "the frontier soldiers were forced to defend themselves and injured two stowaways," said the source. One injured person died later in hospital due to oxygen shortage on the 6,200-meter high land, while another injured person received treatment in the local hospital. Preliminary interrogations showed that it was a large-scale and premeditated illegal stowaway case. Further investigations into the case are underway.

There were several give-away clues in the Xinhua's official statement about the incident on the Nangpa La. In reality, the event had created an internal rift in the agency. Several of the younger journalists had been shaken by the story and didn't want to issue a brazen denial of the facts at hand. A source inside the news organization reported that senior generals in the PLA ordered the State Council Information Office to release the official statement. "A lot of people at Xinhua and even in the publicity department were very angry about having to tell a blatant lie," the source said. With little choice, reporters ran the story but purposefully retained its ungainly language—language that strongly suggested the hand of Communist Party Officials.

The Chinese didn't think there would be evidence to contradict their version of events. The reports in the newspapers and the radio were insignificant. With few climbers willing to bear witness and those who did insisting on pseudonyms there was no hard proof. The story of Kelsang's death was fading from the international headlines.

Yet, unbeknown to the Chinese authorities, a Romanian climber was making his way out of the mountains with incontrovertible evidence.

—·—·—

Sergiu Matei downed his fifth beer of the night. The alcohol in the gloomy Kathmandu bar helped deaden his nerves. Since leaving Cho Oyu, Matei had carried his video of the murder in a travel pouch secured tightly around his waist.

As he had waited to get off Cho Oyu, Matei had felt deep waves of paranoia. He imagined PAP soldiers seizing the tape and arresting him. He'd begun to feel resentful of the film and what it might cost him, were he to be caught. His life perhaps? His freedom? The dark security machine in Tibet had a way of instilling a feeling of self-censorship. Matei had begun to obsess about destroying the tape and imagined hurling it into a crevasse. The killing wasn't his problem, he reasoned. This was something between the Chinese and the Tibetans. As he walked off the mountain with the yaks, he caught sight of a tangle of silver handcuffs hanging from a wooden post outside the Chinese camp. As they glistened in the sunlight, he had begun to feel nauseous with apprehension. But he kept the tape with him at all times. He had to get the story out.

In Kathmandu, Matei was desperate to get home. He considered mailing the tape to Romania but worried that the package would be opened en route and lost forever. Matei did another telephone interview with PRO TV from the rooftop of his hotel.

Safely in New Delhi airport, Matei was approached by an official who claimed he was from the airline and began interrogating him. Convinced the man was working for the Chinese, Matei sweated with fear. "What is your job?" he asked. Matei thought quickly, anything other than news cameraman. "Dentist," he lied. Almost as soon as he did, he wished that he hadn't. What if the man asked him to prove it? "So you were climbing?" the man said. "In Tibet?" Matei nodded. "Which mountain?" Matei paused. "Annapurna," again, he lied. The man nodded.

Then it became too much. "Look, why are you asking me all this stuff?" Matei spat angrily. "This is customs' job, not yours!" The man nodded curtly and disappeared. Once on the plane, Matei clutched the pouch around his waist and smiled gratefully when the jet arced into the sky.

— . — . —

On October 14, a day after the official Chinese denial in front of the world's media of any foul play on Cho Oyu, Matei touched down at Bucharest International Airport. He went straight to the PRO TV headquarters where a team of producers awaited. Matei handed over the evidence that he had guarded with his life.

In the darkened TV studios, Tibet's snow-clad mountains appeared blisteringly white. The sound of gunshots echoed eerily in the editing booth. A reverent hush descended as Matei's colleagues drunk in what their eccentric coworker had captured on film. Three hours later, on Bucharest's 5 p.m. news, the edited tape of Kelsang Namtso's murder was broadcast.

The Chinese version of the event that had taken place on the Nangpa La was contradicted by Matei's horrifying coverage. Soon after airing the segment, international news organizations besieged PRO TV with calls. Within a day, BBC and CNN had purchased footage from the murder tape to broadcast.

The U.S. government was the first to act. State Department officials watched the footage—irrefutable evidence of China's violation of Tibetan human rights—with mounting concern. Ambassador Clark T. Randt, the longest serving U.S. ambassador to China, issued a démarche—the highest form of diplomatic protest—to the Chinese government.

Three European Union countries issued a démarche at the E.U.—China Human Rights dialogue in Beijing. The same day, the Dutch foreign minister Bernard Bot declared that the Chinese should identify and punish those responsible for the shootings and described the video as "horrible and very shocking." In London, in the House of Commons, Harry Cohen, M.P., condemned the shooting, deeming it in violation of the United Nations' policy regarding firearms and demanding an investigation by China into the incident and assurance that such "abhorrent and unacceptable acts" would never be repeated.

—·—·—

As the international furor over the shooting intensified, it became imperative that the Nangpa La group be hustled out of the Tibetan Refugee Reception Center in Kathmandu on a bus bound for India. Staff at the TRRC were well aware that Tibetan spies—at the behest of the Chinese embassy—often circulated in their midst.

Kathmandu was a dangerous city, a netherworld where those who fell between the two superpowers of India and China were consigned to purgatory. There were Tibetans who had served in the PAP or the PLA who were refused entry to India, smugglers of animal skins, and spies for both the Chinese and Indian governments everywhere. No one could be trusted. The Chinese had pressured the Nepali government to close all Tibetan offices in the country as well as the Tibetan Refugee Reception Center.

A few days before she left, still photos from Pavle Kozjek's iconic pictures of Kelsang in the snow were pinned up on the notice board outside Dolma's dormitory. Kelsang's body was a black dot against a white hill of snow. As children from the dormitory crowded round, Dolma could only look at the image for a few seconds before running back to her room, distraught. That evening, the footage was shown on a video recorder in the center. Dolma watched as Kelsang's murder slowly played out from the vantage point of the Western climbers.

Dolma was issued a document that allowed her to cross from Nepal into India. Under international law, she was considered an illegal immigrant, but there was a "gentleman's agreement" in place between UNHCR and the government of Nepal whereby Tibetan refugees were not arrested, but must depart as soon as possible. Even so, the refugees were constantly harassed and sometimes arrested as they made their way out of the country.

After thirty-eight hours, the coach lurched into New Delhi. The vast sprawl of streets was chocked with traffic and smog, and huge cranes blotted the horizon. Dolma had never seen such a vast skyline. They turned down Raisina Road, the sweeping avenue lined with manicured lawns and the grand facades of embassies and Indian ministries, to the Press Club of India where the Tibetan Government in Exile had organized a press conference.

At the Press Club, a media frenzy awaited. Dolma sat between Choedon and the monk Thupten Tsering around a table bristling with microphones and tape recorders. Beyond were batteries of TV cameras. Dolma, in a pink jacket, her long hair tied back, looked demure as she regarded the onslaught of reporters.

The conference began with an extended clip of Matei's shocking footage. Thupten Tsering spoke excitedly, as he poured out the story of their dramatic escape from the PAP. Dolma gazed down at her hands as flashbulbs flashed and reporters raised their voices to be heard. When one journalist asked Thupten why he'd made the dangerous journey, he responded proudly that he'd been seeking a proper Tibetan education.

As Dolma sat in the glare of bright lights and dozens of questioning eyes, she understood that talking about what she had seen and appearing on television would make it difficult—perhaps impossible—to return to Tibet. She was, she decided, going to tell the world what had happened to Kelsang. "I cannot express all my emotions," she stammered. "Kelsang died on the spot, and I'm shattered by her death."

The press conference was the first time the Tibetans had spoken to a free media about human rights abuses in China. Finally, it was Choedon's turn to speak. The shaky image of the farmer hiding terrified in the toilet tent had been shown earlier. "It was the most frightened I have ever been in my life," he admitted. When a journalist asked him if he'd ever return to Tibet, he paused before shaking his head. "Even if I wanted to go back, I couldn't now," he said. "My photograph has been all over the news."

———

Choedon's wife, Yeshe Dolma, was at home with their children when the PSB arrived in the weeks following the press conference. The PSB interrogated her, demanding to know where Choedon was. Had she known what her husband was attempting? The children looked on, terrified at the fear in their mother's face. "I don't know where he is," she insisted. "He went away on business and didn't say when he was coming back." After several hours of relentless questioning, the men left.

Days later, a relative with connections in the local government appeared with a dire warning. Yeshe Dolma must leave her home at all costs. The PSB were returning to arrest her. Gathering up a few possessions in a matter of hours, she said goodbye to her in-laws and left with her children in the night. In Lhasa, a friend helped her find an illegal guide. In order to pay the man, she agreed to sell the family's farmland.

After the attention on the Nangpa La, guides in the Tibetan under-ground were quick to adjust their routes out of the country. They refocused on barren and remote gorges between Nepal and Tibet. Choedon's wife and children walked for a day with their guide before reaching a village above a deep gorge. From there, they were led to the edge where a pulley system had been hastily set up. In recent months, smugglers had perfected the ropes across the gorge to transfer everything from illegal animal skins to counterfeit electronics to currency and drugs.

The family eyed the trembling rope, swaying in the wind and dark-ness. A hook was slung over the rope. Yeshe Dolma gripped it tightly. She swung out above the gorge, while a man on the Nepali side of the rope pulled her across. The rope creaked as it swayed above the gorge far below. Once she was safely across, the rudimentary pulley was sent back to the Tibetan side. As her young son and daughter were jerked across the chasm, Yeshe Dolma fought the urge to shout encouragement as she bit down on the fear rising in her throat.

— . — . —

In Juchen, word was beginning to filter back that something had happened to Kelsang and Dolma. Lhundrup had called Kalsang Chonjour, Kelsang's uncle to tell him that his niece had died on the escape from Tibet. Lhundrup hadn't told the uncle that she had been shot dead. Instead, he had mumbled something about stomach problems.

JONATHAN GREEN

And in turn, after Lhundrup's call and the monk digested the news, Kalsang Chonjour hadn't had the courage to call his sister in Juchen with news that her only daughter had died. He agonized for days, chanting mantras in the temple and burning incense in offering while praying for direction.

But worse, a few days later, he began to hear rumors that his niece had in fact been shot by Chinese border guards. At first, the soft-spoken monk didn't believe the story; it sounded so outlandish. Kelsang, as he remembered, was a self-effacing, quiet young girl. She didn't know how to fight, so why would she have been shot? Still he didn't make the call.

News of the shooting erupted as Indian TV reported the story with Matei's footage. Thousands of monks in the Tibetan settlements at Bylakuppe in southern India sat glued to television sets as they saw the Nangpa La, which many of them had crossed themselves. Kalsang Chonjour swallowed hard as he saw the images on the TV. Finally he made the difficult call to Kelsang's father, relaying the news. The monk tried to console his brother-in-law. "She died very quickly on the spot. She didn't suffer."

There was silence on the other end of the phone and then great crying.

Kelsang's parents knew they would never get the answers they wanted from the authorities in Tibet. No one would ever be brought to justice for the murder of their daughter. Distraught, they asked why their daughter was the only one out of upwards of seventy people who had been killed? Why Kelsang?

A few weeks later, a package arrived at the local police station for Kelsang's family. Even the police couldn't bring themselves to deliver the parcel. A local man was assigned the task of delivering the money Kelsang had had in her pocket at the time of her death. Also inside the parcel was a photograph of Kelsang's bloodied corpse. After handing over around 1,000 yuan, he quickly headed back to the village. He couldn't bring himself to give them the photograph.

Kelsang Namtso's body has never been returned to her family.

190

17

KUNDUN

_—.—.—_

The world grows smaller and smaller, more and more
interdependent. . . . [T]oday more than ever before
life must be characterized by a sense of Universal
Responsibility.

His Holiness, the Fourteenth Dalai Lama

Fast asleep, Dolma almost missed the stop for Dharamsala, the promised land she and Kelsang had dreamed about. For thirteen hours, the
group of refugees wound north by bus, traveling from Delhi into
the high reaches of the Kangra Valley along spiraling mountain passes
through cedar forests. Lights from houses occasionally flashed out of
the darkness.

Dolma remembered how she and Kelsang had discussed what the
Dalai Lama's home might be like. They had imagined it as a throbbing
citadel rising triumphantly on a broad plain, a sight clearly seen from
hundreds of miles away—skyscrapers, glossy cars going to and fro down
airy avenues beside the Dalai Lama's palace. But how could there be a
city like that up here in the mountains?

As dawn broke, the bus came to a halt in a small, deserted square
with a squeal of brakes and a cloud of dust. The bus driver shouted from
the front seat in Hindi, not bothering to turn around. The forty or so
Tibetans looked out the windows at a forlorn city; scavenging dogs and
idling taxi drivers lingered outside. There was no way, Dolma mused, that
His Holiness could live in this rickety town.

Unceremoniously, they collected their belongings and disembarked
under the watchful eyes of policemen. Here they were alone in a strange
country where they didn't speak the language. A young Tibetan boy who

was walking by took pity on them and stopped to show the group the way to the Reception Center for new arrivals.

After a short walk down a narrow street with shuttered stores, they arrived at a gloomy building on a steep hill. The building's heavy gate was unlocked, and a figure motioned the refugees inside. They followed him up a darkened stairwell as he led them to the rooftop. Several attendants returned with steaming tea and *tsampa*. The Tibetans reclined on their bags. As morning broke, Dolma looked out at the terraced hillsides wreathed in early morning mist. Brightly colored streams of prayer flags fluttered in the wind. Ruby-faced monkeys scampered along the roof to scavenge food. Barely had the new arrivals finished their tea when a swarm of journalists arrived.

"How was the nun shot?" one reporter demanded. "What's life like back home? Why did you run away?" And on it went.

After a brief lunch, the refugees were whisked away for more interviews. Leaving the Reception Center, Dolma spied a billboard declaring: "One World, One Dream, Free Tibet." Below it was an image of a pair of hands manacled with Olympic rings.

Dharamsala was a cramped, makeshift town, equal parts holy and kitschy. Khampa youths wearing wraparound sunglasses and cowboy boots roared around on Royal Enfield motorcycles. At roadside cafés, tourists sipped cappuccinos with chocolate lettering—"Free Tibet"— drizzled into the froth. Everywhere—behind the counters of grocery stores, cybercafes, on racks outside tourist shops selling pashminas and Indian prayer bowls—were images of the Dalai Lama.

Unlike the huge open spaces of Tibet and towering mountain ranges where one could walk for eighty days in uninterrupted solitude, Dharamsala's narrow streets thronged with nuns, monks, and tourists. Notice boards advertised "Guerilla Yoga Classes" and Tibetan cooking schools, massage, astrology readings, and traditional Tibetan medicine. Inside the Peace Cyber Café, one of many Internet cafés, monks sat alongside tourists hunched over computers, Skype-ing with faraway friends and family.

In lower Dharamsala, the Tibetan Government in Exile departmental offices—a dismal collection of mildewed, yellow buildings full of ancient furniture and Bakelite telephones—stood around a muddy square with a stupa at its center. In front of the entrance to the Department of Finance was a still-used telegraph wire box.

While tourists basked in the rare proximity to the Dalai Lama, racial tensions simmered between Tibetans and Indians. For its part, China sent waves of spies into Dharamsala. "They used to send thieves, murderers, and rapists," one former bodyguard of the Dalai Lama noted. "These were Tibetans who were serving long sentences in Tibetan prisons and had been given the chance of shorter sentences if they went to India and spied on the Dalai Lama and the government in exile." Today, China routinely sends agent provocateurs with military backgrounds to whip up animosity between the Tibetans and their Indian hosts.*

—·—·—

News of Kelsang's murder had electrified Dharamsala. Free Tibet supporters had moved quickly to spread the news in October 2006.

Tibetans reacted profoundly. Thousands had made the journey over the Nangpa La. Sergiu Matei's video of Kelsang slumped in the snow was heartbreaking, yet at the same time, the Tibetans in the group had pushed on, refusing to stop for the soldiers. It was the first footage of a human rights murder in Tibet since the Chinese invasion in 1950.

Since 2002, when meetings between the Dalai Lama's envoys and China had started, the Government in Exile had asked Tibetan activists not to mount protests, at the risk of embarrassing the Chinese. The hope was that the Dalai Lama's approach, the so-called "Middle Way" that favored autonomy under Chinese rule, would succeed. But some young Tibetans in exile dismissed the Middle Way as a placatory measure. A rift had grown in the Tibetan exile community between those who supported the Dalai Lama's approach and those who didn't. The latter

---

* Former PAP officers are often used as undercover agents. Former soldier Lei Xun had been thrown out of the PAP and was forced to atone by undertaking spying missions against the Tibetan Government in Exile. He attempted to entrap Tibetan officials by trying to enjoin their help in supposed plots to assassinate Hu Jintao or to bomb the railway line. Tibetan officials for the Government in Exile made clear their dedication to Tibetan liberation through nonviolence. Xun was eventually caught in 2008. Tibetinfo.net, January 20, 2009.

were sometimes branded as anti-Dalai Lamas—a terrible epithet for a Tibetan that made one an instant social pariah in Dharamsala.

"The shooting changed everything for us," Tenzin Tsundue, a long-time Tibetan activist, recalled. A high-level Tibetan delegation was meeting with a Chinese delegation in Beijing when the news hit China. "Here we were [representatives of the Government in Exile] meeting with the Chinese and talking and yet they were killing us in the mountains. It was like a provocation. This was the beginning for a new protest movement for Tibet." For the first time in years, hundreds of Tibetans took to the streets, ignoring the Government in Exile's calls for a softer approach.

Lodi Gyari, the Dalai Lama's representative to the Americas and chief negotiator with the Chinese, had been through days of talks aimed at greater Tibetan autonomy. The Chinese procrastinated, wanting to discuss which luxury residence in Beijing the Dalai Lama would take if he were to consent to live in China.

The Chinese betrayed no emotion as Gyari, impassioned, told them of the murder. "Not just as a Tibetan but as a human being, it was very sad," he recalled. "But it was also very inspiring. It gave Tibetans a sense of courage and a sense of self-respect." Kelsang's sacrifice was increasingly powerful: The Tibetans pushing on to freedom under fire, the world's response of outrage.

Before, the chronic human rights abuses heaped on Tibetans for more than fifty years had caused compassion fatigue. The world had grown inured to the horror stories of Tibetan religious prisoners tortured in places like Drapchi Prison. But Matei's film forcefully brought the issue of Chinese human rights abuses to light. "You hear about these things, but you do not see them," said Gyari. "But with this, we were all witnesses."

In 1989, a single man had blocked a convoy of tanks in Tiananmen Square to become a hero in the face of overwhelming force and suppression. To Tibetans, Kelsang's murder had the same effect. Here was one seventeen-year-old girl from rural Tibet willing to defy the might of modern China for freedom and His Holiness the Dalai Lama.

In Dharamsala, the streets that led down to the Tsuglag Khang, the central cathedral, transformed into roiling rivers of yellow candlelight and song as hundreds convened for a vigil. After holding themselves in check for years, Tibetans were at last openly expressing their anguish. Silence descended when Matei's footage was displayed on a makeshift screen on the cathedral steps. Dozens of onlookers wept as they watched. Some beat their chests and howled when Kelsang's body fell in the snow.

Hours later, Dolma made it back to the Reception Center, her head a whirlwind of interviews. Back in the dormitory, Dolma whispered to the nuns, "I never thought people would care so much about the death of Kelsang. I just thought she had been shot and killed for nothing. I never thought people would pay such attention." The nuns murmured in agreement.

In the morning, an official suddenly appeared at the Reception Center to inform the Nangpa La group that they would be granted a special audience with His Holiness. Dolma fussed over her appearance for hours in the cramped bathroom at the center. She borrowed a clean, pale-red *chuba* from one of the nuns, washed her hair, and fastened it with a cheerful pink hair clip.

In preparing for the meeting, Choedon cursed himself for failing to bring His Holiness a gift from Tibet. But when he had been in Tibet, the thought of meeting the Dalai Lama had seemed like such a far-off proposition. He spent 150 rupees on a *kata* (a white ceremonial scarf), the best one the shop had, and then looked at the remaining 1,350 rupees he had left. He sealed 1,000 into an envelope as an offering for His Holiness.

The streets of McCleod Ganj were bustling as the members of the Nangpa La group, conspicuous by their serious expressions—pink-cheeked and freshly scrubbed, the aroma of soap clinging to their skin—were led down the hill on Temple Road toward the Dalai Lama's compound. It sat behind a high wall around which Tibetans performed daily perambulations. First they came to a checkpoint with a walk-through metal detector guarded by Indian soldiers in puttees—tightly wrapped protective cloth strips from their ankles to their knees—cradling submachine guns. They were frisked lightly before proceeding through the gates and past a small guardhouse and along a paved road that swept gently upward.

Inside the compound, Dolma and the others left the hustle of Dharamsala and the rigors of the brutal journey. The mountaintop was ringed with a thicket of trees. The smell of pine hung in the air. Larks dipped and wheeled overhead, and birdsong filled the air.

Beyond a small stone rotary, decorated with roses in clay pots, loomed a grand-looking building with a green roof. Tibetan bodyguards with concealed weapons beneath their jackets were dotted about. The group was ushered through a large set of doors. On a luxuriant crimson carpet, they tiptoed deferentially. Some of the boys from Driru started to remove their shoes until a smiling monk indicated that they didn't need to. They were led into a lavish, wood-paneled room where they were welcomed to sit down, cross-legged, in two lines.

A single empty chair faced them.

In silence, they waited in trepidation, just an occasional cough or whisper. The walls of the room were covered with the most opulent *thangkas* Dolma had ever seen. One depicted the Buddha receiving enlightenment at the Bodhi tree. A large, decorative wooden cabinet to the left of the empty chair displayed a brightly lit gold statue of Maitreya, Buddha of the future.

To the right of the cabinet was a half-open door with panes of glass covered in net curtains. Beyond, they could see the scarlet outlines of monks silently scurrying back and forth. Dolma tried not to look through the door, but her attention, as her heart thumped, kept being drawn back to it. Choedon didn't hide his interest. He craned his neck so much to see round the door that his muscles ached.

Not a word passed as they waited reverentially and tensely, some of the group trembling with anticipation. In this same room, heads of state and international celebrities had sought an audience with the Dalai Lama. Dolma's mind raced as she thought of her mother, of Kelsang's murder, of her childhood in a tranquil village that now felt far away.

After half an hour, there was a brief commotion on the other side of the door, and a flash of crimson robes swept into the room. Suddenly, Dolma was face to face with the fourteenth Dalai Lama, Tenzin Gyatso. Dolma felt that she was looking into the face of a divine being, the very soul of her country. The world slowed to an infinite dimension where no time or any other constraint existed.

The Dalai Lama had a broad face, limpid eyes, and rosebud lips etched into a smile. His expansive features radiated every emotion that whisked through his mind with perfect clarity.

The Dalai Lama smiled, surveying the room.

Dolma's brain could not process the information fast enough. She felt that His Holiness was like the mountains they had passed through on the Nangpa La. She couldn't tell whether he was really big or really small, just that his presence was unbelievably strong. Dolma wept tears of happiness and extreme sadness. "It was both the happiest and saddest day of my life," she later said. "It was the kind of feeling I never had before." She cried for her mother, who she wished was here now and who she would likely never see again. And she cried for Kelsang, who was meant to be here. She thought about the times she and Kelsang had hidden pictures of His Holiness in the mountains overlooking Juchen. And now, here he was in the flesh. Kelsang had paid for this meeting with her life.

Dolma sobbed as His Holiness went glassy in front of her tear-filled eyes. Others gasped in incredulity, attempting to muffle their sobs. The emotions came tumbling out from those around her. Among all of the refugees, there was an overwhelming feeling of unity in the Dalai Lama's presence. Dolma felt that all the petty enmities that had developed among the group as they traveled here—the arguments, fights over eating meat or which direction to go—had melted away. Many were so awestruck they wouldn't raise their eyes to look at the Dalai Lama directly. Dolma felt a gentle tap on her shoulder. Dawa Dorjee from the Reception Center whispered, "Pay attention. Look at His Holiness." He was worried the moment would pass, and Dolma would remember nothing.

The Dalai Lama offered comfort and solace as he soothed them. "It's all going to be alright," he said, nodding in sympathy. As both head of state and the spiritual leader of Tibet, the Dalai Lama not only is supreme leader of a unique 2,500-year-old religion but also deals with twenty-first century governments all over the globe on a daily basis.

Shortly, he was to depart for a state visit to Italy. Most important to him was personally greeting the thousands of Tibetans who risked their lives crossing the high Himalaya, as he himself had done, in the vague chance of an audience with him.

He knew, as they knew, that the briefest flash of time with His Holiness was worth immeasurable spiritual benefit for this lifetime and lifetimes to come.

The stooped seventy-one-year-old standing before the group—and the power of devotion that he inspired—struck fear into the emerging superpower China. Despite a highly sophisticated and omnipotent Chinese police and military, the Dalai Lama inspired a death-defying faithfulness and allegiance among Tibetans. He was living proof that China could not eliminate what lay within Tibetan hearts, no matter how much force they exerted over Tibet.

Today, the Dalai Lama smiled, urged everyone to relax, and took a seat on the simple wooden chair, while the Nangpa La group sat cross-legged around him. Dolma was amazed that he would simply sit with them. In his rapid, quick-fire speech—which veered from falsetto excitement to basso profundo gravity—the Dalai Lama asked who was from Amdo, Lhasa, Nagchu, Utsang.

Choedon couldn't even raise his eyes when His Holiness asked who came from Kardze; he just raised his hand and stared at the floor. Before the meeting, Choedon had sworn to himself that he would tell His Holiness about all the hardships he had faced to get here and how tough the journey had been, and, of course, the terrible murder that the Chinese soldiers had carried out. As he listened to the Dalai Lama, his head bowed reverentially, Choedon caught sight of the Dalai Lama's bare arms. His Holiness's skin was old and wrinkled. Choedon, who had protected the children on the journey, was now overwhelmed with loving kindness and a protective feeling for His Holiness.

At first, Choedon didn't hear when the Dalai Lama asked who he had seen hiding in the toilet tent in the film. Hesitatingly, Choedon raised his hand again. His Holiness asked him to stand. He rose, hands crossed in front of him. His head bowed, Choedon broke down in sobs.

The Dalai Lama consoled him. "It's OK, it's OK," he soothed, his features softening. "Don't be afraid. These tragic incidents have happened before, but we have never had evidence," he said. "But thanks to the attention of the international communities and Tibet support organizations, this murder has been made known to the world." His Holiness paused. "Say what happened, but be honest in your telling of the story." The Dalai Lama knew that Tibetans often embellished Chinese horrors, and he tried to make Tibetans aware that honesty was always best. Choedon sniffled and nodded.

With a kind smile, the Dalai Lama told the assembled group to study hard at school and, for those who wanted to join the monastery, to be good monks and nuns. He turned to the officials hovering behind him, instructing them to make sure that this group in particular was taken care of.

The Dalai Lama turned next to his gray-robed private secretary, who commanded a squadron of assistants to hand out auspicious gifts to the group. They waited in turn for the Dalai Lama to lay his hands on their heads in blessing. When it was Dolma's turn, His Holiness was informed that this was the girl from Kelsang's village. The Dalai Lama smiled and beckoned her over.

Dolma bowed. She felt His Holiness's soft touch on her hair. As she straightened, he addressed her, "It's OK now, you don't have to worry about things. You are here." She looked into his face. "Everything is going to be alright. Now, you must study hard." Dolma nodded. The Dalai Lama smiled.

After their reception, the refugees were given manila envelopes containing pictures of the Buddha and sacred pills that had been blessed by His Holiness. When it was Choedon's turn, he attempted to proffer the envelope of money to the Dalai Lama, but His Holiness shook his head. "There is no need," he said, his kind eyes assessing Choedon. The farmer nodded in assent, stuffing the money back in his pocket. Some officials organized individual pictures with His Holiness. The monks in the group were bent double at the waist in reverence. The monk Thupten Tsering got a picture of just himself and the Dalai Lama. He was ecstatic, trying unsuccessfully to conceal a wide grin.

After the blessings, the Dalai Lama suggested they all go outside to have a group picture taken. As they were walking out, Dolma turned behind her. Pressing hard on her heels was the Dalai Lama. Awkwardly, Dolma hesitated, not knowing whether to step aside or quicken her pace. An official gently pushed her. "Go quick," he said.

Outside, the group formed two lines under some straggly saplings and posed for one last shot of the group that had successfully made the arduous journey from their remote towns to Dharamsala. And then, even before it started, it was over. The group found themselves outside the palace, dazed and unbelieving.

The following day, Dolma called her mother with her news. It was dangerous to talk about such things on the phone, but her excitement could not be contained. Nyima was spellbound. She sighed in relief, "It's all worth it now. It's all been worth it."

18

DETERMINATION

—.—.—

Never give up
No matter what is happening,
No matter what is going on around you
Never give up
His Holiness, the Fourteenth Dalai Lama

After two weeks, Dolma packed up her few possessions at the Reception Center and boarded a bus with eleven others from the Nangpa La group. The vehicle squeezed down the narrow streets in Dharamsala, past buses crammed with tourists. Driving southeast, they passed tea plantations worked by dark-skinned women dressed in bright yellow and lilac saris. The colors stood out in vivid relief against the green hills.

After fifty miles, Dolma and the others arrived at the Tibetan settlement of Bir. Beyond the cramped colony with its rubbish-strewn streets and Indian farming villages was the Tibetan children's school at Suja in the foothills of the Himalaya. It was one of a number of Tibetan Children's Villages (TCV), schools established by the Dalai Lama's sister, Mrs. Yabshi Tsering Dolma in an effort to educate young Tibetans in their culture.

As Dolma was led to the school's offices, she saw hundreds of children, some shouting and playing on the basketball court. Confident and radiant, they displayed a self-pride that transcended their status as refugees.

Dolma was issued a blue shirt and gray slacks before being led to the girl's dormitory, a two-story building that contained chipped wooden bunk beds, four to a room.

The following day, for the first time in her life, Dolma began her formal education. She joined 861 Tibetan children who had traveled from their homeland in search of a Tibetan education. In class, Dolma sat alongside children who had lost limbs to frostbite on the Nangpa La. The painful separation between parents and children was difficult. Often parents called the school or got word to friends and relatives to see if their children had made it over the Nangpa La, only to be told that they hadn't arrived. There are no accurate estimates on the numbers of children who have died on the Nangpa La attempting to reach India.

Dolma adjusted well to the punctual rigors of school. She rose at 5 a.m., began morning prayers at 6 a.m., and then attended classes starting at 9.

Many of those Tibetans who were raised in India and had never been to Tibet saw the *sanjor*—newcomers—from Tibet as a source of intrigue. Their scruffy, coarse compatriots who reeked of the rural life in Tibet embarrassed them. Repeatedly, Dolma was asked whether she had ever seen a television, a cell phone, or a car.

For the first time, Dolma had access to unfiltered news on what was happening around the globe and how the world really worked beyond Chinese-occupied Tibet. In Tibetan history classes, Dolma learned about the kings of Tibet and discovered that Tibet had once had its own currency, administration, and, of course, sovereignty. She learned of the abduction of the Panchen Lama and the true nature of the Dalai Lama's standing in the world as a Nobel Peace Prize winner.

On occasion, members of Gu Chu Sum, an organization comprising former Tibetan political prisoners, came to the school to give talks on the brutality they had endured. Dolma met several of the so-called singing nuns. There was Nyima, twenty-eight, who had been thrown into prison and incarcerated in a steel box for twenty months when she refused to sing songs in praise of Chairman Mao. In all that time, she had no shower and had only once left her cell. "I undid my belt and knotted it into a rosary so that I could say prayers," she told Dolma. "I felt sorry for the prison guards that they had to do work like that." When she was released, she fled over the Nangpa La.

A few weeks into her new life, Dolma saw a hunched figure, his hands stuffed in his pockets, slouch into school and head to the administration office. From a distance, she thought she recognized the spiky black hair but couldn't be sure. When the figure approached, she recognized the insolent grin. Bruised, tired, and emaciated, Jamyang Samten cracked a triumphant smile.

Dolma's spirit soared. She had assumed Jamyang to be dead.

— . — . —

Two months earlier, Jamyang had been on a military bus approaching a dismal prison southwest of Shigatse in Dechen Podrang, Tibet. In 2003, the Chinese had converted the headquarters of a construction company into the Snowland New Reception Center—a reformatory of sorts for anybody caught escaping from Tibet. Jamyang, who had been released from Tingri in the morning, bounced in the back of the truck along with forty-odd captured refugees. There had been no court appearance or judicial proceedings, just summary detention. At Snowland, the fifteen-year-old was led into a sterile room where PAP officers took his money and belongings before he was photographed.

Jamyang and eighteen other males were taken to a cell where they had to remove belts and shoelaces. A row of iron-barred windows ran around the top of the walls. A single toilet stood in the corner of the room.

After the interrogations in Tingri and now beginning their time at the prison, most of the refugees were in dreadful shape. Every day, Jamyang was marched out either for work or for punishment. The guards delighted in humiliating and brutalizing their captives. During the first month of his incarceration, for a period each day, Jamyang was forced to stand in the courtyard under a blazing sun, supporting a chair on his outstretched arms and a bottle on his head. The first time he collapsed and the bottle tumbled to the ground, the guard put him back in position warning him, "If you fall again, there will be consequences." He lasted less than three minutes. When the chair tumbled to the ground, he was beaten before being forced back in place.

After roughly a month, Jamyang was sent out to work long hours in the fields harvesting, repairing roads, and laboring at a construction site. At around noon, he and the other prisoners were each given a ladle of barley and a cup of black tea and perhaps a small bowl of noodle soup.

Many collapsed as they attempted the backbreaking labor under the beating sun. When Jamyang realized that he could escape punishment in the fields, he pretended to pass out. With the door of the cell firmly locked, the prisoners ministered to each other's wounds and tried to buoy their spirits. "OK, the Chinese have locked us up and they mean to punish us," one youth said. "But we have to stay optimistic."

Somehow, their strength of spirit triumphed over their captors. At night, they sang about the girls, sequestered in the cells for females. The girls would angrily shout out of the windows of their cells for the boys to be quiet, but they did so happily. Emboldened, the girls would sing in response, knowing by heart the words of the old Tibetan folk song about a swain and the beauty of his paramour. When the girls' singing died out, Jamyang would lead the group in a refrain that made fun of the Chinese prison guard who came to check on them. Luckily, he didn't understand Tibetan.

Over the next few weeks, the parents or relatives of the captured children arrived at the prison to treat some of the officials to lunch and to pay 100 yuan ($15) to release them. (Many had learned of the children's whereabouts from officials who had tracked them down.) At Shigatse Prison, the release fines increased to 500 yuan ($80). There were around thirteen children aged four to fifteen who were slowly released as relatives came for them. All were forced to sign documents declaring that never again would they attempt an escape. Were they to do so, their parents would be imprisoned in their stead.

After forty-five days in the Snowland Prison, Jamyang, along with thirty other inmates, was finally released. After handing over all of his remaining money—purportedly to cover a fine—he was warned by a senior official that if he was caught trying to escape again, he would be executed.

Jamyang was dumped in the middle of Shigatse along with several other boys. All he had were the clothes on his back. His face was cracked and bruised. His only hope was to head to Tashilhunpo Monastery where he might beg the monks to help him.

He approached the first monk he saw and explained his desperate situation. The monk nodded. He let Jamyang use his cell phone to call his uncle in Lhasa. After he'd spoken to his uncle, Jamyang was escorted to the bus station by the monk, who bought him a one-way ticket to Lhasa.

Several hours later, Jamyang arrived at the bus station. As he was about to step off the bus, he asked the driver how to make his way to the Jokhang Temple. The Chinese driver, who had sneered at Jamyang's disheveled state when he boarded, told him matter of factly to get lost. After the horror of the Nangpa La, and his weeks of torture, Jamyang became enraged. He kicked the gearshift of the bus, raining curses down on the bus driver. The bus driver, shocked, slapped Jamyang across the face. As the fight erupted, one or two monks on board jumped up to restrain Jamyang. In moments, two PSB officers arrived on the scene. The galvanized Tibetan wasn't holding back. "I don't like you people in my country," he declared rashly. Such unguarded insults could easily earn Jamyang another prison term. The monks escorted him to the back of the station before he could do more damage.

At the Jokhang Temple, Jamyang circled the Barkhor a few times before making his way to his uncle's house. When he arrived, his uncle was furious. "Your parents know what you did," he raged.

Jamyang spent the next few days wandering the streets of Lhasa in a funk. He yearned to escape, just to prove that he couldn't be defeated. He wanted to beat the Chinese at their own game, to have his revenge. But he didn't want to put his parents through more anguish.

Jamyang's father was journeying to Lhasa on his motorcycle to retrieve his son when he was swept off the road by a landslide. He was killed almost instantly. Upon hearing the devastating news, Jamyang returned to the Barkhor and walked circuit after circuit, his hands thrust deep in his pockets, biting back tears. How could he face his mother with the knowledge that ultimately he had caused his father's death? With nothing else to lose, he decided that he would escape one last time.

He told his uncle of his decision. Knowing that his stubborn nephew had made up his mind, his uncle paid 500 yuan ($73) to corrupt officials for a permit to get Jamyang to India. Jamyang and a guide set off in a truck to Dram.

In Dram, Jamyang hired a second guide to take him to the Reception Center in Kathmandu for a further 3,000 yuan ($450). Jamyang was overjoyed. A few days later, he was driven to Dharamsala.

Jamyang had washed off the smell of prison and the road in the freezing waters of the Bhagsu Falls, a dramatic waterfall that roared behind McCleod Ganj. The freezing water reminded him of Tibet. He thrashed his clothes in the water to clean them for his meeting with the Dalai Lama.

His Holiness spoke for half an hour before the main temple, Tsuglag Khang, to a new group of arrivals from Tibet. The Dalai Lama looked up and asked who in the audience had been arrested after the Nangpa La shooting. Jamyang swallowed and rose to his feet. The Dalai Lama knew the stories of torture only too well, and his eyes filled with sadness when he looked at Jamyang, wasted but alive. "You have paid to be here with much suffering," said the Dalai Lama with compassion. The Dalai Lama said that it was hard to understand peace when one had been treated in such a way but that Jamyang should try to forgive his tormentors and let go of the pain. "Now you are here, the suffering is over," said the Dalai Lama. "Now you must try to study hard to become a good, strong Tibetan." Jamyang nodded. Jamyang would, if offered the chance, join a fight for liberation. It was hard not to harbor thoughts of revenge, but he tried. "I will try to forgive," he said, hopefully.

—·—

Around the same time, November 2006, Choedon's wife, Yeshe Dolma, stepped off a bus at the Dharamsala terminal with her son, Tenzin Dorje, four, and daughter Lobsang Youdon, two. Choedon enfolded them all in a hug. They were safe, finally.

Choedon and his young family found housing in a cramped two-bedroom apartment near the bus station, part of a jumble of small concrete houses with tin roofs on a terrace overlooking the town. It was a big change from their expansive farm on the Tibetan grasslands that had remained in their family for generations. Proudly, they decorated their cramped apartment with huge posters of the Dalai Lama and the Tibetan flag.

But there was no farming work to be had, and the family lived from day to day, depending on money from the overstretched Government in Exile's coffers, about 700 rupees a month ($15). Compared to the money Choedon might make in Tibet selling caterpillar fungus, the allowance was a pittance. On occasion, a TV crew would arrive to interview Choedon about the Nangpa La murder, throwing some money his way.

At night, the children were kept awake by the constant howls of the wild dogs that roamed Dharamsala. It was said that they were naughty monks who had broken their vows in their past life and were reborn as dogs for punishment.

The family mixed with swarms of tourists who descended on the hillside town. Westerners reserved their seats for His Holiness's teachings days in advance, often pushing Tibetans out the way. Many of the newly affluent Indians arriving in Dharamsala swanned around the swank new air-conditioned hotels catering to them. Although they knew who the Dalai Lama was, they knew nothing about Tibet. At the stores with "Free Tibet" signs in the windows, they went in asking for "Free Tibets," thinking, as one storekeeper said, it was free soap or something.

Technically, as refugees, Choedon and his family were unable to buy property. So as the Indians developed the tourism infrastructure around the Dalai Lama, the Tibetans could not advance with their own enterprises and investments. To do so would be admitting that they were not about to return to Tibet and that their stay in India was permanent.

Choedon had few regrets though. He was proud of the children he had saved on the Nangpa La, and he was proud of the contribution he could make to the world in understanding Tibet. But none of this could disguise the fact that life in exile was bleak, with little promise of work or a prosperous future. Choedon and Yeshe Dolma attempted to find Western sponsors who might help their children with education and some sort of future as long-term opportunities were nonexistent. The family joined a town of 140,000 exiled Tibetans living side-by-side, all looking for the golden ticket to escape to America, Australia, or Europe.

—·—·—

In the weeks that followed their audience with the Dalai Lama, most of the forty-one Tibetans who had traveled with Dolma returned to Tibet, some via the Nangpa La. Lhundrup and several other monks and nuns headed to the Tibetan settlements in southern India at Bylakuppe, near Mysore. For many, it was enough simply to have had an audience with the Dalai Lama.

Roughly half of the thousands of Tibetans who journey to Dharamsala return to Tibet, encouraged by the Dalai Lama and the government to bring back the knowledge of their education, language, and culture, lest it die in what the Dalai Lama terms "cultural genocide." For many Tibetans in the younger generations, raised in the rapidly modernizing city of Lhasa, life in India proves too harsh for them, despite the promise of a true education. Many last a few short months at the school and then return to Tibet.

Jamyang joined Dolma's class and quickly forged ahead in his studies. When Jamyang rolled up his sleeves in class, Dolma could see the scars on his arms from his torture in detention. His long interest in singing found root in India, and before long, he was performing in front of the whole school at the Monday morning presentations and, later, for the Dalai Lama during an official visit to the school.

After a week of settling in at the Suja School, Jamyang related to Dolma the shocking experience of seeing Kelsang's body for the last time. That night, Dolma sobbed, out of sight of the others. Jamyang's testimony had finally given Dolma some sense of closure on her friend's death. Still, she wondered if Kelsang might have lived, had she been by her side. Would she have made it?

Increasingly, Dolma had difficulty falling asleep and lay awake in her bottom bunk, staring out the window beyond the dormitory to a street lamp outside that cast a gauzy glow through lace curtains. Over and over, she replayed Kelsang's murder, blaming herself for leaving her side when the shooting started. What might have happened had she grasped Kelsang's hand and pulled her on? Would she have made it?

While she nursed her hurt sorrow in private, outwardly Dolma became an altruistic and revered figure to the children in the school, often lending a willing ear and a kind word to children who were suffering emotionally. But the psychological wounds suffered in the journey across the Nangpa La ran deep. Samdhup, the mentally ill girl, had become withdrawn, isolated, and agitated. At night, she began to hyperventilate, terrified when Dolma moved to turn the light off in the dormitory. She became increasingly dependent on Dolma as she spoke about Kelsang's murder. The teachers at the school took her to some lamas who prayed over her. Samdhup's condition improved afterward, then her mental state collapsed again. Eventually, Samdhup returned to Tibet, but her fate today is unclear. Rumor has it she was detained at Friendship Bridge or got lost trying to cross the Nangpa La.

—·—·—

In the run-up to the 2006 Olympics, a roiling restiveness was building inside Tibet. In the months after Dolma's arrival in Dharamsala, the number of refugees arriving over the Nangpa La slowed to a trickle. The ramifications of the shooting were powerful and enduring. "The Nangpa La shooting changed everything," a security officer for the Government in Exile admitted. The monthly stipends that PSB and PAP units paid to informants were doubled and, in some cases, tripled. Village meetings were held between nomads and Chinese officials in the border areas. Police increased the bounty for turning in runaways. Cell phones were distributed to everyone in the villages around the Nangpa La with quick-dial numbers for the PAP and a text-messaging facility to report refugees. Towers were built in the middle of the pass for spotting refugees. The Nepalese meanwhile were under increasing pressure from China to close Tibetan institutions in Kathmandu and to arrest refugees entering Nepal.

Publicly, the Chinese did nothing to appease world outrage at the atrocity. A Hong Kong Information Centre for Human Rights and Democracy report stated that Lieutenant General Meng Jinxi had been criticized over the incident and was forced to step down from his post. It said that Meng, a member of Communist Party's Central Committee, was punished by not being named a delegate to the party's congress, held every five years. It was likely he was censured, not for the incident itself, but for the fact that Westerners had witnessed it.

Inside Tibet, in the wake of the shooting and the looming Olympics, any suspicious parties, snakeheads in particular, were taken into custody. Climbers at Cho Oyu on October 18, 2007, a year after the incident, heard gunshots when PAP soldiers opened fire on approximately thirty Tibetans crossing the Nangpa La. Around seven escapees, including three monks from eastern Tibet, were captured. The rest made it to Kathmandu. This time the soldiers had opened fire out of sight of the climbers. Again, China denied the reports. "We have been in touch with the relevant authorities regarding news about Chinese police opening fire on people crossing the border," Liu Jianchao told a press conference. "It's a piece of fabricated news," said a Chinese spokesperson. "It's groundless."

For centuries, the Nangpa La had acted as a release valve for Tibetan unrest. The abrupt crackdown contributed in small part to mounting anger and frustration at increased Chinese suppression in the months before the Olympic Games. A deadly pressure was building.

19

THE RAZOR'S EDGE

—·—·—

If you have attachment to this life,
You are not a religious person.
If you have attachment to existence,
You do not have transcendent renunciation.
If you have attachment to your self-interest,
You do not have the spirit of enlightenment.
Manjushri's Revelation to
Sachen Kunga Nyingpo

Benitez was juggling his cell phones while simultaneously reviewing equipment and food lists, when an important e-mail arrived. It was March 2007, six months after the Cho Oyu shooting, and he was preparing to help lead a trip to Everest.

The e-mail invited Benitez to Dharamsala where the Dalai Lama wanted to thank him for what he had done. Benitez sighed. Secretly he wished the issue would stop drawing him into the spotlight. The confrontation on the mountain between Brice and Todd had largely been put behind him, and Benitez had worked hard to make it up to Cotter in an effort to secure his long-sought partnership in AC. More publicity on the issue of Tibetan refugees wouldn't keep his profile low, particularly when he would be dealing with Nepalese and Chinese border security on Everest in a few weeks, and, besides he was frantically busy. Benitez wrote back and politely declined the offer, saying he would like to when he had more time.

Benitez had returned home from Cho Oyu in October 2006 a deeply conflicted man, torn between the moral need to tell about the murder and a sense of the costs thereof. His vow to tell the world what he had witnessed and his love of the mountains clashed. He declined several major interviews on Kelsang's murder—with CNN and the BBC—that he felt would jeopardize his career.

As he returned to packing, Benitez began to realize the opportunity he had turned down. He e-mailed back and accepted the invitation.

Benitez flew to Nepal a week early to give himself time to meet the Dalai Lama. When Ang Tshering heard that Benitez would be meeting His Holiness, he drove him straight to the market to fill shopping bags with religious trinkets for the Dalai Lama to bless for the sherpas. A day later, Benitez took a train to Dharamsala where he was invited to talk as part of a press conference hosted by the Tibetan Center for Human Rights and Democracy. Inwardly, he was annoyed that he had been caught in another "media ambush," but he spoke when asked. Shortly after, he met His Holiness. Looking directly at Benitez, the Dalai Lama advised him simply, "Just be honest, tell the story, and remember to help people on your journey to telling the truth. We are not alone here."

After the meeting, Benitez was rattled. His abiding philosophy as a climber was to use the experience of tackling mountains as a trans-formative, character-building tool. He began to think that he himself needed to take succor from this very lesson. "Somewhere along the way, I took a wrong turn," he admitted. He realized he had gotten lost in the big business of climbing and had grown insensitive to the politics of the countries he operated within.

From Dharamsala, he went straight to Everest. For the sixth time, he stood on the summit of the mountain that had defined him. This time he surveyed the world with a profound sense of unease.

Looking at the joyous climbers around him, he wondered what the point of it all was. "I realized I'm not a fireman or a policeman, someone who is dedicated to saving lives," he said. "All I amounted to was a mountaineer, a substratum of society, something that people can't peg. Because really there is no point in doing what you are doing."

—·—·—

Benitez returned from Everest and his audience with the Dalai Lama more confused than ever. Seeking stability, he decided to get married to his American girlfriend. Cotter flew over from New Zealand to be one of his groomsmen. Cotter made it clear that Benitez was not going to be offered a partnership in the company anytime soon. After Cho Oyu, Benitez's meteoric career was flatlining. He started to scout for other career opportunities.

Nine months after the incident on Cho Oyu, Benitez decided to go public in a *Men's Journal* article on the murder of Kelsang Namtso and how Brice and Todd had adopted a code of silence.*

It was the first time Benitez had consented to be named in major US media in connection with the shooting. And it was the first time a guide had broken silence in the tight-knit mountaineering community. Benitez was guiding on Ama Dablam in Nepal when the story ran. Todd was also guiding a group on the mountain. Word went up the mountain that Todd was furious. Benitez expected his forceful stand to galvanize the climbing community behind him, a debate about the murder of a Tibetan refugee and perhaps, what he termed 'meaningful change.' But to his surprise, many climbers considered that Benitez was posturing as a "glory hunter" who had pitched his story from the mountain.

Benitez's critics pointed to the young guide's obsession with the media. They said his decision to lead Erik Weihenmayer up Everest was seen as more stunt than altruism, and his constant blogs from the mountains highlighting his involvement in rescues was regarded as little more than self-promotion.

After the article, Cotter, who had supported Benitez's stand in discussing the murder, felt that Benitez was reveling in the attention and drawing focus away from the murder of Kelsang to himself. "He became too much part of the story and diluted the real story," Cotter surmised. Some felt that Benitez had inaccurately depicted himself as a whistleblower, while Matei, who garnered international accolades, had been the true hero. Benitez argued that Matei was a journalist and simply doing his job. He, on the other hand, could potentially lose his career by speaking out. He could be banned from the Himalaya, where the largest percentage of his income was derived. It was a vicious dilemma. He told

---

* Jonathan Green authored the story, which appeared in October 2007.

friends that he felt he would have to give up his only profession and what he loved most in the world if he kept talking publicly about the murder. It would take a lot to make up for such a loss.

For their part, the sherpas didn't like the media attention Benitez was drawing on the mountaineering industry and how it conducted business. Ang Tshering was skeptical about publicizing the murder: "Yes, important to talk about these things but if there are no expeditions, we make no money. And sherpas must have jobs."

Cotter instructed Benitez to focus on his job and not do any more media interviews in the wake of the article. Benitez was also taken off a trip back to Cho Oyu. Tibet was now off limits. He carried on at AC, but his criticism of Todd and Brice began, as he saw it, to make his job almost impossible. Within the symbiotic climbing world, Benitez had effectively turned on AC's business partners. The company depended on Todd for oxygen and sometimes used Brice's connections with the Chinese for permits and equipment in Tibet. Cotter understood that Todd was angry because Benitez had dragged him into the public arena. In January 2008, shortly before leaving for another trip to Everest in March, Benitez resigned from AC. The partnership talks had foundered, and he disliked being told not to talk to the media. Benitez declared the business of big mountain climbing as "morally bankrupt."

Meanwhile, he had lined up another job at Outward Bound in a corporate outreach program. Immediately, Benitez began to build a platform as a motivational speaker using "ethical leadership" as his keynote. He started to court the media and attempted to get attention by speaking out on the murder of Kelsang Namtso. "By the time he was ready to be interviewed on camera, it was difficult to place him because the news cycle moves so fast," Kate Saunders of the ICT recalled.

The climber joined a prestigious speaker series, Brooks International, to give talks on responsible business practice and ethics. One of his speeches, "Murder at 19,000 feet," focuses on the incident on Cho Oyu. His fee is between $5,000 and $10,000. Benitez soon found that while corporate clients thrilled to motivational talks on "finding their own Everest," few wanted to pay him to come to their offices to talk about the murder of a seventeen-year-old Tibetan refugee in the mountains.

Midlevel executives were not going to bond in team-building exercises over the grim story.

Still, when given a chance of magazine interviews or other media appearances, Benitez wasn't shy of responding to media interest. By the same turn, he grew angry and bitter when the media didn't portray him in the same light as he viewed himself. "He has this side that is publicity seeking," wrote Jeff Jackson in *Rock and Ice* magazine. "He might be a little too comfortable with the limelight."

But Benitez pressed on. In 2009, he gave evidence at Spain's High Court in Madrid in a case under the principle of "universal jurisdiction," which attempted to prosecute Chinese leaders for crimes against humanity. The Nangpa La shooting was used as evidence. Matei was also invited but had turned down the opportunity. Benitez wept as he gave testimony. He teared up again when documentary makers interviewed him.

Privately, though, despite talking about the murder whenever asked, Benitez sometimes resented the paradox he found himself in and what he had lost. "It was like being royalty and then having the crown ripped right off your head," he complained. But critics pointed to the fact that he had left AC voluntarily when he wasn't offered his sought-after goal of a partnership. "He can get caught up in being driven too much," said his brother David.

The more Benitez was asked about Cho Oyu, the more complicated it became to him. Eventually he insisted modestly that the e-mail from the mountain, "was just a private e-mail to ExWeb." Later, he said defiantly that he had wanted to "get the word out." It was as if Benitez was still stuck on Cho Oyu, his ego battling with his conscience.

As controversy engulfed Benitez, he yearned—simply—to be back in the mountains as part of what he termed his "unique tribe." "I missed being part of that upper circle, that really elite echelon of people. We're playing with millions of dollars; we're climbing the biggest mountains in the world. We're rolling around, hobnobbing with really wealthy people. It's very egocentric," he said. "The ego side of me missed that exclusivity." At home he walked past his gear closet, jammed full of jackets from his old sponsors. He got "a whiff of nostalgia" when he pulled the down jackets out, the trappings of past glories.

The mountains still had him in thrall. At high altitude, Benitez ruled over powerful corporate executives who entrusted their lives to him. But in New York boardrooms, executives' dependence on him was not as intense. He needed them to experience the threatening majesty of the 8,000-meter peaks. He told them, "There's a lot of stuff you can hide behind in a boardroom and a classroom, but out there is nothing to hide behind. Out there, it gets very real, very quick."

As Benitez yearned for the mountains, his marriage ended and he and his wife divorced. He tried in vain to resecure his job with AC, but got no reply from Cotter. He began to question the stand he had taken. "From a business perspective, I get it," he said. He was only a guide, after all, and not running a business, he reasoned. "Being fiscally responsible and morally responsible is a very difficult choice. In my naïveté, even though it cost me a lot, I could afford to be idealistic."

Russell Brice maintains a position of silence and refused to be interviewed for this book. Over email, he said, "I will continue to support Tibetan and Nepalese people in my own way, others do it their way, but sometimes the media is in too much of a rush to make a balanced opinion."

In 2006, Dolma and Luis, two people from two very different lives, shadowed each other across the Himalaya for several days. Their paths converged at the Reception Center in Kathmandu where both were free to choose their fate. Dolma chose to bear witness to the murder of Kelsang. She summoned her courage as a starving, physically exhausted refugee with a dangerous, uncertain future in a country she did not know. There she stood up against the repressive might of the Chinese government to break the code of silence and tell the world about her friend's murder.

The ramifications of the meeting affected Benitez for years to come. He finally saw the reality of the mountains where he had cheered and shepherded his wealthy clients. The six-time Everest summiteer came face to face with what defined real courage in the mountains. As he was ushered through the door to the meeting in Kathmandu, he realized overpoweringly that he was, above all else, simply insignificant in a far bigger story. "They didn't care who I was," he recalled.

In the years afterwards Benitez wrestled with questions of morality and his definition of freedom from the knowledge he had been imparted. For centuries, narcissistic Western adventurers have sought conquest, fame, and riches on the highest points of the globe. They have also looked for transformative revelation on the top of mountains. But what some climbers discovered, instead, was that the realization of knowledge was a painful shadow road, an anonymous and difficult solo journey; it meant surrendering the ego in a process that was far from glorious. Younghusband had set out to conquer Tibet for the glory of the British Empire and returned a mystic after his bloody invasion of Lhasa. The lamas in Tibet have long been puzzled by Westerners who risk their lives to climb the peaks.[1] The lama at Rongbuk Monastery admitted, "I was always filled with compassion that they underwent such suffering in unnecessary work."

Years later, Benitez's understanding of freedom reflected the highly individualistic Western concept that was about one's personal liberty. In his case, Benitez defined freedom as his right to return to the business of mountaineering, albeit as a changed man aware of his flaws.

Ultimately, though, he always chose the mountains. "That's where I'll always be the most free."

—·—·—

Safely out of Tibet, China's long reach haunted Sergiu Matei as he tried to get back to his life in Bucharest. The paranoia he had experienced on Cho Oyu never left, even though he was home and allegedly safe.

He did, however, exalt when he heard that Choedon had made it to Dharamsala, punching the walls of his apartment with such force he cracked the plaster. Yet the exhilaration of Choedon's successful escape couldn't eradicate Matei's own gathering demons.

Romania was wrestling with its communist past. The country, in the vacuum left by communism, was infested with corruption and organized crime. The constant threat of surveillance began to grate on Matei. He became a slave to the impulses of dread and fear he had first experienced in the Himalaya. He was convinced that Chinese agents were going to capture him.

Journalists came to interview him, and he never refused, but each time he grew paranoid about the consequences of speaking out. Once or twice he got calls from men asking him specific details of how he got the tape out, at what time, which borders he went through. He assumed they were journalists but when he asked, they would mumble thanks and hang up. He suspected China was collecting information on how such a breach in security had occurred.

The Romanian Ministry of Internal Affairs issued him a Walther P99T that fired rubber bullets. Not satisfied, he went out and bought a handgun.

Matei's bosses declared that in the interests of the cameraman's safety, it was best to lock up his explosive video of the Nangpa La shooting. The single videotape contains never-seen footage of the climbers' reactions to the shooting, as they told others not to say anything about what they had witnessed, according to Matei. Others angrily told Matei not to save Choedon lest he get them all into trouble. PRO TV has licensed the original two-minute, ten-second clip to television channels and a documentary maker, but the entire video archive of the incident has never been seen. Attempts to access the full footage have been rebuffed. And rumors circulate that the Chinese control the rights.

Yet the power of the video cannot be contained. As soon as it aired, it was put on YouTube by an unknown individual. It quickly spread all over the Internet to computers worldwide, making anyone with an Internet connection a witness. Although it cannot be watched in China or Tibet, the Chinese censors cannot contain the powerful clip and its message, as it plays in a viral loop all over the world to this day. Matei helped immortalize Kelsang Namtso.

Although the film was locked away in a nameless vault, the memory of what he had witnessed and Kelsang's death played through Matei's mind in an endless loop in haunting symmetry on the Internet. At night, he woke up in cold sweats, his heart racing. It was the same horrific image over and over again, just before he had turned his camera off: Kelsang's body folding in half with the force of the bullet and then slumping forward on her right side. And then, worst of all, her attempt to crawl before collapsing. The nightmare would sometimes be accompanied by Choedon's eyes—saucer-wide and brimming with fear—when Matei found him in the toilet tent.

The incident had brought back the rigors of growing up under communism in Romania during the bloody tyranny of Nicolae Ceauçescu. Matei remembered that when he'd been a boy, officers from the *Securitate* (secret police) had arrived at his home to interrogate his father after he had publicly thrown a handful of oats at a painting of Ceauçescu. His childhood had been marked by hours of waiting in long food lines for bread, oil, and sugar rations.

The Himalaya, which represented freedom and the potential for fame and fortune to some, had become to Matei a sort of Berlin Wall. "I'm never going back to climb in the Himalaya, because I'm not going to pay money to the PLA to kill people," he said. "You're investing in murder. And I'm not going to encourage it."

The fact he had never reached the summit of an 8,000-meter peak didn't bother him. He had learned one of life's valuable lessons. He had no desire to return to the mountains. Westerners raised in democratic countries define freedom as the right to be able to make money and to run their businesses. Climbers on Cho Oyu from former Eastern Bloc countries, who suffered under repressive regimes, define freedom as a right to which everyone is entitled. Kelsang's murder is a threat to their own liberty as much as to that of the Tibetans.

It was in contrast to the Westerners who still refuse to talk about what they witnessed. "Freedom to me means something different than to someone that was raised in a free country," Matei says. "I know what it costs."

Many Eastern Europeans boycotted the Himalaya after the shooting. Pavle Kozjek knew that attaching his name to the pictures of the soldiers who carried out the killing would likely damage his climbing career. Kozjek told ExWeb, "I think that China is closed for me. Even if they let me in, I'd be worried about getting out. Although I've climbed all 8,000-meter peaks, I'm kind of sorry for that. In general, I kind of like the people and the country, but I can't agree with treating their own citizens like that."

Kozjek added later, "I've been climbing for thirty years and things have changed in that time. Climbing has become a commercial business like any other. Commercial expeditions take people to the top and down again, making fame. For real climbers, if there is a human life at stake, everything is less important—including success on the mountain." Tragically, he died two years later attempting the Muztagh Tower on K2 in August 2008.

Matei was nominated for an International News Emmy for his footage in 2007. He didn't win, but it didn't matter. The decision to film the shooting may well have played to his knee-jerk news-cameraman's instincts, he admitted. But then, earlier, he couldn't bring himself to film Kelsang dying, which went against his training. "There was something sacred about the Himalaya that I couldn't film something like that there," he said. His story of redemption began when the camera was turned off, and he had reflexively moved to save Choedon.

In the years since the shooting, PRO TV lost funding for foreign coverage, and Matei has battled to make ends meet. As Western countries struggle to support objective, free media, China has invested $6.6 billion in the overseas development of its party-controlled media like Xinhua and the People's Daily with which to promote its "soft power" image to the world.

—·—·—

In December 2008, the Dalai Lama and Matei met in Warsaw. His Holiness and his entourage rushed an ambassador from an audience to greet the Romanian warmly. "You managed to do in two minutes what it has taken me fifty years to do," said the Dalai Lama, according to Matei, as he grasped the Romanian's hands warmly and smiling with enthusiasm.

Matei beamed and added, "Yes, it really shafted the Chinese in the ass!"

The Dalai Lama, puzzled, turned for guidance to his horrified entourage.

"What does he mean?" said the Dalai Lama.

A nervous aide, head bowed in veneration, ventured forward a step, his hands clasped nervously, "Your Holiness, he said that it quite embarrassed the Chinese to see this footage."

The Dalai Lama drank in this information and patted the Romanian on the arm. "Yes, yes absolutely."

As they talked, Matei beamed and then impulsively lunged for a hug with His Holiness. The Dalai Lama chuckled and tugged the Romanian's ginger-red beard.

Later, the Dalai Lama counseled Matei about the tragedy. "You must get over it," the Dalai Lama said. "She didn't die for nothing. There is a reason here." Matei nodded and in the months that followed has begun to take solace. His nightmares have stopped altogether. And, piece by piece, he has begun to let go of the fear that gripped him.

20

THE RESTLESS HIMALAYA

— . — . —

*In the beginning they put their words like honey on
a knife. But we could see, if you lick the honey, your
tongue will be cut.*
Takster Rinpoche, the Dalai Lama's eldest brother

On March 10, 2008, Dolma and Jamyang were at morning assembly when the headmaster announced that there was trouble in Tibet. It was an auspicious date, marking the forty-ninth anniversary of the failed 1959 Tibetan uprising against Chinese rule.

After evening class, the entire school was summoned to a special prayer session. The headmaster reported that widespread protests had broken out in Tibet and were turning ugly. Students panicked, desperate for news of their loved ones.

Tibetans had found their breaking point. The deep resentment that had been building for decades since the Chinese arrived in 1950 had finally erupted with deadly force. The Nangpa La shooting was an open secret in Lhasa. While footage had not been shown within Tibet, the story of Kelsang's murder fuelled the burning resentment at China's oppression.

Protests had begun at Drepung Monastery in Lhasa when monks, fed up with patriotic reeducation campaigns in the run-up to the Olympics, protested, demanding the release of monks who had been arrested for celebrating the Dalai Lama's U.S. Congressional Gold Medal in 2007. An angry mob of monks from Sera Monastery descended on the Barkhor, flying the banned Tibetan flag and shouting the forbidden words, *Bo Rangzen!* (Free Tibet) and *Gyawa Rinpoche kutse trilo tenpa sho!* (Long live the Dalai Lama). Either phrase uttered publicly could earn them a jail sentence. They distributed illegally printed pamphlets calling for a free Tibet. They were beaten and arrested.

On March 11, protests intensified. Hundreds of monks from Sera, Ganden, and Drepung marched to the Barkhor area demanding the release of the arrested monks. Three days later, protests at the venerated Ramoche Temple in northeast Lhasa turned violent. Tibetans ransacked Chinese-run stores, burning the looted contents in the street. Yet while all Han Chinese-run stores were smashed and looted, Tibetans tied white *kata* scarves to the door handles of Tibetan-owned businesses. These were left untouched. Rumors circulated that the shops and hotels most vehemently targeted were fronts for the PSB, the very establishments where escaping refugees were entrapped or informants passed on their details to the police.

Han Chinese taxi drivers were dragged from their vehicles and killed, while official PSB and PAP cars, fire engines, and government vehicles were torched. Schools in Lhasa, long the target of Tibetan anger for indoctrinating children with Communist rhetoric, were set ablaze. The Chinese flag was burned in the streets. Police informants were beaten and, in some instances, killed.

As news of the gathering wave of protests spread to Tibetans in outlying regions, the entire plateau erupted in protest. Government buildings were attacked, and the Chinese flag replaced with the Tibetan flag. Authorities feared full-blown revolt just months before the Olympic Games.

The entire plateau was sealed off in the days that followed. Tourists were deported from the country, along with all foreign media. No journalists were allowed in. All Internet, telephone, and cell phone services were jammed. NGOs were warned that anyone caught sending information about the protests to the outside world would be arrested and their organizations dismissed from the country. Authorities announced a reward of 1,000 yuan ($146) for anyone caught leaking news outside Tibet. In Beijing, users turning to Google News China were unable to search for any news of Tibet.

From India, the Dalai Lama called for peace.

From Chengdu, PAP command center, a military counterattack was launched. Unhampered by Western observers, the Chinese security forces went to work. The PSB raided the homes of former political prisoners, taking computers and cell phones. The PAP, which had long been trained to raid monasteries, attacked. Two thousand PAP officers, dressed in black fatigues and ski masks, descended on Sera Monastery firing tear gas at the protesters. Troops and heavy armor were loaded onto the Qinghai Tibet railroad, bound for Lhasa. The BBC, before it was ejected, reported seeing well over 400 troop carriers containing 4,000 troops mobilizing in Tibet.

A war of propaganda erupted online as Chinese nationalists and Tibetan exiles attacked each other. Several posts by bloggers claiming to be Tibetan—who offered their support of terrorism—were discovered to be plants by Chinese nationalists.

On March 16, 2008, almost 3,000 monks at Ngaba Kirti Monastery in Amdo were joined by local townspeople. The police opened fire in the main square, killing at least ten and possibly as many as twenty individuals. Locals rushed the bodies to the monastery to be photographed. The images were smuggled out of the area and e-mailed to monks in monasteries in Dharamsala.

Thunderous protests erupted throughout Dharamsala as the images were displayed around town. An image of a dead Tibetan male in his twenties lying supine showed a deadly accurate gunshot wound to his heart. "CHINESE MURDERERS!" someone had scrawled over the picture. In another, a sixteen-year-old schoolgirl, Lhundup Tso, had been photographed lying dead in a pool of blood.

— · — · —

The same day that Tibet erupted in protest on March 10, all climbing expeditions on Everest and Cho Oyu were officially banned. An official notice offered myriad reasons including "heavy climbing activities, crowded climbing routes" and "environmental pressures will cause potential safety problems." In truth, China didn't want to invite criticism from climbers about the outbreak of widespread protests in Tibet. A Chinese team was soon to make an ascent of Everest with the Olympic torch.

Russell Brice hoped that his assiduous courtship of the Chinese would save him. Brice had admitted after the shooting on Cho Oyu that he didn't want to turn on his Chinese business partners by talking about the killing. "We're in a privileged situation being able to go to Cho Oyu, which is a fairly delicate area," he was reported as saying.[1] "We don't want to abuse that or we won't be able to go back; the Chinese won't let us. We've been building up that trust for years." He admitted he had treated soldiers for snow blindness but he declared that it was an act of compassion. He said: "They were human beings who were suffering."

But Brice was to find out that the Chinese were no respecter of their business partners, no matter how far you went to appease them. Brice and Himex were forbidden from climbing from the north side of Everest like everyone else.

Some expeditions applied for permits to climb in Nepal instead, lest their clients demand their deposits back. Shortly after the Chinese banned climbers on the north side of the Himalaya, the Nepalese Tourism Minister Prithvi Subba Gurung announced that the south side of Everest would also be closed—to ward off the possibility of more trouble as the Chinese made their way up Everest with the Olympic torch. The Nepalese government was paid an undisclosed sum by the Chinese government for the loss of revenue from closing Everest.

China was persistently courting Nepal, while providing billion-dollar soft loans and military training (cooperation between the PAP and the Maoist military). There were plans for an extension of the railway into Kathmandu. Meanwhile, the Chinese increased pressure on Nepal to eradicate humanitarian organizations devoted to the Tibetan cause. In the run-up to the Olympics, they called in their debts.

The highest peak in the world suddenly became a highly militarized zone. Chinese jets screamed over the summit; snipers and military units were placed in high camps. Climbers' satellite phones and laptops were confiscated. Memory cards were snatched from cameras. All communication from the mountain was closely monitored.

Climbers were discouraged from wearing or uttering any pro-Tibet sentiment. Expedition leaders turned in an American climber to authorities when he confided that he had a "Free Tibet" flag in his backpack, which he intended to fly from the summit. Journalists were unceremoniously banned from the mountain. The Chinese had learned from the Nangpa La shooting that Western witnesses could be enormously damaging to their interests.

While the Chinese climbers charged with carrying the Olympic torch to the summit were filmed for numerous publicity reels, the bloodshed in Tibet continued behind a media blackout. At 9:18 a.m. on Thursday, May 8, a Chinese team carried the Olympic torch to the top of Mount Everest. The flame flickered in the jet stream at 30,000 feet as Nyima Cering, the third torch bearer, shouted, "One World One Dream."

The following month, the torch returned to Tibet after it had been carried through six continents in the "Journey of Harmony," to increasing controversy. The only other time there had been an international torch relay was in 1936, when the German Nazi party carried the Olympic torch from Greece to Germany as part of Adolf Hitler's Nazi propaganda before the start of World War II. The Chinese made sure the torch went everywhere with a detachment of blue-track-suited runners, the so-called Sacred Flame Protection Unit. China originally claimed they were volunteer students. But, after protests and arrests erupted in London, they were discovered to be PAP from the Dignitary Protection Unit.

On June 23, the Olympic torch was marched through Lhasa, an empty, shuttered city heavily patrolled by military police. As many as a thousand Tibetans, held without trial, lay in prison in uncertain wait. Two weeks earlier on June 10, over the border in Nepal, Nepalese police, under pressure from the Chinese government, had raided the home of Tibetan Refugee Reception Center director, Kalsang Chung (the man who had introduced Luis Benitez to Dolma and the Nangpa La group). They also raided the homes and arrested Ngwang Sangmo and Tashi Dolma of the Regional Tibetan Women's Association in Kathmandu. All were taken and held for several weeks until foreign embassies and the UN negotiated for their release.

In August 2008, the world cheered as the most expensive Olympic Games in history started with fanfare and a $100 million opening

ceremony in Beijing. Reporters at the games were prohibited from men-
tioning Tibet, which was now under the most brutal crackdown since the
Dalai Lama fled in 1959.

Mao's dream of an all-powerful China was partially realized with the
torch on Everest and the Beijing Olympic Games, totemic of China's
power in the twenty-first century. Climbers who had been on Cho Oyu
at the time of Kelsang's murder saw the Olympic Games in China as further proof of the Western complicity in China's grand narrative. As one
British climber put it: "The entire international community was saying
to China by sanctioning the games in Beijing, by continuing to trade, by
being pragmatic and continuing to ignore certain human rights issues
because you're too important to our economies . . . because the world is
making decisions, these were all reflected in the way that the climbers
behaved. We didn't feel anything would change by speaking out."

This appeasement serves China. With few governments willing to
challenge China's portrayal as a peaceful, quietly emerging superpower,
it has become emboldened in its suppression. Human rights around the
globe are being rolled back. As China becomes increasingly active in
developing countries in Africa and South America, building roads and
offering money as they did once in Tibet, China's influence grows.

Meanwhile, American soft power erodes.

— · — · —

As the Olympic games occupied the world's media, violence in Tibet
continued.

According to the Tibetan Government in Exile, two hundred-twenty
people were killed.* The real figure is impossible to determine, largely
because the bodies were disposed of in secret. There were reports that
many corpses were disposed of at a new crematorium behind Yabda
Township in the Toelung Valley. One witness claimed to see a truck, blood
smeared on its sides, leaving Lhasa with fifteen bodies piled high in the
back. The bodies were generally not returned to the families.

---

* According to the Chinese, only nineteen individuals were killed in Lhasa, while
sixty-one police officers had been wounded.

The Chinese state media reported that 4,434 Tibetans had been detained. According to one report, in the weeks after March 14th a member from every Lhasa household disappeared in raids.[2] Monasteries underwent such intense patriotic reeducation that a number of monks committed suicide. At Ngaba Kirti Monastery in Amdo, Lobsang Jinpa left a suicide note by his body: "I do not want to live under the Chinese oppression even for a minute, leave aside living for a day." Suicide is reviled in Buddhism as it greatly jeopardizes a good rebirth.

In 2008, the horrors of the Cultural Revolution were eerily recalled in scenes across Tibet. In Ngawa, Sichuan province, film footage showed a group of PAP officers standing behind a row of Tibetans, bending them double, as their crimes were displayed on placards hung around their necks. A warehouse at the railway station in Lhasa was used as a holding center for prisoners. In late April 2008, 675 monks, along with hundreds of other prisoners, were herded onto the train at gunpoint to labor and reeducation camps in the barren wastes of Qinghai where China once tested its nuclear weapons and offered nuclear waste-dumping facilities to the West.[3]

Lobsang Gyaltsen was sentenced to death for "setting fire to two garment shops in downtown Lhasa on March 14 that killed a shop owner, Zuo Rencun." Another defendant, known only as Loyar, was sentenced to death for his part in setting fire to a motorcycle dealership where the owner, his wife, and two sons died in the blaze. According to Xinhua, the two Tibetans "have had to be executed to assuage the people's anger." The sentence was carried out by a PAP execution squad in October 2009.

China meanwhile began to publicize its version of the uprising as it had done with the Nangpa La shootings. They released 'official' footage of monks hurling stones and raiding shops while suppressing any footage of the security forces shooting and hunting down Tibetans. With no independent observers to film the events, unlike Cho Oyu, the Chinese representation went unchallenged. The TV station CCTV (Chinese Central Television) broadcast scenes of victorious police raiding Tibetan homes. The commentary read: "The Central Government has invested much money and manpower to help develop the Tibet

Autonomous Region since its peaceful liberation in the 1950s. Since, things have been the most prosperous in the region's history. It is the Tibetan people's unanimous conclusion that unity and stability mean a happy life whereas splitting off the region from China can only spell disaster."

Once again, a veil of secrecy descended over Tibet. China denied UN High Commissioner for Human Rights Louise Arbour entry into the country. Inside Tibet, patriotic reeducation was made compulsory for all citizens. The most rigorous crackdown ever on free speech and contact with the outside world began. A special task force of PSB and 108 PAP was established to combat "rumor mongering"—a euphemism for contacting the outside world or spreading information.

In the years that followed, a Tibetan filmmaker was sentenced to six years for making a documentary in which he interviewed ordinary Tibetans on their views of the Chinese in Tibet. His subjects bravely spoke openly on camera choosing not to disguise their identities. Others were jailed for putting up pictures of the Dalai Lama on the Chinese version of Facebook. Any expression of Tibetan national identity was criminalized. Folk singers who sang Tibetan songs were imprisoned. And, over the course of the year following the uprising, 2,300 officials were dispatched to 505 monasteries and nunneries.

21

THE PRICE OF FREEDOM

—.—.—

During times of universal deceit, telling the truth
becomes a revolutionary act.

George Orwell

During the uprising in Tibet, Dolma took refuge with the nuns
Lobsang Samten and Thinley Wangmo at Dolma Ling nunnery. Here
was a refreshing respite from the reports of violence and the protests.
A beautifully tended lawn lay between the boarding house and the
nunnery proper. Flowering vines crept up the building's walls.

Despite riots in Nagchu, Driru—already heavily patrolled by
military—was relatively unscathed. Although she'd successfully reached
her mother on the phone days after the uprising, Dolma was set on
edge when, the following week, the phone line went dead. Each day,
news of fresh horrors of the violence in Tibet emanated over Radio Free
Asia and Voice of America. Then news of what was happening slowly
dried up.

A few days after the uprising started, Dolma and I met in the pastures behind her school. Dolma sat cross-legged, twirling a clover leaf
between her fingers. The cries of children in the playground faded as
class resumed.

Dolma is maturing into a woman: Her face has lost its girlish fullness,
and she smiles with confidence and compassion. She grows more like her
mother, Nyima, every day—fiercely independent yet with a soft, intuitive
kindness. Her hands are no longer callused by the hard work in the fields
in Juchen. She takes pride in her clothes, her mother's influence still

strong. Today she wears stylish Delhi fashions purchased with whatever money Nyima can afford to send.

Yet her true home is lost to her forever. As a result of her outspokenness about Kelsang's murder to the world's media, she is forbidden to return to Tibet. The Chinese secret services would pounce were she ever to cross the border. She said frankly, "Even if I went home to see my mother, I am sure I would spend the rest of my life in jail because the Chinese [authorities] know everything."

When Dolma started doing media interviews, she used to call home to make sure there were no repercussions for her family, but she suspected that they had paid a price for her outspokenness. In later years, Nyima asked her daughter not to telephone too often (calls from India are monitored).

Still, Dolma has never wavered from her vow to talk about the murder of her friend. Dolma said, "Her [Kelsang's] death highlighted Tibet. It made more and more people understand that similar things have occurred and gone unnoticed. Every time I talk about it, it hurts," she admitted. But now she has grown stronger. "I used to cry when I spoke about it. Now I don't. I am hard."

Dolma heard about the climbers who preferred to adopt pseudonyms, and many who refused to speak up about the murder they had witnessed. Dolma isn't angry. "I don't blame them for not speaking out," she said simply. "I just feel sorry for them that they only think about themselves. Because of that, their world is very small. Instead of helping others, they don't have the courage or the determination to understand others. And the more they think of themselves, the more they will find themselves stuck in a circle. That is the price they pay."

Dolma paused contemplatively. "Yes, I feel sad because the sadness feels endless," she said. "Kelsang's death on the Nangpa La, my being unable to return home because I have spoken her story." She coughs, demurely putting her hand in front of her mouth. "But on the other hand, after I told the story of Kelsang, people came to know her tragedy. So if my telling her story helps, it no longer matters if I can go home or not."

Dolma's childhood ended abruptly on the Nangpa La. Still she has few regrets:

> After I came here to India, in a place where I know nobody, many times I had a really tough time missing my mother, missing home, but on the other hand I feel I am lucky to have this eye-opening opportunity. Back home I never really knew what sadness was. I never knew how to take responsibility and how to lead a life and engage in society, I never thought of standing on my own feet. Maybe that is because I am from a small village. Sometimes I am happy and sometimes I am sad and that is what life is all about. And that is what I learned when I came here.

She paused to think, "So much of what you think in your mind, and the way you look at things, rather than what is here in the physical world, is what makes you happy."

It's a lesson she tries to live by each day, when she misses home and the soft embrace of Nyima, the geshe Kalsang, and the powerful mountains above Juchen where once she played with Kelsang.

Dolma wonders how her mother looks with the advancing years: Does she have gray hair and wrinkles? Will it be ten or fifteen years until she sees her family again? Or perhaps never? Might Tibet be free then?

A monk traveling from Juchen brought a picture of Nyima and Dolma's sister Kyizom, which Dolma keeps next to her bed. In the image, the women are both smiling. Kyizom, in a heavy yellow down jacket, is petite and fine-boned. Nyima, who is clutching a prayer wheel, grins proudly. Strong women both. Dolma takes heart and solace in the image of her mother and sister.

Each month, children from the Suja School return to Tibet. Dolma wishes she could return, but she keeps her desires quiet. When pressed, she admitted:

> Tibet is where Tibetans belong, that is where our culture was born and where it flourished. My home is beautiful,

the grasslands, the snow mountains, the pure and unpolluted waters, they were all designed for the Tibetans living on the high plateau. Tibet is precious. If I had the choice, I would rather live there.

For Dolma, the future in India is not assured. Despite a growing eloquence born of talking about her experience on the Nangpa La, Dolma struggles with learning English. After three years at the Suja School, she will have to leave to begin her vocational training, perhaps as a cook.

Dolma's freedom is contradictory. The price she has paid for freedom in India is her own captivity. Straddling the civilizations of East and West, Dolma finds herself torn between two political ideologies. Free speech is encouraged in Western democracies. To speak freely as a member of a closed society has resulted in Dolma's lifelong sentence.

Yet Kelsang's and Dolma's dream and their single-minded pursuit of the concept of freedom—something they had never known, but sensed was on the other side of the Himalaya and represented by the Dalai Lama—was worth the risk. Two girls from rural Tibet defied a super-power by refusing to believe what they had been told about the nature of freedom and the Dalai Lama. They set out to find truth in defiance of China and it's propaganda, whatever it might cost.

In doing so, Kelsang and Dolma, untainted by the great evil of our age, cynicism, acted as a perfect prism refracting the human condition. Their quest and its outcome shone a powerful light on how the West often acts only in self-interest. Climbing outfitters, escorting the wealthiest and most pampered members of Western society to Himalayan peaks, secretly disdain their Chinese hosts but outwardly act as apologists for them.

Dolma's decision to tell Kelsang's story whenever the opportunity comes her way makes her proud. "We are showing that the Chinese design for Tibet is not what we want," she said. Dolma, who was perhaps reluctant to leave home originally, has absorbed some of Kelsang's trenchant spirit. In exile, she has accepted the responsibility thrust on her young shoulders. Ultimately, the definition of freedom to Dolma is that knowledge—no matter how painful in its acquisition and realization—is liberating. And indeed, a new generation of young Tibetans, both outside and inside Tibet, are defending democratic values and free speech, with the conviction that what happens inside Tibet must no longer remain secret. The struggle for Tibet has begun from within.

As we spoke, Dolma gazed at the mountains reflectively. Behind the school, emerald green terraced fields swept northward, to the forest and the white-capped mountains of the Dhauladhars, sometimes knows as the Outer Himalaya. The glazed peaks set boldly against the horizon offered a serene backdrop. Beyond them lay the turmoil, bloodshed, and violence of Tibet. On this side of the Himalaya, all seemed peaceful and fragrant. Red, blue, and yellow paragliders dipped lazily and wheeled beyond us, soaring freely on mountain thermals like dandelion seeds.

Dolma enjoys the company of her nun friends, but deep down, she questions whether the clerical life is her calling. To date, she hasn't taken her vows as a nun and is vague about when she will be officially ordained. Yet even beyond her friend's death, Dolma has stayed true to her promise to Kelsang to stay with her on her journey to spiritual salvation. Even death won't stop that.

As we spoke, a smile played on Dolma's lips. She had had one more audience with His Holiness the Dalai Lama in which he told her about Kelsang and the karmic reason for her death. "His Holiness said to me that Kelsang would have a good rebirth," Dolma paused. Her eyes twinkled, as she pulled at another tuft of clover. "Because I spoke out about her death, people prayed for her. And His Holiness prayed for her. Because of that, she had a good rebirth. And she's back. She's somewhere in Tibet."

EPILOGUE

—·—·—

Frostbitten and dusty, knots of Tibetan refugees swarmed past us as we climbed barren mountain trails toward Tibet's border. One man, whose eye had frozen in the sub-zero temperatures, stopped and begged for eye drops. He winced in pain when I dropped the liquid in his eyes, before scurrying down the trail, mumbling thanks.

It had been two months since Kelsang Namtso had been killed on the Nangpa La. My magazine editor at the *Mail on Sunday* had asked me to investigate further.

Within days, I was in the foothills of the Himalaya in Nepal with Kunchok, my Tibetan translator, and Ramesh, who would be my guide through the mountains. We did our best to pose as tourists as we trekked to Tibet. "You don't tell anyone who you are or what you are doing," whispered Kunchok, as we slogged upward through the hamlet of Phakding. "You can't trust anyone here."

My aim was to follow the refugees' route from the border with Tibet and the Nangpa La, all the way back to Kathmandu and then on to Dharamsala, India.

The higher we climbed, the more I noticed a striking disparity between the tourists and adventurers and those headed the other way—refugees who looked as though they were escaping conflict. It was hard to reconcile the fact that people were vacationing in a country where a Maoist insurgency had left 13,000 dead.

Beyond Namche Bazar en route to the Nangpa La, we did our best to avoid Maoist insurgents. We gasped for oxygen in the thin December air as we neared Thame. When we arrived in the village, a Nepalese man, hunched in the cold, his hood pulled up over his head and white wires from an iPod jammed into his ears, stood by a low stone wall. As he shifted his weight from foot to foot, he made a poor attempt at feigning disinterest at our arrival.

"Don't look at him," Kunchok warned me in a whisper. "He's police. Probably paid by the Chinese."

As we entered our guesthouse in Thame, several young women wearing face masks stood warming themselves around a stove. At the sight of us, they disappeared into the chill night. Kunchok waited a few moments before following outside. An hour later, he returned. Later, the girls would meet with me.

At around midnight, Kunchok led me from our guesthouse to a circle of tents in the middle of the village. "Move quickly," he said, scanning his surroundings as he held open the tent flaps for me. Hurriedly, I crawled into the cramped interior. A dozen shrouded figures sat in the gloom of a smoky yak-dung fire.

As Kunchok translated, I learned that two brothers were escorting their three sisters into Nepal. They wanted to be nuns in India. The sisters grinned at me uneasily and tittered when I raised my camera. They'd never met a Westerner before.

The brothers, tough-looking men in filthy anoraks, had been working as porters for a Western expedition on Cho Oyu when Kelsang Namtso was shot. By their account, none of the climbers had done much at the scene of the crime. A few years earlier, the brothers had also been porters on another expedition on Cho Oyu when a Tibetan refugee had fallen down a crevasse and climbers with the means to help had done nothing. Westerners, as these men saw it, didn't really care all that much for Tibetans.

Days later, we reached the Tibetan border before returning to Namche. Along the way, we encountered other refugees hiding out in safe houses, biding their time, before they pressed onward for another dangerous leg of their journey to India.

It took almost a month to follow the trail and to finally, arrive in Dharamsala where I, along with forty or so newly arrived Tibetan refugees met the Dalai Lama.

"We have one generation coming into exile and another generation passing on here," the Dalai Lama said warmly. "It is important to understand what you must do in exile. I stress the importance of education." His goal is for the next generation of Tibetans to receive the benefits of an education so that they can stand up for their rights inside Tibet.

The Dalai Lama discussed how he felt personally duped by Mao, who had promised to modernize Tibet. After the invasion of Tibet in 1950, the Dalai Lama had traveled to Beijing to meet him. He was impressed with Mao's ideas of progress and equality for all. "He said to me, 'Now you have joined the motherland; in time the Tibetans will help the Chinese.'" The Dalai Lama paused, rocked back on his heels, and broke out in gales of laughter. "Maybe Mao was just joking with me! Or maybe he really felt that!"

These days, modern China, as the Dalai Lama sees it, is only interested in making money. "On paper they are communists, but in reality they are capitalists." He paused and then laughed again at the absurdity. "It's a very strange situation!"

Following his talk, the Dalai Lama greeted each Tibetan in welcome.

After the assembled group had filtered out of the temple, the Dalai Lama's assistants beckoned to me. I turned to the Dalai Lama in the now-empty room to ask him about the murder of Kelsang Namtso. Immediately, his features darkened.

"This shooting is not a new thing!" he railed with disgust. "Just this time, it was seen by Westerners. They have been killing and shooting like this for years!" The Dalai Lama made little attempt to hide his rage. His voice thundered around the temple.

It was the first time I had met the Dalai Lama. I didn't expect him to be angry. As he vented his frustration, he suggested we head outside to a balcony behind the main temple.

Outside, the Dalai Lama relaxed, but his words were more insistent. At a discreet distance, a Tibetan bodyguard in a leather bomber jacket cradled a submachine gun. Before I'd been allowed entry into the compound, I had had to walk through a metal detector and had been patted down.

As he began to speak, it became clear that Kelsang's death had unleashed a powerful, personal sense of injustice within the Dalai Lama.

The circumstances of her murder had highlighted Tibet's plight to the world. The Dalai Lama was furious that it had taken a young woman's murder to illuminate the injustice served by the Chinese to the international community. The West's apathy with regard to Tibet was, as he understood it, the result of racism and blatant self-interest. "In the sixties, seventies, and eighties, we went through incredible suffering," he explained. "But they [the West] all looked at Russia and not China." His chest was heaving as he spoke. "Perhaps it is because we are Asian, they don't care!" he snorted, giving a dismissive flick of his wrist. "So you see, there is even discrimination in human rights!"

He checked himself and tried to soften. "It has to change. Look what happened in Russia. The same will happen here. In the short term, I am pessimistic, but in the long term, I am optimistic."

Before I took my leave, the Dalai Lama offered me words of advice. He told me what he told everyone else he had met who had been connected to the Nangpa La incident. "Just be honest and tell the truth." It seemed strange advice at the time. Why wouldn't I?

Two years later, I reflected on the Dalai Lama's words when Tibet exploded in protest and shortly thereafter the global economy crashed. Then, too, the West looked to China for help. And then, too, Westerners turned a blind eye to the bloodshed in Tibet when they celebrated the Olympics. The truth, it seemed, was too ugly to confront.

When I met him, the Dalai Lama had been amused at the paradoxes. The world's largest Communist nation had become the world's banker and supplier. When I began to investigate the story of Kelsang Namtso, I found that almost everything connected with Tibet was a mass of contradictions.

I was struck by the clash of privileged Westerners with poverty-stricken Tibetans on the roof of the world. The juxtaposition of cultures highlighted to me an uncomfortable moral dilemma about what the West is willing to accept in order to get what it wants.

My quest to discover the truth about Kelsang's death began with two magazine articles and has ended with the publication of the book you now hold in your hands. What I found along the way challenged and constantly surprised me.

From the outset, there were problems gathering information. I began my research by making perfunctory telephone calls to Sinologists and Tibetologists at American universities and think tanks. Few returned my calls or e-mails. Talking about human rights abuse in Tibet can result in being permanently blacklisted from China.

The representatives of a number of Himalayan charities and NGOs also refused interviews. They too worried that the Chinese would shut them down if they were caught entering what the Chinese see as the political fray.

A surprising number of human rights NGOs know relatively little about Tibet. For one, it is vastly complex. In large part, it is simply too expensive and dangerous to get information about Tibet out of the country.

Even the International Campaign for Tibet, dedicated to extracting information, faces a Sisyphean task. Kate Saunders of ICT noted, "We still don't know what really happened with the March 2008 protests. It takes months, if not years, to really find out what is happening. And most often, sadly, we don't find out at all. Court cases are held in secret, people just go missing. We'll never know everything."

Beyond the tourist areas of Tibet, very few people have been to the remote reaches of the plateau or the Himalaya. Those who have are often proprietary about their knowledge—preserving it for speaking engagements and commercial enterprises in which they stand to make a buck. "I wouldn't exactly call it an atrocity," one well-known climber insisted in his staunch refusal to talk. "It was just one person."

The people who did agree to talk to me anxiously insisted that they not be named or quoted, and that their respective organization not be highlighted in my book.

Aside from how difficult it is to obtain information about Tibet, I was shocked by the levels of paranoia I encountered in my research. Climbers who had borne witness to Kelsang's murder feared not only that they would be refused reentry to the country for more climbing, but that speaking out could affect their careers at home. "Please don't use my name, as my company works in China," was a common refrain. Others attempted to abnegate their responsibility through denial of the importance of what they had seen or were deliberately vague. "It was the altitude," said one. "Hard to remember what happened."

The growing paranoia and fear surrounding China appears to be ever increasing. "There is a network of Chinese informants in the United States, and other countries, so there is a level of fear everywhere," said Ben Carrdus, a researcher at ICT. Rampant Chinese nationalism is being fanned among the youth in expatriate Chinese communities around the world.

In my quest for information, I looked for Mandarin-speaking researchers. As soon as the word went out among Chinese communities that my book was about a human rights abuse in Tibet, all communication with the translators I had been in contact with abruptly ceased.

I also began to notice increasingly that pro-Tibet protests in countries were met with extremely well-organized pro-Chinese demonstrators. "The Chinese embassies pay Chinese students and organize buses them for them to go to these things," Carrdus explained. "It's a standard way for the party do business." The United Work Front Department is the liaison between Beijing and Chinese consulates and student organizations in the United States and Europe.

I drove to Canada and met the Chinese dissident writer Sheng Xue, an eloquent and fine-boned woman who had escaped Tiananmen Square with her husband. At her suburban home in Ontario, she had organized an interview for me with Han Guangsheng, a defector to Canada who had once run a prison in Shenyang and had been a vice chief in the PSB (Public Security Bureau) in the city. After the interview, Sheng Xue showed me the daily assaults she and her husband live with each day. Their answering machine and e-mail inboxes are jammed with incriminating messages. To young Chinese nationalists, Sheng Xue is seen as a traitor to the motherland.

At the same time, I found a growing network of China watchers—academics and journalists alike—obsessively collecting hard-won data on China's so-called peaceful rise. Desperately, they want the world to know that the rise is anything but peaceful.

As facts are so difficult to come by, conspiracies abound. I met a number of people who had stood up to China, with grave results. Brian

McAdam, a Canadian diplomat who had served thirty years in consulates around the world, the last in Hong Kong as an immigration control officer, had blown the whistle on corruption in the Canadian consulate when he discovered gangsters with connections to the Chinese government were buying visas. Overnight, he lost his job and his reputation. Today, from his home in Toronto, he passionately campaigns against China's rise. All the windows of his house are constructed with bullet-proof glass. "I probably sound like a paranoid conspiracy theorist," he said, sitting in his basement. "But that's because I am."

Even those who work in the field of human rights have become tainted and conscious of a dark specter of surveillance and paranoia. When Carrdus showed me around the NGO's townhouse headquarters in Washington, D.C., on one of my frequent visits, he pointed out the window of a facing building that looks directly into ICT's conference room. "That's where we think they do their surveillance on us from."

Carrdus, a ten-year veteran of the Tibetan cause, said he has to curb himself sometimes from rampaging paranoia. "Sometimes I get home after work and think my light switch has been tampered with or someone has been in my apartment." He grinned uneasily. "Then I have to check myself."

Because information on Tibet is so sparse and, after cross-checking, much of it proves to be misinformation, the task of this book was difficult. I'd research only to discover that what I had written was disguised propaganda from one side or the other. Nearly every aspect of modern-day Tibet is contentious, a quagmire where facts are distorted.

Even among established figures in the exile Tibetan community, it is sometimes difficult to elicit information beyond anything but the broadest generalizations, even if they do consent to meet. They trust no one and are notoriously enigmatic or obtuse.

I'd set up interviews, and subjects would grow scared and not show up. Or, as happened on several occasions, they would begin to talk hesitantly, realize what it might cost them or their family back in Tibet, and then grow silent. It took months to win people's trust to get them back again. Interviews with some members of the Nangpa La group were vague and distant. "Tibetans grow up used to keeping their mouths shut and not saying anything at all," said Carrdus. "It's difficult for us in the West to understand what it's like to grow up in an oppressive country and how one might be conditioned not to ever say anything that could get yourself or others into trouble."

The Dalai Lama's advice to simply tell the truth often felt like an impossible, Herculean task. Yet, slowly the book evolved. And the truth, always incomplete and often imperfect, was never, ever, really what I thought it might be.

ACKNOWLEDGMENTS

—·—

This book exists because of the help and support I have had from a bewilderingly long list of people who graciously gave their time when I frequently asked for it. Apologies to anyone I have omitted.

My deep gratitude, first and foremost, goes to Dolma Palkyi, who has never, ever strayed from the responsibility of telling about what happened to her best friend, Kelsang Namtso. She's an inspiration to me.

Thank you to the dedicated and tireless Tibetan researchers and translators in Dharamsala and in the borderlands of the Himalaya— lifelong friends all—Tenzin Loesel, Karma Spirit, Kunchok Chodak, and Ngawang Sangdrol.

The assistance of all those at the International Campaign for Tibet has played a crucial role in bringing out this story. They deserve recognition for the increasingly difficult job of extracting the truth about Tibet. My particular thanks go to Kate Saunders, who read the manuscript for accuracy and to prevent repercussions for people in Tibet. And thanks to Chris Ratke and Ben Carrdus, who have been ever patient with my list of demands.

Robbie Barnett at Columbia University gave much of his time and access to his impressive archives.

I was extraordinarily lucky to work with an editor whose wisdom, guidance, and, above all, compassion can be found throughout this book. My heartfelt thanks to a champion of this story and the greatest teacher I have ever had, Morgen Van Vorst. And my gratitude to Clive Priddle, Melissa Raymond, and the fantastic staff at PublicAffairs. I could not have wished for better support on this, my first book.

And special thanks to writer friends who read early drafts and offered support and counsel when things got rough, as they often did: Todd Pitock, Mikel Dunham, Brendan I. Koerner, Gabriel Cohen, Matteo Pistono, and Torty Conner—the latter for the Kingfisher beers and searing insight while I was in Dharamsala, but in which order I can't remember.

And a special thank you to Rachel Oldroyd and the team at *Live* magazine, *Mail on Sunday,* who first drew my attention to the story and sent me on my first assignment to Nepal. Also, to Brad Wieners at *Men's Journal,* who commissioned me to write about the conflict among the mountaineers on Cho Oyu. That piece led to this book.

Luis Benitez tirelessly answered all my questions on mountaineering and Cho Oyu and gave much of his time to the book.

My agents Jody Hotchkiss and Gay Salisbury were instrumental in helping bring this story to the wider world.

My gratitude to the organizations that gave grants to make the investigative work on this project easier: Investigative Reporters and Editors and the Fund for Investigative Journalism. Their altruism is now more important than ever as budgets for investigative journalism continue to shrink.

And also thanks to Lobsang Choedon, Jamyang Samten, Jamie Pastor Bolnick, Francesca Eldridge, Michael Kodas, Guy Cotter, Bob Thurman, Edwin Bernbaum, Karma Rinchen, Kunga Tashi, Manuel Bauer,

Rebecca Novick, Mike Fagin at West Coast Weather LLC, Amy Goldsmith, and Maria Savio.

And to all those who helped but cannot be named—the list is extremely long—thank you for trusting me.

NOTES

_.-._

INTRODUCTION

1 A $44 million report by China's Ministry of Land and Resources, started in 1999 and using 1,000 researchers who worked in secret for seven years, revealed that there was an estimated $128 billion worth of metals to be mined, after 1,000 Chinese surveyors had swarmed the plateau for seven years. And that was only half the plateau.

2 According to Communist Party officials and reported in "Mining Tibet: Mineral Exploration in Tibetan Areas of the PRC," by the Tibet Information Network.

CHAPTER 1

1 "A wolf wrapped in a monk's robe, a monster with a human face but the heart of a beast." Zhang Qingli, quoted by Paul Lin in the *Tapei Times*, April 25, 2008.

2 Xinhua quoting *Tibet Daily* on June 1, 2000.

CHAPTER 3

[1] Weihenmayer, Erik, *Touch the Top of the World: A Blind Man's Journey to Climb Farther Than the Eye Can See*. New York: Plume, 2002.

CHAPTER 4

[1] Congressional Executive Commission on China Special Topic Paper 2008–2009.

[2] International Commission of Jurists, *Tibet: Human Rights and the Rule of Law*, 1997.

[3] Avedon, John F., In *Exile From The Land of Snows: The Definitive Account of the Dalai Lama and Tibet Since the Chinese Conquest*. New York: Random House, 1984.

[4] Congressional Executive Commission on China Annual Report 2009, footnote 26.

[5] Shakya, Tsering, *The Dragon in the Land of Snows*. London: Penguin, 1999.

CHAPTER 5

[1] Hopkirk, Peter, *Trespassers on the Roof of the World*. New York: Kodansha America, 1995.

[2] Hopkirk, Peter, *Trespassers on the Roof of the World*. New York: Kodansha America, 1995.

[3] Isserman, Maurice and Stuart Weaver, *Fallen Giants: A History of Himalayan Mountaineering from the Age of Empire to the Age of Extremes*. New Haven and London: Yale University Press, 2008.

[4] Isserman, Maurice and Stuart Weaver, *Fallen Giants: A History of Himalayan Mountaineering from the Age of Empire to the Age of Extremes*. New Haven and London: Yale University Press, 2008.

[5] Alexander, Carol, "Greatest Mountaineer." *National Geographic*, November 2006.

[6] Buchanan, Rob, " Why David Breashears Cannot Let Everest Go." *Men's Journal*, June 2006.

[7] Achenbach, Joel, " The Man and His Mountain." *Washington Post*, June 1992.

[8] Fickling, David, "We Knocked the Bastard Off." *The Guardian*, 2003.

[9] Author interview with Detective Greenslade

CHAPTER 6

[1] Qi Jinfa, China's vice minister of Agriculture, to Xinhua, March 1998.

[2] Kristensen, Hans M., "Extensive Nuclear Missile Deployment Area Discovered in Central China," *FAS Strategic Security Blog*, Washington, May 15,

2008, http://www.fas.org/blog/ssp/2008/05/extensive-nuclear-deployment-area-discovered-in-central-china.php.

3 Spencer, Richard, "Pollution Kills 750,000 in China Every Year." *Daily Telegraph,* July 4, 2007.

CHAPTER 7

1 Isserman, Maurice and Stuart Weaver, *Fallen Giants: A History of Himalayan Mountaineering from the Age of Empire to the Age of Extremes.* New Haven and London: Yale University Press, 2008.

2 Tichy, Herbert, *Cho Oyu: By Favour of the Gods.* London: Methuen, 1955.

3 Hopkirk, Peter, *Trespassers on the Roof of the World.* New York: Kodansha America, 1995.

CHAPTER 19

1 MacDonald, Alexander W., "The Lama and the General." *Kailash: A Journal of Himalayan Studies,* 1973.

CHAPTER 20

1 Heil, Nick, "King of the Hill," *Outside,* May 2008.

2 International Campaign for Tibet. "Authorities acknowledge 4000 detentions: thousands disappear in ongoing Lhasa crackdown," press release. April 14, 2008.

3 International Campaign for Tibet, "Nuclear Tibet: Nuclear Weapons and Nuclear Waste on the Tibetan Plateau." 1993.

BIBLIOGRAPHY

—·—·—

Avedon, John F., *In Exile from the Land of Snows: The Definitive Account of the Dalai Lama and Tibet Since the Chinese Conquest* (New York: Random House, 1984).

Baker, Ian, *The Heart of the World: A Journey to Tibet's Lost Paradise* (New York: Penguin, 2004).

Barber, Noel, *From the Land of Lost Content: The Dalai Lama's Fight for Tibet* (Boston: Houghton Mifflin, 1970).

Bernbaum, Edwin, *Sacred Mountains of the World* (San Francisco: Sierra Club Books, 1990).

Bernbaum, Edwin, *The Way to Shambala* (Boston and London: Shambala Publications Inc., 2001).

Bishop, Peter, *The Sacred Myth of Shangri-La* (London: Adarsh Books, 2000).

Chan, Victor, *Tibet Handbook: A Pilgrimage Guide* (Chico: Moon Publications Inc., 1994).

Chang, June, and Jon Halliday, *Mao: The Unknown Story* (New York: Anchor, 2005).

Coffey, Maria, *Explorers of the Infinite* (New York: Penguin, 2008).

David-Neel, Alexandra, *Magic and Mystery in Tibet* (New York: Dover Publications, 1971).

Dunham, Mikel, *Buddha's Warriors: The Story of the CIA Backed Tibetan Freedom Fighters, the Chinese Invasion and the Ultimate Fall of Tibet* (New York: Penguin, 2004).

Dowman, Keith, *The Power Places of Central Tibet* (London: Routledge & Kegan Paul Ltd., 1988).

Fishman, Ted C., *China Inc: How The Rise of the Next Superpower Challenges America and the World* (New York: Scribner, 2005).

French, Patrick, *Younghusband: The Last Great Imperial Adventurer* (London: Harper Perennial, 2004).

French, Patrick, *Tibet, Tibet* (New York: Vintage, 2003).

Goldstein, Melvyn C., Dawei Sherpa, and William R. Sienbenschuh, *A Tibetan Revolutionary: The Political Life and Times of Bapa Phunsto Wangye* (Los Angeles: University of California Press, 2004).

Goldstein, Melvyn C., *The Snow Lion and the Dragon* (Los Angeles: University of California Press, 1997).

Hanbury-Tracy, John, *Black River of Tibet* (London: Frederick Mueller, 1938).

Hawley, Elizabeth, *Himalayan Database: The Expedition Archives of Elizabeth Hawley* (Golden:The American Alpine Club).

Hilton, Isabel, *The Search for the Panchen Lama* (New York: Norton, 1999).

Hilton, James, *Lost Horizon* (New York: Pocket Books, 1933).

Hopkirk, Peter, *Trespassers on the Roof of the World* (New York: Kodansha, 1982).

Iyer, Pico, *The Open Road* (New York: Viking, 2008).

Isserman, Maurice, and Stuart Weaver, *Fallen Giants: A History of Himalayan Mountaineering from the Age of Empire to the Age of Extremes* (New Haven and London: Yale University Press, 2008).

Kaulback, Ronald, *Salween* (New York: Harcourt Brace and Company, 1939).

Kodas, Michael, *High Crimes: The Fate of Everest in an Age of Greed* (New York: Hyperion, 2008).

Klesiath, Michelle C., *Heavy Earth, Golden Sky, Tibetan Women Speak About Their Lives* (Lulu, 2007).

Kurlantzick, Joshua, *Charm Offensive: How China's Soft Power Is Transforming the World* (New Haven and London: Yale University Press, 2007).

Krakauer, John, *Into Thin Air* (New York: Villard, 1997).

Lee, Dick, and Colin Pratt, *Operation Julie: How the Undercover Police Team Smashed the World's Greatest Drug Ring* (London: Hutchinson, 1978).

Lopez, Donald S., *Prisoners of Shangri-La: Tibetan Buddhism and the West* (Chicago: The University of Chicago Press, 1998).

Lustgarten, Abraham, *China's Great Train: Beijing's Drive West and the Campaign to Remake Tibet* (New York: Henry Holt, 2008).

Marshall, Steven, *Hostile Elements: A Study of Political Imprisonment* (London: Tibet Information Network, 1999).

Meyer, Karl E., and Shareen Blair Brysac, *Tournament of Shadows: The Great Game and the Race for Empire in Central Asia* (New York: Basic Books, 1999).

Navarro, Peter, *The Coming China Wars* (New York: FT Press, 2008).

Palin, Michael, *Himalaya* (London: Thomas Dunne Books, 2004).

Seth, Vikram, *From Heaven Lake: Travels through Sinkiang and Tibet* (New York: Vintage, 1987).

Shakya, Tsering, *The Dragon in the Land of Snows* (London: Penguin, 1999).

Tendler, Stewart, and David May, *The Brotherhood of Eternal Love* (London: Panther Books, 1984).

Thurman, Robert, *Essential Tibetan Buddhism* (New York: Harper-Collins, 1995).

Tichy, Herbert, *Cho Oyu: By Favour of the Gods* (London: Methuen, 1955).

Weihenmayer, Erik, *Touch the Top: A Blind Man's Journey to Climb Further Than the Eye Can See* (New York: Plume, 2002).

Hutton, Will, *The Writing on the Wall: China and the West in the 21st Century* (London: Little, Brown, 2007).

Smith, Warren W., Jr., *Tibet's Last Stand* (Lanham: Rowman and Littlefield, 2010).

Reports from Tibetan Center for Human Rights and Democracy

"Death Penalty in China: 2005 Special Report."

"Uprising in Tibet 2008."

Reports from the International Campaign for Tibet

"Like Gold That Fears No Fire: New Writing from Tibet," 2010.

"Tracking the Steel Dragon," 2008.

"Dangerous Crossing—Conditions Impacting the Flight of Tibetan Refugees," 2003 Update, 2004 Update, 2005 Update, 2006 Report.

"Tibet at a Turning Point: The Spring Uprising and China's New Crackdown," 2008.

"A Great Mountain Burned by Fire: China's Crackdown in Tibet," 2009.

INDEX

—·—

Jonathan Green is an award-winning author and journalist. He has reported on jihadist militias from Sudan, on the cocaine trade from the guerilla-controlled jungles of Colombia, on corruption in oil-rich Kazakhstan, on the destruction of the rainforest in Borneo, and on human rights abuses connected to gold mining in West Africa. He has received the Amnesty International Media Award for Excellence in Human Rights Journalism, the American Society of Journalists and Authors award for reporting on a significant topic, and been named Feature Writer of the Year in the Press Gazette Magazine and Design Awards. His work has appeared in *Men's Journal,* the *New York Times, Fast Company,* the *Financial Times, British GQ* and *Esquire,* and the *Mail on Sunday* among many other publications. Green lives in Massachusetts with his wife.

PublicAffairs is a publishing house founded in 1997. It is a tribute to the standards, values, and flair of three persons who have served as mentors to countless reporters, writers, editors, and book people of all kinds, including me.

I. F. STONE, proprietor of *I. F. Stone's Weekly*, combined a commitment to the First Amendment with entrepreneurial zeal and reporting skill and became one of the great independent journalists in American history. At the age of eighty, Izzy published *The Trial of Socrates*, which was a national bestseller. He wrote the book after he taught himself ancient Greek.

BENJAMIN C. BRADLEE was for nearly thirty years the charismatic editorial leader of *The Washington Post*. It was Ben who gave the *Post* the range and courage to pursue such historic issues as Watergate. He supported his reporters with a tenacity that made them fearless and it is no accident that so many became authors of influential, best-selling books.

ROBERT L. BERNSTEIN, the chief executive of Random House for more than a quarter century, guided one of the nation's premier publishing houses. Bob was personally responsible for many books of political dissent and argument that challenged tyranny around the globe. He is also the founder and longtime chair of Human Rights Watch, one of the most respected human rights organizations in the world.

· · ·

For fifty years, the banner of Public Affairs Press was carried by its owner Morris B. Schnapper, who published Gandhi, Nasser, Toynbee, Truman, and about 1,500 other authors. In 1983, Schnapper was described by *The Washington Post* as "a redoubtable gadfly." His legacy will endure in the books to come.

Peter Osnos, *Founder and Editor-at-Large*